PRAISE FOR *AMER*

"Tomasulo's memoir gives a voice to tl one. It reaches into the very heart of wnat is possible when people are given support, compassion, and an opportunity to thrive."

Scott Barry Kaufman, author of *Ungifted* and *Wired to Create* (with Carolyn Gregoire)

"Dan Tomasulo's tale of hope and grit explores a dark blemish in American history, re-framing the narrative—both of his own life and that of his patients—through hard work and compassion, and irrevocably altering the civil rights discourse about how we care for the most severely intellectually disabled in this country. If you want people to change for the better, you have to change their situation. *American Snake Pit* shows with courage and compassion how this can be done. From my viewpoint, this is the formula for hope."

Philip Zimbardo, Ph.D., Professor Emeritus, Stanford University, and author of *The Lucifer Effect*

"A compassionate, funny, fictionalized (but no less real) account of what happened when newly minted psychologist, 'Dr. Dan,' was put in charge of transitioning six intellectually disabled people from an abusive, overcrowded institution to a community home. But who is really in charge? Earnest and clueless Dr. Dan? The challenging and crafty residents? The ex-con cook? The wise-cracking sexy secretary? The no-nonsense seasoned staff? Or the mayor and fire chief who scheme to get the home out of their town? High jinx and pathos ensue as these disparate characters learn to get along."

Marie Hartwell-Walker, Ed.D. and author of *Unlocking the Secrets of Self-Esteem*

"Equally harrowing and transcendent in its telling, Tomasulo's revealing tale balances on the boundary of what it is to be human, and to endure with dignity and compassion."

Barnet Bain, Core Faculty, Spirituality Mind Body Institute, Teachers College, Columbia University; author of *The Book of Doing and Being*; and producer, *What Dreams May Come*

"Tomasulo has done something remarkable in *American Snake Pit*. He has given voice to the voiceless. The book is about making courage and hope and kindness happen. The courage to be the change for a broken and dysfunctional system, the hope to see an invisible but somehow better future among clouds of impossibility, and the kindness to want to prioritize and champion that unspoiled, sacred spot that lies deep inside every human being. Tomasulo given us a gift. Don't just read it. Don't just treasure it. Allow yourself to be forever changed by its wisdom."

Ryan M. Niemiec, Psy.D., Education Director and Psychologist, VIA Institute on Character, author of *Character Strengths Interventions* and *Mindfulness and Character Strengths*, and co-author of *Positive Psychology at the Movies* and *Movies and Mental Illness* (with Danny Wedding)

"Tomasulo reminds us that first and foremost we must never lose sight of our humanity. People with intellectual disabilities have often been victims of a myth that they are less able than others to access the human qualities in all of us that help us to thrive. The stories of Willowbrook survivors and their staff provide a lens into the power of community, hope, humor, and strength of character."

Joan B. Beasley, Ph.D., Research Associate Professor, University of New Hampshire Institute on Disability/UCED, and Director, Center for START Services

"Tomasulo is a gifted clinician, a gifted writer, and a deeply compassionate human being. He challenges our implicit bias against severely intellectually disabled by revealing his own. We watch 'Dr. Dan' move from graduate student to polished clinician as he leverages his creativity, curiosity, and kindness in finding a way to reach people that others thought were unreachable."

Shannon Polly, Master of Applied Positive Psychology (MAPP), and co-author of *Character Strengths Matter* (with Kathryn Britton)

"In a place others label hopeless, Tomasulo finds hope. In a place others see rejection, Tomasulo discovers resilience. In a place others find gross, Tomasulo uncovers grit. *American Snake Pit* grabbed me by the throat from the first sentence and wouldn't let go. Brilliant. Period!"

Margaret H. Greenberg, MAPP, PCC, and *New York Times* bestselling co-author of *Profit from the Positive* (with Senia Maymim)

"Engrossing, moving, and inspirational, *American Snake Pit* is a tour-de-force. We couldn't put the book down! Tomasulo's memoir beautifully depicts the transformational power of kindness and compassion, even for those in the direst of situations."

Suzann Pileggi Pawelski, MAPP, and James Pawelski, Ph.D., co-authors of *Happy Together*

"Gripping, haunting, shocking, and gorgeous, *American Snake Pit* explodes off of the page like fireworks, shining a brilliant and long-overdue light on one of the most infamous institutions in American history."

Daniel Lerner, New York University Clinical Instructor, and co-author of *U Thrive* (with Alan Schlechter)

"American Snake Pit is very much Tomasulo's story, but it is also the modern history of the intellectually disabled in the United States. Unlike the textbooks I grew up reading that attempted only to cram facts into my brain, Dan's stories drew me inside of them. Even as I set the book down for the last time, I wanted more of Dan, whose honesty and humor will connect with anyone interested in learning how to be a human being. This is a book that should be on the shelf of every mental health clinician, every politician, and all lovers of a great memoir or good history."

Alan Daniel Schlechter, MD, Assistant Professor, Department of Child and Adolescent Psychiatry, NYU Langone Health; Director, Outpatient Child and Adolescent Psychiatry, Bellevue Hospital; and co-author of *U Thrive* (with Daniel Lerner)

"Tasked with integrating a group of discarded individuals into the very community that rejected them, Tomasulo leads us on a journey to understand what connects us as humans. We're reminded of the fundamentals: our need for safety, our need to be heard, and our need to have hope. Even in the most difficult of circumstances, Tomasulo shows us that these fundamentals have the power to heal and transform. What is best in us emerges."

Cory Muscara, MAPP; Long Island Center for Mindfulness; Assistant Instructor, University of Pennsylvania; and Teaching Staff, Columbia Teachers College

"In this gripping and sometimes heartbreaking memoir, Tomasulo brings to life an unforgettable cast of characters, all of them plagued by demons, all of them trying to make the best of their harrowing circumstances. An eye-opening exploration of how mental illness can undo a life—and how love and friendship can put it back together."

Emily Esfahani Smith, author of *The Power of Meaning*

"Tomasulo tells the thoughtful and sometimes poignant stories of an incredible group of people who live with severe mental illness and behavioral problems. By the end of this book, you'll be cheering for this group of underdogs as though they were all people you knew and loved—much like each is loved and cared for by underappreciated and underpaid staff. If this book doesn't inspire you to think about group homes more empathetically and more humanely, I'm not sure what will."

John M. Grohol, Psy.D., founder and CEO of PsychCentral.com

"Tomasulo's accounts of working with patients from the 'Snake Pit' will jolt you and remind you to be grateful that clinicians like Tomasulo give their hearts and lives to helping those who can't represent themselves. And the huge surprise at the end of the book pulls the stories together in an amazing way. Bravo!"

Caroline Adams Miller, MAPP, and author of *Getting Grit* and *Creating Your Best Life* (with Michael B. Frisch)

"With humor and bold honesty, *American Snake Pit* takes us on the decades-long spiritual path of a courageous and faithful healer."

Lisa Miller, Ph.D., Professor and Founder, Spirituality Mind Body Institute, Teachers College, Columbia University

"By turns heartbreaking, inspiring, and humorous, this deeply personal book gives voice to people who are far too often voiceless, and forms a clear call for more individual and collective compassion."

David Bryce Yaden, Research Fellow, Department of Psychology, University of Pennsylvania, and editor of *Being Called*

"A poignant reflection on the horrors found within the walls of the Willowbrook Institution and the potent resiliency of individuals who are subjected to extreme and deplorable conditions in the 'snake pit' that our public policy has created. This should be a 'must read' for both the professional and lay community."

Robert J. Fletcher, DSW, Founder & CEO Emeritus, NADD, and former Willowbrook Class Case Manager

"Tomasulo brings a serious and timely issue to light in a non-serious way. His story serves as an important reminder that all people, irrespective of physical, behavioral, or emotional attributes, must be offered the same opportunities to become positive, productive, and fully integrated members of society."

George Contos, Chief Executive Officer, YAI / National Institute for People with Disabilities

"Honest, funny, and insightful, Tomasulo empathically describes the lives of developmentally disabled individuals transferred from the infamous Willowbrook State School in ways that are poignant and whimsical—and clinically valid."

George E. Vaillant, M.D., Professor of Psychiatry, Harvard Medical School, and author of Triumphs of Experience and Spiritual Evolution

AMERICAN SNAKE PIT

Hope, Grit, and Resilience in the Wake of Willowbrook

"To remain silent and indifferent is the greatest sin of all."
—commonly attributed to Elie Wiesel

stillhouse
press
CRAFT PUBLISHING FOR ARDENT SPIRITS
Fairfax, Virginia

Copyright © 2018 by Dan Tomasulo.

FIRST EDITION
All rights reserved.

No part of this book may be reproduced without written permission of the publisher.

Note to the Reader: In the service of confidentiality, I have disguised the identity of certain characters and, on occasion, incorporated parts of other clients' histories. Occasionally, I have fictionalized scenes in order to protect the persons described herein.

The author's proceeds from the sale of this book will be donated to YAI/National Institute for People with Disabilities. For information about using this book as a fundraiser for your organization, please contact media@stillhousepress.org.

Terms and references used in the book may be found at:
www.stillhousepress.org/american-snake-pit

All inquiries may be directed to:
        Stillhouse Press
        4400 University Drive, 3E4
        Fairfax, VA 22030
        www.stillhousepress.org

Stillhouse Press is an independent, student-run nonprofit press based out of Northern Viginia and established in collaboration with the Fall for the Book festival.

LIBRARY OF CONGRESS CONTROL NUMBER: 2017956893
ISBN-13: 978-1-945233-02-9

Designed and composed by Douglas Luman.
Cover art: Mateusz Nowakowski.

TABLE OF CONTENTS

Foreword

"Things do not change; we change."
—*Henry David Thoreau*

It is hard to explain my reasons for writing this book. All I can say for sure is that there was something disturbing about my feelings for a very long time—and that the book needed to be written. Something happened when I saw someone with a disability—an innate reaction, a distancing that sealed me off from them. It was almost as if I needed to protect myself from their infirmity. Their disfigurement, crudeness, unusualness, dullness, or pitiful presence kept me from reaching out, making a connection, or inviting friendship. I now understand this as a form of prejudice, and my life's work grew out of trying to understand that response.

I was embarrassed by my reactions as a teenager to people with emotional disabilities. I could feel an initial distancing, a type of repugnance that pushed me back—that somehow shut me down. I became quieter—avoiding, ignoring, or turning away from the individual. I didn't understand this reaction, but it troubled me. What was I so afraid of? What jammed my normal way of being? While I first noticed this reaction with people whose emotions seemed off, who yelled too loud, or who were socially awkward, I found the same thing happened when I encountered people with physical disabilities. It troubled me—an embarrassment of sorts. And nothing else in my adolescent experiences created this effect.

There was a man in my hometown, Richie, in his late 20s or early 30s, who was intellectually disabled and mentally ill. He often mumbled to himself, stared off into space, or tapped his eyebrows with the tips of his fingers. He was slightly disfigured, with a very large nose, and walked with unusual speed. He was made fun of by students, shunned by parents, and hidden from by children. Yet Richie was a fan of all the high school sports teams. He always seemed unfettered by the antics of others, and he said hello and waved to you if you made eye contact. His constant presence at the high school football, basketball, wrestling, and baseball events brought on ridicule, unflattering mimicking, and derogatory statements: "Go home, idiot!" "Loser!" The cruel mimicry and constant taunts of teenagers seemed to follow him everywhere. On occasion, a parent or teacher or coach would yell, "knock it off," but it never really got better. Richie would show up, yell for his team: "Come on, you can do it, you can do it!" He also had a slight lisp and occasionally stuttered, which made even his cheering into something that caused offensive remarks or reactions. When I saw Richie at these events, I wondered why he was there. Why would he put himself into such a vulnerable and exposed circumstance? I felt bad for him, but I also wished he wouldn't make himself a target. Why not stay home? Or be quiet? Or sit somewhere else than the middle of the bleachers? In other words: why don't you make my life easier by not being you?

As Richie made his presence known, people either shut down, like me, or acted out, like those mocking him. His presence caused people to react. Even the parents and teachers and coaches trying to keep the peace were affected. People were not neutral around him. What I didn't notice was any sweetness toward him. No one said hello, no one smiled, no one shook his hand. I noticed people's reactions, but I never did anything sweet or kind toward him, either.

Richie was ubiquitous. It didn't matter if we were dropping my sister off for dance lessons or getting Friday-night pizza or food shopping. Richie was there, and he always seemed to be in a good mood—and always walking off in a hurry. On occasion, he tried to start a conversation with a teenage girl—but this almost always ended with the young girl turning away without saying anything, or leaving after a polite, but curt, hello. A few of these encounters ended with the girls saying awful things to him about his appearance or speech, but never once did I see a mean or negative reaction from him. In fact, the only thing I ever heard Richie reply to anything ever said to him was: "That's okay, that's okay." There wasn't a mean bone in his body.

Toward the end of high school, I took a job at an ice cream parlor in town and in fairly short order became the manager—helping to make the ice cream, opening up, closing up, and cleaning up. I took some pride in managing it, and the owner and I got along very well. Over time he gave me more responsibilities and pay—and of course there was the added bonus that I could have a helping of anything I wanted at the end of my shift. My friends and fellow students would come in. It was a perfect way to make some money, be around my friends, and eat some terrific ice cream.

One day Richie came in and ordered a cone of rum raisin. I served it up for him, and while I was holding the cone out for him to take, he began the excruciating process of counting out the thirty cents in pennies, nickels, and a dime. He was short by three cents and I told him not to worry about it. A customer saw our exchange and told Richie to put his money away and that the cone was a treat, on him. This was the first act of kindness I'd seen directed at Richie. As the man handed me the money, Richie froze, not knowing what to say or do—genuinely shocked. While I held out the cone, Richie gathered up his change on the counter and stuffed it back in his pocket. His moistened eyes darted back and forth between the customer and me. He took the cone from my hand and vigorously shook his head—a kind of humbled, animated thank you to both of us. In what seemed like one synchronized move he started eating the ice cream, quickly walked toward the door, and muttered: "That's okay, that's okay." Richie had no idea how to receive kindness.

After that, Richie showed up every day. It was as though kindness and good fortune were now linked to the ice cream parlor: he would show up soon after I opened, buy a rum raisin ice cream, and stay long after he was done. After a while the owner realized this, thought it was bad for business, and told me I had to tell Richie he couldn't stay once he finished his ice cream. I did this, and explained to Richie that the seats were for people eating their ice cream and once done he would have to go so someone else could sit. Richie understood, but when he left he stood right outside the door. The owner was not happy about this new turn of events and told me he was going to involve the police. For several days we discussed alternate means of handling the situation, and somewhere along the way I recommended hiring Richie to help clean up. This way he could be connected to the ice cream parlor, I would have help in the evenings, and we could tell him that part of the deal was that he wouldn't hang around during the day. The owner rejected this idea out of hand, and it was clear the police would soon be involved.

Then the unimaginable happened. Out of the blue the owner's wife, only thirty-eight years old, died of a brain aneurism, and we closed the store for a week. Everyone in town knew her and the funeral parlor was packed every night. On the last night, Richie arrived and stood in the back, holding rosaries. When the owner thanked him for coming Richie's eyes darted around. "That's okay, that's okay," was, again, all he could say.

The owner changed his mind and hired Richie, whose efforts cut the time it usually took me to close the shop in half. We fell into a routine of cleaning the ice cream machine, wiping the soda fountain down, cleaning all the dishes, then putting the chairs on top of the tables and mopping the floor. Richie stayed away during the day—yet faithfully showed up at night. As the floor was drying, we would sit and eat a well-deserved ice cream cone. I'd usually have chocolate chip, and Richie loyally chose his rum raisin.

Then one day Richie didn't show. Then again—and again. There were rumors about what happened: he'd gotten hit by a car walking at night; he was hospitalized in an institution; he'd run away. I always wondered what happened to him. Although I tried to find out, I never saw him again. Soon, I left the ice cream parlor for college, after which I enrolled in graduate school—where this book begins.

So, I suppose, this book in many ways is inspired by Richie. He was the first person in my direct experience who struggled with intellectual and psychiatric disabilities. His innocence and enthusiasm for life, willingness to learn, and his desire to form relationships opened my eyes and heart to people I had closed myself off from. What I learned from him and from the people I have worked with is that, in spite of enormous intellectual and psychiatric disabilities, these individuals are not very different from you and me. They crave love; need affection, compassion, and kindness; get hurt when they feel left out; are in need of guidance; want meaningful relationships; get angry when they are betrayed or can't have their needs met; and are generally as confused and uncertain about their course in life as the rest of us.

Writing about my experiences with them required using a style of writing—creative nonfiction—that would allow their stories to be told without invading their privacy. Because I am trained as both a psychologist and writer, I serve at the discretion of these two professions. The first is devoted to the welfare and care of others and to treatment of their condition that respects their humanity and their privacy. Toward this end, though this book is based upon actual events, some of the characters and incidents portrayed herein are fictitious. This includes the name and setting of the group home, Walden House. Readers should not assume that any similarity to the name, character, or history of any person, living or dead, or to any actual event is intentional. Individual characteristics, locations, and other identifying details about the characters portrayed and their circumstances have been veiled and shrouded according to the

American Psychological Association's guidelines for psychologists writing about their clinical case studies. When writing about people I've worked with, I have followed the APA's directives in each and every instance.

But I also have an allegiance to my profession as a nonfiction writer that requires a conscientious attention to detail. To that end, historical facts concerning Willowbrook, including specific names, events, and details are exact and not veiled. They are reported and validated through verified sources.

This story needed to be told while paying homage to both disciplines. The path I have chosen to satisfy these conditions is to use distortions when necessary to disguise an individual, but to always present core elements of personality or condition to establish the path of the character. In other instances, I have kept the individual intact as completely as possible, but have transplanted them from one location or point of time to another so as to preserve their distinctiveness while camouflaging their identity. The result is that my own story is very similar to, but not exactly the same as, what you are about to read. These changes are necessary for me to protect these individuals and yet safeguard the goal of telling a story about their lives while preserving the emotional truth of my experiences with them.

Had I simply identified and wrote about the individuals in the group home or my practice without sufficiently masking them and their location (some of them, I am happy to say, are alive and doing quite well), I would be in breach of the APA's doctrine on the use of case study. Yet if I used fully fictionalized characters, this would no longer be an account of their experiences.

Truman Capote has been credited with creating the nonfiction novel by blending the facts of the situation with novelized circumstances in his classic *In Cold Blood*. This was a wonderful addition to the literary world, but I do not have the same opportunity as Mr. Capote. The details and identities of his main characters, Richard Hickock and

Perry Smith, were public and utilized in the book. In *American Snake Pit*, the main characters (excluding myself, of course) are people whose identities must remain veiled.

Yet exposure is my goal. Derogatory terms such as idiot, moron, imbecile, and retard (once used as actual medical and psychological categories for people with intellectual disabilities) have always occupied a marginalized place in humanity. Over the past thirty-five years I have engaged in the training, consultation and writing of people with intellectual disabilities. These early experiences led to the development of the first book on psychotherapy published by the APA, which was used internationally as a guide for treatment. This is not to diminish the great strides made by the use of medication and behavior management techniques—these have made wonderful improvements in the lives of individuals who have been marginalized—but it does serve to allow meaningful interaction between individuals with severe cognitive and psychiatric disabilities which, as researchers have been able to demonstrate, make lasting and important therapeutic changes in individuals' lives.

I now teach positive psychology at Columbia University in New York City and work for Marty Seligman, father of positive psychology at the University of Pennsylvania in the Master of Applied Positive Psychology program. In these capacities, I work with students to understand what is possible, what allows for hope, and what makes people flourish. My goal in this book has been the same as my other, more academic writings: to increase awareness and understanding of the needs of these individuals by highlighting our similarities rather than differences—and to learn from their extraordinary examples of resilience, hope, grit, compassion and triumph of the human spirit. They are my teachers, exemplars of human potential. They have inspired me deeply, and sharing their courage and transformation with you is my reason for writing this book.

Thank you, Richie, for having the courage to be you, and for helping me become a better person.

Sophia

"I think that particularly at Willowbrook, we have a situation that borders on a snake pit."
—Robert Kennedy, 1965

I never tasted another person's blood before Sophia's.

She emerged from behind the dresser naked, destroying everything in her path, her body marked with jagged keloid scars and burns, a geography of abuse by those who came before me.

Like me, they had also claimed they were there to help.

Sophia used her bare hands and feet to demolish a dresser drawer by kicking and pushing down the sides. It felt like watching an animal dig a shelter to live in. She grunted, panted, ripped apart the wood, and shredded clothes that had been in the drawers. Littered with debris, the room appeared as if a grenade had gone off. One hadn't, but a detonation was coming.

It startled her when I opened the door. She growled and turned away. As I moved into the room, I called to her.

"Sophia, it's okay. Do you remember me?"

Her wiry body seemed an odd combination of raw power and poor muscle tone. She bent toward the dresser and reached down to grab it, the whole thing, with her right hand on the bottom and her left hand holding the top frame where the first two drawers had been. She lifted the five-drawer dresser. I could see the strain in her muscles. Her body looked as if someone had placed iron cables inside pastry dough. She turned toward me, her front covered by self-inflicted wounds: cuts, bruises, punctures, and burns. The largest scar—a discolored, vulgar slash—crossed her heart between her scarred breasts, which were too large for her five-foot, one-hundred-pound frame. They hung down in front of her like distended water balloons. I took in a sharp breath that made a slight sucking noise, a startle-response to the grotesque.

Her strength was a marvel to witness. She let out a long growl and pulled the dresser back toward her, and up over her head. The remaining drawers came out of their tracks, hitting her. The bottom drawer rested on the inside of her right arm, and she rotated toward me, our eyes connecting. I'd seen this look with other patients. A psychotic episode was well underway, and her eyes were engorged and bloodshot. Her black curly hair provided a frame to contain the rage in her eyes. Her breathing was shallow, but harsh, and I half expected to see steam come out her nostrils. She held the dresser above her head and bent her knees. With one long push and grunt, she heaved it toward me.

As it came at me in slow motion, my academic life felt more irrelevant than ever. Every syllabus from every psychology course I'd taken flashed into my brain to no avail. No class had covered this situation. I knew what to do if someone was uncooperative while taking an IQ test; I could handle a child who didn't want to talk during a therapy session; I could mediate an argument that broke out between two inpatients. But no course syllabus included "How to Subdue a Violent Naked Woman."

I wasn't fully inside the room, so protecting myself was the easy part. I stepped back and pulled the door within an inch of its frame. The dresser landed with a dull cracking sound, facedown, behind the door, and I watched Sophia for a moment through the opening. Eventually, I pushed the door and I could feel the weight of the dresser against it. As I stepped inside the room, I could see that Sophia had already destroyed the clothes hanging in the wall closet behind me.

"Sophia, it's okay. You're safe here. This is your home," I said, as clearly as possible without screaming.

Sophia's breathing became rapid, her eyes darted, and she took short, halting steps like a caged animal. I couldn't imagine what she was planning.

She turned away from me, facing the window. I felt glad the institute replaced all the windows with plexiglass—this was exactly why. A decorative railing outside provided triple reinforcement to prevent any possibility of someone falling or jumping out. Sophia faced the window and for a split second calmed herself. I'd also seen this with others—the time during the rage in which everything stops momentarily before escalating beyond comprehension.

She stood about four feet from the window and made a twisting motion with her body, hurling her fist, like a torpedo, into the plexiglass. It cracked at the point of impact, and Sophia's fist, wrist, and elbow went through not one, but both panes. Her bleeding was immediate and profuse.

I instinctively ran toward her—exactly the wrong thing to do. Sophia looked over her left shoulder at me, and I saw her fear mixed with rage. She pulled, tugged, and yanked her arm, but it was stuck in the plexiglass and, since it didn't shatter, the rigid edges grabbed hold of her flesh. I tried to grab her shoulders to prevent her from pulling, but my action made her more agitated, and she made repeated, frantic attempts to free herself. Finally, with one violent jerk, she tore her arm free.

Her veins became fountains of blood, and she grunted and breathed heavily. Nothing I did calmed her. Blood, more than I had ever seen in my life, gushed out of her. I tried to reach for her arm and it splattered into my face. My leather jacket, white shirt, and light blue tie were saturated, and I could feel the salty thickness of her blood in my mouth. She pulled away from me and tried to run out of the room, but the dresser now blocked the door. She grunted and shook her arm, as one does after banging a finger with a hammer, and blood spattered onto the walls, floor, and ceiling. I couldn't catch her, and the thought occurred to me that anyone watching this scene—a man in a shirt and tie chasing a naked woman around a room that had been the scene of obvious violence—would conclude that I, not she, was the person responsible for the bloodshed. When I got too close, Sophia hit the right side of my head with her arm, and I could feel the blood settle in my ear. At one point, I had to wipe my eyes because I couldn't see.

I had my back to the door and didn't realize someone had entered. A small, stocky woman straight-armed me with her left arm and bear-hugged Sophia, bringing her to the ground. Sophia was on her back while this woman sat on Sophia's stomach. She grabbed a piece of the clothing from the floor and wrapped Sophia's arm, tourniquet style, as she spoke.

"Sophia, Sophia, Sophia, what did you do? I go to the bathroom for two minutes, and look at this. How did you do this to yourself?"

The woman looked up at the window and quickly surveyed the damage in the room. To my great surprise, Sophia had calmed down and smiled. The woman kept her hand on Sophia's right arm and spoke to me. "She's going to need a lot of stitches. Who are you? What are you doing here?"

I found a clean part of my shirt and wiped blood from my face. "My name is Dan. I'm the new manager for this program."

"Dr. Dan," she said. "I heard about you. Welcome to Walden House. You're the expert on how to work with folks like Sophia."

"I'm not actually a doctor yet, and I sure don't know about the expert thing."

"I'm Taimi." She took her hand off Sophia's arm and extended it toward me. "Nice to meet you. First day on the job, eh?" She still held onto my hand.

"Yeah." I surveyed my jacket, shirt, and tie.

"You know what I think your first official duty will be?"

"What's that?"

"Call 911 and tell them to get an ambulance here—and quick."

I ran out the door and down the stairs. I stopped abruptly at the landing and ran back up, just as quickly, to the room. Taimi was gently wrapping Sophia's arm with clothing to soak up the blood. I was out of breath.

"What's the address?"

Taimi lifted her eyebrows and cocked her head. "Just tell them to come to the group home for the Willowbrook inmates. Believe me, everyone in town knows who, and where, we are."

Incurables

The 1960s were a time of liberation from oppression. The generations before us, our parents and grandparents, had set the bar high. They defeated Hitler and released the inmates from concentration camps like Dachau, dropped the A-bomb on Nagasaki and Hiroshima to end World War II, and conquered diseases like polio through rigorous medical science.

All of these challenges were from the outside: foreign dictators, distant enemies, and devious viruses that would have to be defended against and defeated. But our challenges as the baby boomers would come from within: husbands, sons, and brothers returning from Vietnam were ostracized; mothers, daughters, and sisters universally subjugated by not having equal rights; and those among us with mental illness, chemical imbalance, or developmental delay were locked away in institutions to be abused and forgotten.

The fight against the Vietnam War and the struggle for returning veterans took place in the streets, on university campuses, and on TV. The women's liberation movement took place in the car, at the kitchen table, and in the bedroom. But the other war was much more localized. The revolution happened at one place, a type of hell on earth, in Staten Island, New York—at an institution known as Willowbrook State School. But it was never a school of any kind, and it grew to become more like a concentration camp. Sophia was the first, but there would be six other very challenging people coming to live with her. Some would come from the community, some from other institutions. But all of them would come to this experimental group home, Walden House, because of the neglect, abuse, mismanagement, mistreatment, and deaths that happened at Willowbrook.

It was bad right from the start, and controversy and misery hung over the campus like a stalled cyclone. The 375-acre campus was designed in 1938 and built over the next four years for the objective of housing intellectually disabled children. Yet the needs of returning veterans from World War II usurped this intention, and it was converted into a US Army hospital through 1947. The New York State Department of Mental Hygiene then reclaimed it for its original purpose—but only after a series of bitter negotiations. Over the next four years the veterans left, and in April 1951 it was given its name—Willowbrook State School. No one then would have imagined it would be uttered in the same breath as Auschwitz and Dachau.

The official capacity was for 2,950 residents, but within four years, over 3,600 were crammed inside its walls. By 1963, it had become the largest state facility of its kind in the United States, forcing over 6,000 residents into a space for 4,275. Imagine being in a space designed for 100 people—like a subway car—then imagine fifty more people shoved inside with you. But you are not getting off in one or two or ten stops—you are to live together for the rest of your life.

It was also understaffed (at one point with nearly one thousand vacant jobs) and medical personnel were composed largely of refugee physicians from Hitler's Germany and third-world countries. In 1964, a New York legislative committee toured the facility and was horrified at the abuse, neglect, and "vile stench." Their confidential report highlighted the cruelties and mismanagement, but it wasn't until the violent deaths, which all took place in the first half of 1965, that the institution made the news. A man and, later, a ten-year-old boy, were scalded to death by a shower as a result of poor plumbing and unsophisticated attendants. One resident died from a punch in the throat by another inmate, and a twelve-year-old strangled himself struggling to get free from a restraining device. These deaths and the resulting concerns made it into the local paper.

In the fall of that year, the charismatic Robert Kennedy, then US senator from New York, showed up unannounced. He saw firsthand the conditions and told the press, "I think that particularly at Willowbrook, we have a situation that borders on a snake pit . . . living in filth and dirt, their clothing in rags, in rooms less comfortable and cheerful than the cages in which we put animals in a zoo." It is from this quote that this book gets its name—yet it is the resilience of the human spirit to transcend these conditions for which it was written.

Although the bad press activated the politicians, the conditions actually got worse, not better. How did seemingly good intentions and responsiveness go awry? Treatment goals were the problem. The biases and medical model used by psychiatrists at that time in history shaped how the people of Willowbrook were viewed. The psychiatrists' approach created an environment and a treatment protocol that fueled systemic abuse and neglect and eclipsed a more client-centered method. A physician with limited resources was taught to triage patients by separating acute from chronic, treatable from untreatable, and, for practical purposes, those for which there was hope—from those considered hopeless. Psychiatrists were looking to gain status in the medical profession at that time and felt they had to do as their physician colleagues did. Under this prevailing attitude, Willowbrook had become a repository for chronic patients. Other state institutions jettisoned the worst of their inmates by discharging them there. As one historian put it, Willowbrook had become "a dumping ground, receiving discards as in a draw poker game."

The distinction between the potential for rehabilitation and the need for custodial care informed psychiatrists' treatment decisions. This approach was translated into a "solution" by politicians. Then-governor Nelson Rockefeller and the New York State Department of Mental Hygiene revealed a plan and a budget for a 1965 Comprehensive Mental Health and Mental Retardation Program, touting it as "the most comprehensive and extensive in the nation." It looked like a response to the mess at Willowbrook by preaching to provide high-end treatment for those able to profit from it, and better, more humane institutions for those who couldn't.

However, $500 million of the allocated $600 million immediately went into the construction of new buildings and state schools. These facilities were identified for use to help those for whom there was hope. But the money, almost all of it by the time it was spent, went for construction and trade jobs—not for providing direct services. By 1969, most of the buildings had been built, but nothing got better in Willowbrook: no better custodial care, no better treatment, and no better staff.

The overcrowding, insufficient and poorly trained workforce, and prevailing insolent attitude that the lower-functioning residents should get only custodial care was still dominant. This added to excessively high absenteeism and low morale among the staff. Not a dime was given for improving care. With the attitude, the lack of funds, and the illusion that the problem was being addressed, Willowbrook sank to the bottom of humanity. It became nothing more than a warehouse for the "incurables."

However, two physicians tried to change all that. Dr. Michael Wilkins and his friend, psychiatrist William Bronston, joined the staff and systematically began reporting the deplorable conditions to the director, Dr. Jack Hammond, along with specific plans for improvement. Instead of a cooperative response and proactive leadership, Wilkins and Bronston found Hammond defensive, ignoring their written and in-person reports.

The unresponsive and uncaring reactions sparked a reaction. The two activists now possessed very clear goals, nationally and locally. At the national level, they fought to get the U.S. out of Vietnam. At the local level, they worked to transform Willowbrook.

In 1971, New York State imposed a job freeze on the Division of Mental Health (DMH). As a result, staff members who quit were not replaced. At one point, there were twice as many openings as there were nurses at Willowbrook and the institution remained unable to hold on to custodial staff. The cuts in the New York state budget were directly linked to the skyrocketing cost of the Vietnam War. Wilkins and Bronston wanted to fight back as the war literally took food out of the mouths of the inmates and clothes off their backs. Bullets, tanks, guns, and mortars were made from the trust fund meant for human dignity.

Just as the various moments of the sixties worked to unite blacks and whites as brothers, and all women as sisters, Wilkins and Bronston hoped to bring physicians, social workers, nurses, and unskilled direct-care workers together as "health care workers." They wanted to be the Willowbrook delegates to the annual state medical convention and tried to galvanize support for their perspective. They attempted to rally the Willowbrook doctors to improve the conditions of the institution by "upgrading all employees' status, wages, working conditions, and service skills." They attempted to unite physicians to denounce the cutbacks causing the freeze and to embrace this new point of view about everyone being part of a larger whole and being a "health care worker." They also asked their fellow physicians to "call for the immediate withdrawal of all US troops from Southeast Asia."

They were ignored and then alienated by their fellow physicians. Undaunted, Wilkins and Bronston took their platform to the parent association of Willowbrook, the Benevolent Society. They found partners with a few social workers (Ira Fischer, Elizabeth Lee, and Tim Casey) and were offered help from Mary Feldt and her husband, Robert, who was then head of the Staten Island Legal Aid Society.

The Benevolent Society began demonstrations to protest the cuts by the DMH and heated up the demands against Hammond, even threatening lawsuits. Hammond responded by trying to intimidate Wilkins and Bronston by forbidding them to hold any meeting with parents on the campus. He also began questioning an inmate, Bernard Carabello, about his involvement with the physicians. The intent was to create a scandal by implying there was a homosexual relationship between Wilkins and Carabello. The strategy backfired when the story of the interrogation was leaked to the press, and the Legal Aid Society got involved. The parents of the children in Willowbrook were outraged. By December 1971, they were protesting regularly.

At Willowbrook. Hammond couldn't deal with all the protests. On January 5th, he unceremoniously fired Wilkins and Elizabeth Lee.

The next day, Wilkins, still undaunted, called another activist friend whom he'd worked with in the sixties at a charity treating children with lead poisoning. His friend was a lawyer who provided legal advice when Wilkins offered free medical consultations. Now his friend, Geraldo Rivera, was a TV news reporter and Wilkins thought Rivera might be interested in doing a story. He was.

"What conditions?" asked Rivera.

"In my building," said Wilkins, "there are sixty retarded kids with only one attendant to take care of them. Most are naked and they lie in their own shit."

Wilkins met Rivera at a diner on January 6 and gave him the keys to his building. They illegally slipped a camera crew inside a building on the grounds of Willowbrook and within ten minutes they were in and out. The videos were aired on the New York Channel 7 news and the atrocities captured by the images created a public outcry that shoved the legal system into action. The news reports became the basis of the Willowbrook Consent Decree, a major contributing factor to the passage of the Civil Rights of Institutionalized Persons Act of 1980.

This was the point in US history when mental health treatment became a civil right. Before Willowbrook, the right to treatment for mental health issues wasn't considered important enough for society's investment. People could be treated as poorly or as well as the authorities would allow—and protection for the most vulnerable among us wasn't a consideration. What would be learned from Willowbrook is that when people are given a chance to feel safe and the opportunity to learn, they can thrive. Oddly enough, these opportunities would cost only a percentage of what it was to leave people untreated in the deplorable conditions of a poorly run institution.

The tragic impressions informed Americans about how evil replaces indifference: the public and lawmakers were both disgusted and motivated. In the end it would take more than twenty years, and over one hundred court hearings, to bring lasting changes.

But there were other problems. Deinstitutionalization, the effort to help people with mental illness move out of institutions into the community, didn't always have the high-profile legal and financial backing of the Willowbrook Decree. When people were moved out of institutions without follow-up and follow-along service, rates of homelessness increased, as did the rates of crime and joblessness. It was estimated that approximately one-third of the homeless were people with mental illness. The cost for institutionalization for taxpayers was high, and the quality of life for the inhabitants was low. But simply getting people out of institutions doesn't improve lives or the bottom line. Getting them out into viable community placements and training programs does. Deinstitutionalization didn't cause homelessness or criminal activity, but how it was carried out often did. In other words, dumping people into communities without training and services to help them had the potential to make things worse, not better.

Because of these issues, there were mixed reactions in New York during the late 1970s. People wanted to help, as long as "those people" weren't going to live in their neighborhoods. Deinstitutionalization was a noble concept, but neighborhoods bristled at the thought of the intellectually and psychiatrically disabled living next door. Some communities had stronger reactions than others. In a few instances where group homes were opening, townspeople tried to burn the homes down.

But those who wanted to help didn't have many tools. The very young science of psychology only offered some rudimentary behavioral techniques to help habilitate people into the community, and psychiatrists during this time regularly engaged in something called overshadowing, a term coined by Dr. Steven Reiss to describe how intellectual disabilities cause other symptoms of mental illness to be overlooked. Rather than try to properly diagnose and treat, the heavy tranquilizers prescribed for people moving into the community were little more than chemical restraints. But the decree demanded that the process continue.

By 1979, those patients from Willowbrook with the best-perceived chance of success in the community had moved out years earlier. These were people with lesser disabilities and the highest capacity for learning. The second wave out needed many services to function beyond the hospital. These patients struggled with coexisting intellectual and psychiatric disabilities, trouble seeing and hearing, and difficulty with, or no capacity for, speech. Little was known about how to work with such severely disabled individuals, but the hope was that the combination of behavioral techniques and psychotropic medicine would help them lead more productive and meaningful lives. As this was happening, a handful of unique experimental group homes were funded by the Young Adult Institute (YAI), one of the major human service agencies serving people with intellectual disabilities in New York City, to help with the deinstitutionalization. These homes were set up to work with "the worst of the worst." The residents selected for these homes were people with overwhelming physical, psychiatric, and intellectual disabilities for whom there was little hope of living outside the walls of an institution. But, again, because of the decree, an effort had to be made to move them into the community. The idea was to determine what the residents needed and whether it could be provided. However, the stakes were high. If we could demonstrate that the residents of the home were able to reside in the community, then they would stay out of the institution. If the homes didn't work, they would be re-institutionalized. We were the experiment. Given the circumstances, this was the equivalent of a life-or-death sentence.

No one expected these patients to do well outside of an institution. These individuals had profound intellectual impairments, which meant most had IQs below forty. Statistically, a person like Sophia was as rare as a bona fide genius. The rarity of her condition also involved astounding acts of violence committed to her—and by her.

Sophia was one of the inmates targeted for placement. As the alleged offspring of two inpatients, she was born and raised in Willowbrook. She had never seen the outside world. At twenty-eight years old, she would be the first resident to come to the experimental group home from that institution. Her history included being raped in the institution by other inmates, and even by orderlies. It is also very likely that she had to fight off Andre Rand, an orderly assigned to her building. It was later discovered that Rand was a convicted child kidnapper and murderer who had buried one of his victims in a shallow grave on the grounds.

Sophia wasn't always the victim. She could be combative and assaultive. She learned to fight off her attackers by tapping into her rage. She also had a variety of self-inflicted wounds. One of these came about when she tipped over a large kettle of boiling water onto herself. In another instance, she stabbed herself in the chest with a knife she had wrestled away from an attacker. Fragments of information suggested she was often straitjacketed or, as one chart entry described, "chemically restrained." It appeared they flooded her system with Thorazine, a major tranquilizer, so she couldn't hurt herself or others. Sophia qualified as one of those beyond hope—as did all the others coming to the home.

The lessons from Willowbrook are important because they follow a pattern that happens repeatedly in our society. Psychologist Phil Zimbardo has dubbed this pattern "The Lucifer Effect." Institutions slowly become a place where evil is an accepted practice. Like the Holocaust, the My Lai Massacre in Vietnam, mass suicides in Guyana by the People's Temple, the Branch Davidians in Texas, and the torture of Iraqi prisoners by US soldiers at Abu Ghraib, evil has a slow and insidious process of becoming culture. Little by little, Willowbrook had become a place where evil triumphed and the "incurables" were beyond hope.

All we had to do was prove they were wrong.

Dan

Carrying the last box out to the pickup truck, I felt the unevenness of the frozen mud. The unpaved road suited my wife and me when we moved in. It was one of the things we sacrificed when finding a cheap place to live in the wilds of New Jersey. But this night, the mud mixed with unbearable cold becoming grotesque sculptures of frozen dirt. Each uncertain step shook loose another tear. The air itself seemed frozen.

I shoved the box in the back and heard the guitar twang as it jostled. I should have worn gloves. Pushing the tailgate up and the cap door down, I locked them. Looking back at the cottage, I saw her—like a window-display mannequin. A motionless shadowy figure frozen in the night, watching.

The truck whined about being started—it didn't want to go. On the third try it sputtered alive and I sat watching my breath fill up the cab. As the windows fogged, I turned on the headlights, revealing a labyrinth of frozen tire marks. At best, I could see thirty feet in front of me—a short tunnel of light in unforgiving darkness.

My fingers were numb on the steering wheel. As I bounced down the road, the headlights guided me to the paved intersection. I put on the left blinker. At two in the morning, there was no traffic, but I wasn't ready to make the turn. After a while, I moved the lever all the way up and the other blinker began. Finally, I moved the control back to the middle, and let my ice-cold hands cover my eyes and tears. A slow, deep laugh began in my stomach. Who was I signaling to? I stepped on the gas and turned the wheel to the left. I was on the way—thirty feet at a time.

I found my way to the A-1, a cheap, seedy motel that boasted hourly rates and free but excessively watered-down coffee. The clientele were the unsavory, the unfaithful, and the unemployed. Paranoid that someone would break into my room during the day, I packed everything I owned and stuffed it into the back of my red Toyota pickup. This way I could drive while keeping an eye on my life in the rearview mirror. This was how I arrived at Walden House when I met Sophia.

The hourly-rate sex-athon people prevented much sleep, and two weeks in I hit the $500 limit on my MasterCard. My new paychecks went to my old address, and cash dwindled at an alarming rate. As a doctoral student in psychology in my final year, I was flat broke. I tried not to panic, but I knew if I didn't eat at the group home, I wouldn't have eaten at all.

When I got the job at Walden House, I became part of a select group of managers chosen by YAI to run these homes. YAI was taking the most ambitious approach to working with residents. The new managers were all trained in psychology and had significant experience in the field. The interviews for these positions were done in stages: a résumé was submitted, followed by a telephone interview.

Then came an invitation for an in-person interview and a tour. First, we went to see a ward at Willowbrook, the feeder for many of our group home residents. Following this, we visited an existing YAI day program. The ward at Willowbrook smelled of urine and was filled with half-naked people who functioned like zombies. No staff greeted us, and it looked like a poorly run prison camp. In contrast, at YAI a number of staff sat with people at different tables helping them create artwork. The clients, or participants, as the staff liked to call them, were showered and dressed in clean clothes. It was more like a well-run school than the Auschwitz-like Willowbrook. YAI earned the reputation for being the leader in moving intellectually disabled residents into the community. They had taken on the challenge. With the money available, they set out to place the inmates with the most difficulties into the community. YAI was eons ahead of what we were doing in New Jersey.

I had been a program manager for a sheltered workshop for adults with severe and profound intellectual disabilities in Haledon, New Jersey, and I was familiar with developing work skills for people who had never worked. The program offered nothing more than the basics: we helped people listen better, develop social skills, and learn routine tasks. YAI, in contrast, was developing intensive client-centered training programs. They had been getting good results, and were now willing to put their effort toward the more difficult cases.

The final stage in the interview process surprised me—a group interview. The facilitator, Gerry (who would later become a wise confidant and friend) met with a dozen or so of the prospective managers. We had been selected to participate in the interview from about two hundred or so applicants. We met in the home at the appointed time and were given a brief tour. Although it wasn't a competition, it quickly turned into something like one of those quiz shows where people tried to be the first to answer. They had us introduce ourselves and asked questions: "How would you handle a participant who didn't want to eat dinner when it was served?" "How would you discipline a client who tried to strike you?" "What if you found two residents kissing in one of their bedrooms?"

Each question was posed to the group and the answers started: "If they don't eat when dinner is served, they don't eat," said one. "I'd bring their dinner plate to them," said another. "I'd check to see if they were medically okay," offered someone else. My take was different: "Is the cook any good?"

Humor had always been my strong suit. It was almost always my first line of thought in answering the questions, but I backed it up with something reasonable. After the laughter died down, I suggested: "If the cook was decent, I would let the resident know they were welcome when they felt ready, but I would make sure a staff person was assigned to keep an eye on them while we ate."

When it came to the question about kissing, some of the answers surprised me: "I'd tell them to stop," said a respondent. "I'd schedule them for sex education as soon as I could," explained another. "I'd ask the one who wasn't supposed to be in that room to leave," someone said. This was followed by a candidate saying, "I disagree with that. I'd only ask one to leave if they were the same sex." I could now see the wisdom of YAI using a group interview. It gave the applicants a chance to reveal their thinking, their skills, and their prejudices. I proposed, "If it was clear that neither of them were being coerced, I'd apologize and close the door."

That night they offered me the job.

Several factors brought me to the interview for the position. My marriage had fallen apart and my financial circumstances were dismal. I needed more money to pay for the separation, living expenses, books, and tuition. Because of my experience and candidacy, I essentially talked myself into the higher-paying position of managing the home. While I may have been the most qualified for the position, I didn't have any real knowledge of what the job entailed. The only consolation was that no one else did either. I was breaking away from a life that no longer worked, but "away" became my only goal. I had no idea toward what.

In many ways, I mirrored our country. We were all still moving away from the scars of the Vietnam War, away from the scourge of Richard Nixon and Watergate. Away from the massacre at the Olympics, away from the Arab oil embargo and skyrocketing gas prices. We were still trying to figure out what to do about Three Mile Island, and how to deal with the aftermath of the images broadcast by Rivera. As a society, we were trying to leave behind what was no longer working, and move toward the unknown.

My journey into psychology was fueled by a deep realization in college, then in graduate school, that I had few other talents. These deficiencies caused my first wife's parents to be uniquely disappointed when their only daughter married me. Her family came from a long line of tradesmen, and when she picked me her parents seemed to go into a period of mourning that lasted our entire marriage. My father-in-law was a master carpenter, and my mother-in-law was a master cleaner, cleaning her home to perfection several times a day. To them I was a perpetual college student who only wanted to work with the unsavory side of humanity. Not only did they despise my goals, they never understood why I would spend good money on graduate school, never mind a PhD.

Her parents tried to coax me into using my hands to make an honest living. This was as foreign to me as graduate school was to them. I explained that my toolbox consisted of a butter knife, a credit card, and a sledgehammer, but they insisted. Reluctantly, I agreed to take the aptitude test for the plumbers' union. This was a sad day for all concerned. The results indicated that I should be able to fill a tub without assistance, but needed supervision when flushing a toilet.

My father-in-law had built his own home and was a perfectionist. He offered to take me on one of his side jobs to teach me the basics of carpentry. I explained that I wasn't as adept in carpentry as I was in plumbing, but he wouldn't take no for an answer. One Saturday morning I went with him to a large home he was framing. On this day I would help him lay down the plywood flooring. I desperately wanted approval from him, but knew the day was doomed from the moment we got coffee. We stopped by a Dunkin' Donuts, and I offered to pay. He was giving me ten dollars an hour, big money in 1978, and I figured my offer would put me on his good side, if he had one. He was very particular about his order: black coffee with three sugars, two jelly donuts and a Boston cream. I have no idea where this food went when he ate it. Ray was as thin as a rail, yet ate like a horse. He never touched alcohol, but smoked like a chimney, and everything in life was good or bad, black or white. Gray and beige were not part of his color scheme.

I didn't know they had already added sugar to the coffee, so I added three more packets. When I gave it to him, he spit it out, took the Lord's name in vain, and told me, "You couldn't pour water out of a boot if the directions were on the heel."

He was right.

I helped him carry the plywood into the house. Not much of a problem. Then came the art of hammering. In the time it took Ray to nail down fifteen sheets of plywood, I was still gently tapping a single nail on my first piece. I hit the nail twenty or thirty times while holding the hammer near its head. The nail would bend; I would pull it out and start all over again. Ray hit each nail twice: the first to center it, the second to bury it. He held the hammer at the very end to maximize the power of its strike. When he saw me trifling away with my tapping, he came over to give me a lesson.

"Stop," he said.

"What's the matter?" I asked, not wanting to know.

"You've got to do it faster if we're going to get finished today," he said.

"Okay," I said, holding the top of my hammer.

"Hold it down here," he said, grabbing the bottom of my handle. "Then grab the point of the nail and put it on the wood like this." He demonstrated. "Then bang it once." He slammed the hammer down squarely on the nail and it went in three quarters of the way. "Then finish it off," he said. And with another bang, he flattened the nail into the plywood.

"Right," I said, knowing there was no chance in hell I could do that.

I steadied the nail with the thumb and index finger of my left hand. When Ray held his nail, it seemed as if he could have willed it into the wood with his bare fingers. The nail behaved as if it had no choice but to stay straight and do exactly what it was told. When I held my nail, it immediately affected an attitude, and behaved more like cooked spaghetti than a piece of steel. I grasped the hammer down near the end of the handle and was amazed at how unsteady I was. The hammer quivered as I raised it, and when I brought it down it missed the nail altogether. I laughed; Ray shook his head. On my second attempt the nail flew from my fingers and across the room. Ray took the Lord's name in vain again.

I got another nail, steadied it, and whacked it about halfway in. But on my second smack the nail bent in half, and went crooked into the plywood. Ray told me to pry it out, get another nail, and try again. When I turned the hammer around to attack the nail, I squiggled the claw underneath it and yanked as hard as I could. The head of the nail snapped off. Ray turned around and walked away. It was the first—and only—time we worked together.

Since the nineteen dollars a day at the A-1 had become prohibitively expensive, two weeks into my new job I began looking for another temporary solution. I considered living at the group home, but I was supposed to be the new manager, not a new resident. I found a boarding home in Suffern, New York for ten dollars a night. It made the A-1 look like the Plaza, but it was all I could afford.

The spindly two-story, eight-room house leaned to the left. Since my room was upstairs to the right, I considered my presence an opportunity for the structure to become balanced.

Everything in the house was gray. Everything. No white trim anywhere—not on the ceiling, the windowsills, the molding, stairs, or chair rails—perhaps the result of a buy-one-get-six-free sale on battleship gray at Benjamin Moore twelve years prior. The color scheme reflected my mood.

The walls, made of a type of particleboard, were now more particle than board. One sheet of this was all that separated my space from the one next to me. They had partitioned a real room into two so both areas could be rented. My room had a bed and a ceiling bulb dangling from exposed wires—no night table, no chair, no rug, no lamp. The bathroom was down the hall, but it lacked the inspired style of my room. The sink, which the owner said regrettably did not work, had murky brown water in it, and a lid-free toilet with a brown-stained porcelain basin would require maximum motivation to even be considered. A completely rusted-out stall shower caused me to wonder about my most recent tetanus shot, and a sliced-open trash bag duct-taped to the ceiling served as the curtain. Water from the corroded showerhead poured out with the enthusiasm and color of urine, but never achieved similar warmth.

Ms. Grimp, the owner, was sixty-ish, and her body resembled a public mailbox. A cigarette, a permanent appendage, lolled out of the right corner of her mouth, and I imagined she had done the voiceover for Linda Blair in *The Exorcist*. Ms. Grimp's distinctive odor reminded me of a forgotten liverwurst-and-onion sandwich (with mayonnaise) left in my car over a three-day vacation. It was the first thing I thought of when I met her.

The mattress swallowed me whole the first time I lay down on it. I wasn't used to a bed that functioned like a Venus flytrap and feared I might suffocate if I didn't sleep on my back staring at the ceiling bulb. Most of the "guests" were alcoholic men who simply stumbled in during the night and passed out in their personal flytraps.

The guy next to me was there when I moved in. I'd only seen him once, walking—well, staggering—toward me on his way from the bathroom, bent and unshaven with doughy eyes. My room was at the very end of the hall and it was not possible for me to walk past him as he caromed off the walls, so I waited until he fell into his room. I doubt he even knew I was there.

He had a horrible cough, with enough phlegm involved to remind me of my old Pontiac, and a long wheeze both before and after the effort. The particleboard provided only a visual barrier and even his slightest sniffle broadcast into my room, down into the canyon of my bed, and into my head. The first two nights were torturous, and I appreciated the brief moments I could drift off temporarily. The intensity and irregularity of his breathing kept me from achieving any serious sleep.

After living there a while, and trying to deal with the setbacks from the first day with Sophia, I thought things might be different. I imagined I'd settle into some kind of routine, but this wasn't the case. It was all over town that the new resident had been to the hospital. There were rumors that she had tried to kill herself or me. The townspeople were suspicious, and in some cases, openly hostile. Taimi had once tried to fill the agency van at the local gas station and was told they wouldn't accept the agency's credit card and made her pay in cash. Nothing was getting easier.

Running the group interviews in search of new staff became a challenge. Lots of people came, but few seemed to possess the disposition or skill needed. I also interviewed new residents so I could learn about their history and disabilities. They had uniquely difficult challenges. The job had become all-consuming.

At the end of one of those days, I felt particularly exhausted. The accumulated catastrophes in my life had reached a critical mass and I felt certain I could let my bed devour me and finally get some sleep. I took a tetanus-phobic shower, and twirled under the dribbling showerhead. After drying off on the other side of the Hefty bag, I walked back down the hall to help balance the structure and ensure the house would stay standing another day. I put on a pair of shorts and let myself be seduced and munched on by my mattress.

Within minutes my elusive roommate moaned in the hallway. His shuffle seemed even more hesitant and exaggerated than the previous nights. I listened as he flopped down on his bed. It sounded as if he had fallen from an airplane onto the beach. He was out.

I waited for the onslaught of phlegm, but all I could hear was shallow breathing, as if he were blowing up a small balloon. It must have lulled me to sleep.

The heavy footsteps and radio voices of the police woke me up. A red light swirled through the room—clearly an emergency. Maybe the house was on fire, maybe a break-in, maybe someone had lost his mind and walked all the way to the left end of the hallway, tipping the house over. Whatever it was, it was serious, and I hopped, or tried to hop, out of bed.

It was as if I were in the deep end of a swimming pool filled with cotton. In my anxiety, I thrashed around trying to step up and out of the bed. I felt like Elmer Fud waking up to a trap set by Bugs Bunny. Finally, I calmed myself, lay back down, and rolled out of the bed onto the floor as I had learned to do in the mornings. As I opened my door, a cop barked into his handheld, "We're just letting the paramedics do their thing, but he'll be DOA."

Two EMS technicians jockeyed a gurney into the man's room.

"Looks like he suffocated in the bed somehow, maybe a heart attack, I don't know," he continued.

"What's happening?" I asked.

The cop looked at me with a bit of puzzlement. I don't think he expected a younger, sober man to be staying there. "The guy next door stopped breathing. I think he's dead."

"Was he face down in the bed?"

"Yeah, you know they'll do an autopsy. Sometimes these alkies choke on their own vomit and suffocate in their sleep."

"And sometimes they get eaten by a Venus flytrap." I turned back to my room.

It was time to go. Taimi and Sophia were asleep when I got to the group home, so I left a note in the office explaining I came in early, and that I was upstairs, taking a shower, getting ready for my appointment with the town fire chief.

I took my duffle bag into the bathroom and turned on the water. It was perfectly warm, the temperature regulated by a device designed to keep the residents from scalding themselves. I found a fresh bar of soap and two large terrycloth towels on the towel bar. A small crucifix mounted to the back of the bathroom door watched over me and, as I stepped into the shower, the surge of heat on my body inexplicably overwhelmed me. I wept in the sanctuary of the steam and the ritual of cleansing.

I was home.

Albert

My room, painted a cream-colored pastel, carried the feel of a monastic life. Thick oak moldings framed a single bed, nightstand, and small sink next to a stall shower. A closet with a heavy oak door, a brass doorknob, and a single six-drawer dresser completed the furnishings. As with every bedroom, a large wooden cross hung on the wall at the foot of the bed. Yet even with the cross watching over me, I often woke up disoriented. I would lie in bed and look around until I could get my bearings. To ground myself, I hung my favorite quote attributed to Thoreau on the wall alongside the bed: "Go confidently in the direction of your dreams. Live the life you have imagined." It seemed to help.

Sophia was our first resident, but six more would be joining us over the next three months. A few had already been slated, but there was one who needed to be evaluated. I first went to see Albert, a twenty-six-year-old man who had been living in Willowbrook but was transferred to an institution in upstate New York as part of the move to a less restrictive environment.

Most institutions are pretty much the same. Cinderblock walls, while more expensive to build, guarantee that inmates will not kick or punch holes requiring repair. High ceilings prevent hangings, furniture bolted to the floor or too heavy to throw keeps the injuries down, and thick plate glass and mesh screens with black wrought-iron railings prevent escape while giving only the slightest suggestion of natural light.

The institution wanted Albert to leave. He was one of the nasty ones. He was nonverbal, violent, and had a disorder known as pica, in which the patient has a desire to eat substances not meant for consumption. Albert was particularly fond of light bulbs: over the past thirteen months, he had eaten twenty-seven of them.

On the day of our meeting there were eight of us: three psychiatrists (two male and one female), two psychiatric nurses (one male and one female), a female psychiatric social worker, and a male psychologist. They were meeting with one purpose in mind: to convince me that Albert would be better off in our experimental program than in their institution. They had had it with him, and it would save the institution over $60,000 if they could get him out into the community. Their job was to sell me on Albert.

My job was to see if we could handle him.

The meeting was in a private room. These were my post-hippie days, but I still had longish hair and a beard. Since I, and everyone else from the 1960s, was going to save the whole damn world, I thought I would start with people with cognitive impairments and work my way to the normal folks. I was very casually dressed. I no longer wore a tie after the Sophia episode, and I didn't want one of the inmates to follow through on their fantasies of choking a psychologist. But I wore my brown leather jacket, which was now sporting darkened stains following Sophia's initiation. It was my way of being professional, but not stuffy. If I had worn my usual denim jacket, I knew they wouldn't have taken me seriously. The leather jacket was, by far, the most expensive piece of clothing I owned, and I treasured it, not just because of the expense, but because it was a symbol that I was a professional. I could still have long hair and a beard, but with a leather jacket, even with its Rorschach-style blots, I would get some respect. At least that was the story I told myself.

I was also careful not to wear any jewelry. I'd already heard horror stories of staff choked by their own necklaces, or having their earrings yanked out. I was never much for jewelry anyway. In fact, the only piece I'd ever worn was my wedding ring. But that was no longer a problem. It had been weeks since I'd left Suzanne, our dog Shamu, and my wedding ring behind. Everything was happening very fast, and in the last month it had been the end of the world as I knew it. They say when God closes a door, he opens a window. In my case, he opened a group home.

We sat in this room and they gave me years of charts on Albert. He was a peculiar little guy—only about five feet four inches, but he was wiry and remarkably fit. He was what they called an elective mute, meaning that he could talk, but usually chose not to, and the pica thing was extraordinary. The list of things he had eaten went on for three pages. As I mentioned, light bulbs were his favorite (particularly the 60-watt variety), but he also enjoyed 3x5 cards, pencils, pieces of a ceramic ashtray, matches, a headband, stones, a credit card, coins, stamps, a battery (AA), an assortment of paper clips, a spool of thread, and an earplug. He had been hospitalized at the institution years earlier after an incident in his home where he broke a bird off his father's trophy for sportsmanship, then broke off, and swallowed, the trophy's rifle—apparently to kill the bird. At twenty-six, Albert had already had numerous operations to remove objects from his stomach.

He was my kind of guy.

Nothing in his chart put me off. If you're going to save the world, you have to save everybody, even the people who are trying to eat it.

I didn't want to let them know that I was predisposed to take Albert, so I kept asking for more information. "Are there other conditions I should know about?"

"Well, yes," said the female psychiatrist, "Albert has encopresis and he has a fascination with his feces. He is an anal expulsive type and has, on occasion, smeared his feces on the walls as an expression of either anger or creativity. But I can tell you we have been working with him on that, and I doubt that it will be a major problem for you. It has been over a year since he has had an episode and most of us are of the opinion that we have achieved extinction with that particular type of behavior."

"So you achieved extinction with what stinked," I said.

"Well I wouldn't put it that way, but I do think we have eliminated that behavior."

"No pun intended, right?" I said, being a wise guy.

"No," she said, exasperated, "no pun intended."

I laughed and began writing a note on the yellow pad in front of me.

"Will this be a problem?" she said with concern as she watched me write my note.

"No," I said, "I am just writing down that Albert may be part of an endangered feces."

She didn't smile a bit, but her colleagues gave me a courtesy laugh. How can they take this all so seriously? Anal expulsive? The guy likes to spread crap on the walls and eat light bulbs. How could they not find this at least a bit funny?

The psychologist spoke up.

"Do you know what synesthesia is?"

"Sure," I said. "Very rare. It's when someone has a cross-modal perspective of the world. They hear flavors and feel colors, something like that, right?"

"Right, something like that," he said.

"And some people have this incredibly heightened ability, like their hearing or their sense of smell or something like that is way beyond what most humans can do. I think I remember something like that, very rare, though."

"Yes, very rare."

"Why, do you have someone here who has that?" I said with excitement.

"Would you like to see a sample of Albert's synesthesia?" he said. "He has something peculiar, we think it is a type of olfactory/personification form, but we're not sure. It might simply be hyperosmia . . ."

"What is that?" I interrupted.

"An abnormally increased sense of smell," he responded.

"Oh," I said. "What is it that he can do?"

"Let me show you," he said, knowing he had my full attention.

I had only read about this condition and at the time it was considered a rare phenomenon. I thought the chance to see it in action was a great opportunity. I was definitely drawn to the bizarre and unusual. This would give me a chance to add to the growing list of conditions I'd seen firsthand.

They had it planned as a way of enticing me to work with Albert. The psychologist took out a new package of pencils and was careful to open the cellophane without touching them. He scattered them on the table in front of me by using his pen to separate and move them away from one another.

"Let me invite you to pick one pencil and hold it in your hand for a moment, and I am going to invite everyone else to do the same thing."

Each member of the team reached over and grabbed a pencil. It was clear they had done this before and each had a telling smirk on his or her face. I picked up one of the pencils and held it.

"Now, if you would," he said, "place the pencil on the table and we will line them up about three inches from one another."

I put my pencil down and was encouraged to remember which one was mine.

"I am going to invite Albert in and introduce you. I think you will be very interested in seeing what Albert can do," he said.

Mine was third from the right, of the eight pencils in front of me.

One of the other psychiatrists got up and made a call asking for Albert to be brought down to the room. Within minutes a large black man escorted Albert into the room. The orderly was holding Albert's right elbow very lightly, as if he were walking him down the aisle to be seated at a wedding. Albert's other hand was busy: with alternating fingers, he was picking his nose and putting the findings in his mouth.

"Albert, this is Dr. Tomasulo."

"Actually, I don't finish defending my dissertation until—"

The psychologist waved off my disclaimer and spoke to Albert. "Can you say hello?" he said.

As I stood up, Albert pulled his index finger out of his nose and stuck out his left hand to greet me. I remembered how long it took to wash Sophia's blood out of my hair. "How 'bout a high five?" I said, hoping to reduce the risk of actually getting a booger on me, and stuck my right hand up in the air. Albert smiled in a very coy way and arched his left hand back and I zeroed in on touching his palm with mine. He made a high-pitched sound that sounded like he was trying to say hi.

"Nice to meet you," I offered.

Albert was standing, rocking and holding his stomach with his left hand and hooking his right hand behind his neck. He was rocking and moaning slightly as the orderly turned and left. I was completely unprepared for what he did next.

Still rocking, Albert walked over to the table and then abruptly stopped. He smiled, picked up the first pencil and ran it lengthwise under his nose as if he were sampling a Cuban cigar. Then he handed it to the male psychiatrist. Could this be?

He put his hand back on his neck and rocked once, picked up the second pencil, smelled it in the same way, and handed it to the female psychiatrist.

The next one was mine. Albert picked it up, drew in a long, deep breath through his nose, sampling it, and then handed it to me with a smile. Each pencil was aromatically savored, then handed to the proper recipient. Never before, nor since, have I seen such a feat. Albert was, indeed, a unique human being.

At the end of it, Albert stuck his hand out and I flashed eye contact with the psychologist to be sure it would be all right for me to return the gesture. With a brief nod, I was given the OK, and I extended my hand. I had been so thrown off by the amazing demonstration I had forgotten about the snot on his fingers. I shook his hand. He abruptly withdrew it, picked his nose, put his hand back on his neck and began to rock and smile.

"Albert likes you," said the psychologist.

I nodded, still smiling at Albert.

"He doesn't normally extend his hand a second time unless he likes you. He shook your hand and smiled, he definitely likes you."

"Good," I said, feeling a bit uncomfortable that they were talking about Albert like he was a child. "I am very glad to have met you, Albert," I said, trying to make eye contact.

They escorted Albert out of the room and the orderly who had brought him was waiting to take him back to his room.

"What do you think?" asked the psychologist.

"Very impressive, man; that was the coolest thing I have ever seen," I offered.

"Albert is an amazing person," he said with some pride.

"I can see that," I said.

We broke for lunch, which, in a state institution, is a very dissatisfying experience. Even the Jell-O looked overcooked. We ate, shared war stories, and I told them about my encounter with Sophia. They all agreed the institute should be given some kind of award for trying to open this kind of home. They were effusive with their accolades for me and the fact that I was going to be running the place. It was clear they were buttering me up.

Then there was the obligatory tour. There isn't much to ogle in an institution. It was as bland as all the others and the olive drab paint didn't do much to brighten it up. The dayroom could have been used as the set for Ken Kesey's *One Flew Over the Cuckoo's Nest*, and the bathrooms were the most barren and least appealing I had seen. No toilet bowl seats or covers graced their top. The bowls were stainless steel and designed to be sat on directly.

When we returned to the original meeting room, I noticed my jacket was missing. This was a secure building and I was certain that someone had simply moved it to a more secure location once we had left. I was wrong.

I wasn't worried until I made a joke.

"Well, it seems like my jacket is missing. Why don't we just find Albert and let him sniff it out?"

I thought this might have been a touch of comic relief, but instead of laughter, I got an uneasy surprise. I watched as each of their faces soured. All but the psychologist kept their eyes focused on the floor.

"That was supposed to be a joke," I said in my defense.

None of the others looked up, but the psychologist looked at me as he spoke. It was as though he was sending me two messages: one with his words, and the other telepathically, a forewarning of some kind. I was definitely too dense to receive it.

"We think that Albert may like you," was all he said.

"I like Albert too, but what does that have to do with my jacket?"

"We think that Albert likes you," he said, choosing his words, ". . . and that he . . . he may have your jacket," he said, staring at me, hoping I would understand.

I didn't. "Why don't we go find Albert and ask him if he knows where my jacket is?" I said, like I was talking to a group of kindergarteners.

Finally, the female psychiatrist looked at me, but before she spoke she glanced around and made eye contact with each of her colleagues. "We think Albert likes you," she began, then quickly added, "and that might create some problems."

"I am really confused," I said. "We are in a secure environment; I just met Albert and took a tour; now my jacket is gone. I would like to get my jacket back—because I like my jacket, and I would like to wear it home, and if I am lucky maybe wear it tomorrow. But I hear you saying that Albert likes me and that this does not seem to bode well for my jacket. Am I getting this right?"

"Yes," said the female psychiatrist. "Let's go find Albert and your jacket."

"Fine," I said, exasperated.

We walked out of the room and down the long corridor from which we had just returned. The mood was somber, as if we were walking in a funeral procession. Finally, the psychiatric nurse began filling in the missing pieces. Her voice was annoyingly high. "Albert has an obsessive-compulsive disorder that is co-morbidly present with his mental retardation, as I am sure you know, but he has the eating disorder where he likes to eat inanimate objects, which, as I am sure you know, can be a real hazard, but as we said he has really cut back on eating inanimate things. He . . ."

"Is he only doing 30-watt bulbs now?"

"That is very funny, Dr. Tomasulo," she said, not smiling. "But these co-existing problems sometimes result in Albert doing some very unconventional things."

"Please don't tell me Albert has eaten my jacket," I said as we neared the staircase.

"Oh no, no, no, no, no," she said as she shook her head. "He may have eaten the buttons, but he wouldn't attempt to swallow a whole jacket."

"Well, good. Buttons are easy to replace," I said hopefully.

"Well, if we're lucky, the buttons will of course be replaced by the institution, that would be no problem at all. It is just that, well, as we've said, Albert likes you."

"Yes, yes. This has been established. Albert likes me. I could use all the friends I can get, but it is still a mystery as to how this might be affecting my jacket."

"Well, it is very complicated, Dr. Tomasulo, but essentially he may have wanted something of yours as a keepsake."

"Oh," I said, not having the faintest idea of what she was talking about.

She took out her seemingly endless key ring. I had a flashback to the Banana Man, a TV clown character from my childhood who would pull impossible things out of his coat all the while making a high-pitched "Whoaaaaaaa." Then, as he paused between lifting things out of his pockets, he would sing to himself, "La-la-la-la-la." With her squeaky voice and her endless key ring, I half expected her to go "Whoaaaaaaa," as she pulled them out, then break into, "La-la-la-la-la."

She finally found the key and knocked on Albert's door. The knock was a token consideration for Albert, but wasn't meant as a sign of respect for his privacy. It was, more or less, an announcement that we were coming in.

This was a small, stark cinderblock room with twenty-foot-high ceilings and nothing but a bed riveted to the floor and a dresser bolted to the wall. I noticed there was one lone, bare light bulb in the center of the ceiling. I wondered if Albert eyed it up the way I stare at crumb buns behind the glass case at the bakery.

Albert was sitting on the corner of his bed. He was smiling and rocking with his right hand behind his neck and his left hand on his stomach. His high-pitched "Hi!" came squeaking out when he saw me.

We all piled into his small room, and as we did, a faintly disagreeable odor seemed to be coming from Albert. My guests became noticeably agitated and seemed to anticipate something I couldn't. The psychiatric nurse/Banana Man began.

"Albert, you remember Dr. Tomasulo, don't you?" she said, not waiting for his response. "Well, I know you know Dr. Tomasulo had a very nice, and, I am sure, expensive jacket, and we were wondering, because we know you like Dr. Tomasulo, if you have his jacket?"

Albert could not have been more excited. He rocked and smiled and bounced on the end of the bed as he chanted, "Hi ... hi ... hi ..."

The smell was now unmistakable.

"Do you have Dr. Tomasulo's jacket?" she continued.

In a furious, nearly epileptic fashion, Albert nodded and bounced right off the bed and onto the floor. He reached under the bed and slid out my jacket. It was inside out with the arms folded across the middle as if wrapping something. I could see at least two of the buttons had been ripped out, creating holes in the leather.

With the reverence of an ordination ceremony, Albert carefully scooped the jacket into his arms and rose from kneeling to standing in front of me. He was smiling and rocking and holding it out for me to take.

"Hi . . . hi . . . hi . . ." he said with childlike exuberance.

Albert rocked back and forth in front of me with his gift. He extended his arms, waiting for me to receive it. I glanced around; no one even pretended to look at me. The moment the jacket slid onto my hands I could feel the warmth and stench of his feces wrapped inside of it. My eyes began to tear instantly from the tang and the realization. As I put the jacket on the floor, Banana Man spoke: "It looks like Albert ate your buttons so he could literally take a piece of you in, and incorporate you into his being, and, well, it looks like he wanted to give you a gift of something that was once a part of him—to remember him by."

In my mind, all I could hear was: "La, la, la, la, la . . ."

The two psychiatrists began snickering; I burst out laughing.

"I would have preferred a postcard," I quipped.

Finally, the group started laughing. Albert rocked and smiled as I looked down on the floor and contemplated the offering I'd just received.

It had been quite a month: I'd been assaulted by a naked woman, roomed with man who'd been eaten by a Venus flytrap, had the buttons from my jacket ripped off and eaten, and a pile of shit gifted to me by a man who thought Thomas Edison was a brilliant chef.

* * *

After Albert moved in, we realized the tremendous challenge that came with someone who eats light bulbs as snacks. In the first six months, Albert became a human lost and found for misplaced small objects. A ring Taimi left at the kitchen sink as she washed her hands, a momentarily unattended spool of thread, and a Canadian quarter plucked from a pocketful of my change and left on the kitchen table all vanished. Miraculously, everything missing eventually was expelled and documented. Failing to find something would mean a trip to the hospital for X-rays, enemas, or exploratory surgery. Albert deciding to take a dump was the signal for the equivalent of a staff flash mob. The closest to him would tell Albert not to flush. Other staff were called with the code "A-bomb" and soon a plastic colander was fetched by one staff member and relayed to another, who deployed the colander into the target toilet. Somehow, the need to locate small missing objects trumped the directive to teach Albert proper hygiene.

"Albert, when you are done, don't flush the toilet," I remember advising him one day.

For this I was getting my PhD.

But it would be Albert, only months later, who would save all our lives.

Mayor Billings

It was hard to believe how much people hated us. I'd come from a sheltered workshop environment tucked away on the outskirts of Paterson, New Jersey, where we were not hassled. I was studying and preparing for an academic career where new ideas, tolerance and understanding flourished. So the sheer hatred, misinformation and unbridled ignorance I'd be exposed to was something I would have to cultivate a tolerance and adequate response to. It was hard to imagine how threatened people felt, but it certainly became a stark reality when I met Mayor Billings. Although it was just Sophia and Albert, more residents were coming and none of our people were going to be an easy fit. I wasn't alone in my struggle: The other experimental group homes around New York were facing similar challenges and protests in their neighborhoods.

I could feel how people looked at me. Sometimes it was overt. If I was outside the home, people would have a sour, disapproving look when they saw me walking in. After a while I started to feel the implied rejection. We were not welcome in town, and everyone did, indeed, know the location of the "home for the retards from Willowbrook," as they called us. The misperceptions about people with intellectual disabilities ran the gamut. People worried about their children being sexually assaulted, about our people doing hard drugs, about the male participants breaking into homes and raping women in the village, and about our residents burglarizing the neighborhood. When we explained that the home provided twenty-four-hour supervision, it was used against us. At a town meeting, someone said the only people he was aware of that need round-the-clock supervision were incarcerated criminals, and that if our group needed it, that's what they were. I tried to make the point that children and the elderly often need round-the-clock supervision, but was told that since that was true, the town didn't need more people to care for.

It was also thought that if the participants mingled with the community, there would be a greater risk of infectious diseases. Regardless of my efforts to refute this, the perception remained.

Mayor Billings had made it his campaign promise to stop "the idiots and misfits" from ruining the municipality. He won by a landslide and was determined to keep us out. But since the church hadn't been able to sell the convent in two years, the institute's offer was accepted. The mayor was livid and tried everything to undo the sale, but failed. The focus of his attack shifted directly to the home, which meant it came straight at me.

Fueled by Mayor Billings' misinformation, people in the town feared their property values would go down—this in spite of the fact the institute provided government studies showing just the opposite. These studies showed that since the group homes were going into the better neighborhoods and into homes that were very well maintained, that the property values in these neighborhoods actually went up and held their value better than surrounding areas.

Legally we had a right to be there, but the law was a double-edged sword. We could move in, but within the year we had to prove we could get all of the residents out of the house in a two-minute fire drill. The laws were new, designed to accommodate the immediate movement of patients into the community while assuring they would be able to survive in their new environment. Mayor Billings had lost the legal game trying to keep us out, but he had a trick up his sleeve we couldn't have anticipated.

His brother-in-law was the fire chief.

The New York State fire inspection code required that group homes be held to a strict standard of evacuation. Regardless of the number of inhabitants or their level of disability, a group home had to demonstrate that all of its residents could vacate the premises within two minutes. We would have to do this within the first year of moving in or lose our temporary certificate of occupancy. This meant all of the participants would have to go back to where they came from. Which, in most cases, meant they would go back to hell: either Willowbrook or another institution.

I was familiar from my previous job with the need to have fire drills. But there was never any time pressure, and we simply had to show a log that said we had one. This was different. The residents' futures, their lives, were at stake.

Before we were all moved in, the mayor had gotten a court injunction to block us from using the town pool because of a fear of hepatitis B. The reason for this stemmed from lawsuits in the public education sector where children coming out of Willowbrook were considered potential carriers of the disease. Federal lawsuits were filed on both sides to protect other children in the classroom from being susceptible, but to also protect the rights of the children coming out of Willowbrook. The problem was that no one knew which of the Willowbrook children had the virus—so they would all have to be tested.

The inmates of Willowbrook were the subjects of a callous and unusual medical experiment by a notable and famous researcher, Dr. Saul Krugman. During the sixties and early seventies, he experimented with the residents of Willowbrook. Parents of these young residents were coerced into allowing their children to be fed the live virus to determine if they would be infected without the protection of gamma globulin, found earlier by Klugman to be an effective immunization against the virus.

The experiment showed that those not immunized with gamma globulin got infected. What is unconscionable is that these results could have been determined in the laboratory rather than by feeding children a live virus.

Judge Bartels, who took over for Judge Judd after his untimely death, had been presented with information that a number of surgeons had also had the virus and were not limited from their practice. He ruled "that the segregation of retarded hepatitis B carriers without imposing a similar restriction on non-handicapped (carrier) persons would constitute unlawful discrimination."

This federal ruling covered our residents as well. Technically, we were allowed to go swimming in the town pool—but the mayor had other ideas. It was April Fools' Day when the mayor's office called and invited me to the town hall to meet him. But this was anything but a joke. I accepted the invitation, and two days later Taimi and I walked downtown. Dave and Tom, two temporary staff members, stayed with Sophia and Albert.

"Thanks for coming with me," I said as we walked along. "Why do you think the mayor called?"

"The town meeting is next week," said Taimi. "I'm sure we are on the agenda. Everybody wants to help the disabled as long as it's NIMBY."

"NIMBY?" I asked.

"Not in my backyard," Taimi said as we crossed the street. "People think property values will go down when a group home moves in. The Princeton study showed that values actually go up and stay up."

"The Princeton study showed?" I said, eyebrows raised.

"I don't have to take classes to know shit."

"Right," I said. "I guess people scare easy."

"I bet the mayor is going to try to get rid of us," she said as we turned toward town hall. "I bet that ruling on hepatitis B pissed him off."

"He's not going to try to close our home now," I said, trying to convince us both.

We found our way through the town hall maze of offices, and stopped at the mayor's secretary's desk. "We're from the group home," I said, introducing us. "We're here to see the mayor."

She glanced at us disapprovingly, and then pressed the button on the intercom. "The people from the retarded home are here," she said dispassionately.

"Intellectually disabled," I said. "The people in the home are intellectually disabled."

"I guess that's what makes them retarded," she said as she rearranged her papers.

The mayor was a dead ringer for Danny DeVito in Taxi, and invited us into his office. We sat down across from his too-large maple desk, and he wasted no time. There were no niceties, no small talk, just bullying. "I admire what you're trying to do, but my constituents, the people who have the right to vote, and pay taxes—"

"We pay taxes," I interrupted, knowing the gloves were already off.

"Yes, but they can't vote, so you're our responsibility. And for safety you must conform to the fire code and stay out of the town pool. It's for your own good," he fired back.

"I certainly understand about the fire drill, but as residents we should be able to purchase pool passes. Judge Bartels' decision allows it."

"Ah, there's the rub, technically," he said, taking a piece of hard candy from a bowl on his desk. "Candy?"

"No, thanks," said Taimi.

"I'm trying to give them up," I said.

He flashed a courtesy smile, unwrapped the candy, and stuck it in his mouth. "Until you are up to code and pass the fire drill, everyone out in two minutes, you're not residents," he said as he tongued the candy.

"What about guest passes?" Taimi asked. "The town has these. We could pay for passes as guests of the mayor. Judge Bartels says we have the right—you could show some decency."

"Thought of that, young lady, but that would be favoritism," he said as he folded his arms, "and as mayor I have to be impartial."

"Know what I think you can do with your pool passes?" Taimi said, ready to launch.

"I was thinking the same thing, Taimi," I said, trying to avert a disaster. "Let's ask the mayor to hold the passes until the fire drill. We have until June 14."

"Barely six weeks, son," he reminded me. "You get three tries. If you fail, you and your misfits go back to where you came from." The mayor crunched down on the candy to make his point.

"I have a copy of the fire code. Can the fire chief help us?" I said, ignoring the slur.

"Thinking ahead, smart boy," he said. "My brother-in-law, Chief Willy, owns the local hardware store. He'll take care of you."

"I'll contact him," I said.

"You do that, son."

I stood and reached across his desk to shake his hand. "Thank you for your time, Mayor Billings," I said grudgingly. "What time is the town meeting Tuesday?"

The mayor stood up; so did Taimi. "If I were you I'd be out having fun, not at a meeting," he said. "Anything important I'll let you know."

"All the same, I might drop by," I said.

"Suit yourself." He shrugged. "Seven p.m."

Taimi and I turned to leave, but the mayor had one more thing to say. "Son, lock your doors at night. We don't want your misfits getting out and into trouble."

Taimi turned back toward the mayor. I knew there would be only one way to defuse her, so I whispered: "Certainly, warden."

Taimi got it, and then smiled at me.

"Pardon?" said the mayor.

"Now he's going to pardon us," I whispered to Taimi.

But Taimi wasn't going to let the mayor off the hook that easy. He'd crossed a line. "Mind if I have some candy?" she asked.

"Help yourself," he said, gesturing with his right hand.

Taimi emptied the bowl into her pocketbook. "Us misfits thank you," she said with an exaggerated grin.

We snickered to each other as we walked down the hallway and out onto the sidewalk.

"We're screwed," said Taimi. "Two minutes is how long we hold on to staff, not how fast we can get out of the house."

"We've got three shots at it," I said, trying to be hopeful. "How bad could it be?"

Chief Willy

I invited Chief Willy over to discuss the procedures.

Although the town fire department was volunteer-only, the chief took his job seriously. Chief Willy was a dull, thick man with a pointy nose and dirty blond hair that gave him a boyish, yet odd presence. He was a local house painter who got his work from political connections rather than his skill. He presented himself as a family man, and he had one eleven-year-old boy, but the reality was that he was a fixture in the local tavern. It was well known that he had had several blatant trysts with a string of luckless, mostly unappealing young women with little direction or self-esteem. His business card, which he handed to you every time he saw you, had a hapless homeowner who had fallen, seated, into a can of paint while attempting to paint his own home. The same logo appeared on the side of his van and was captioned: "Don't Let This Happen to You." Willy was a one-man marketing sensation. How could you forget a business called Paint in the Butt?

I took Willy on a tour of the home to get his advice. His swagger was difficult to tolerate, and as he waltzed through the home it was all I could do to be cordial. He was crude. He made a continual stream of remarks as he walked through the first floor.

"I can't believe a bunch of retards live in a house bigger than mine," he said as he sauntered through the foyer into the living room. "I live right next door to this whack joint with my wife and boy, Jeffery. He's gonna grow up thinking he's only got to be a world-class idiot and he could live in a better house than the one he grew up in."

"I've seen your boy outside. How old is he?" I said, trying to avert a conflict.

"He's ten—no wait, eleven. Damn boy is growing like a weed."

I'd only caught a few glimpses of Jeffery. He seemed sullen. I'd seen other children playing in the neighborhood, but Jeffery was clearly a loner. I'd never seen him bring friends over to his house.

"Well, it seems like this is a terrific town for him to grow up in," I offered. But as soon as I said it I realized it was the wrong thing to say.

"That's just the point. That's why we don't want retards living in some grand home in the middle of town. We don't want to send our children the wrong message."

"Most of them lived in deplorable conditions before this," I responded.

"That shouldn't mean these misfits should hit the lottery and move in here," he countered.

"Well, the hope is that it will be cheaper for the taxpayers in the long run. It costs a lot to institutionalize a person."

"That's a bunch of crap. The bleeding-heart liberals try to make the rest of us hardworking people believe that bullshit. I think it's a crime," he snorted. "Now those nun freaks didn't pay any taxes, but at least they were quiet women and knew their place."

We walked into the kitchen. I could feel myself getting angry and debated with the committee in my head about what, if anything, I should say. "Geraldo Rivera took photos of a place called Willowbrook . . ." I began.

"Yeah, like I'm going to believe some Puerto Rican lawyer."

And so it went.

Willy pointed to the stove and the kitchen ceiling and counter. "There's nothing but violations here. None of this is up to code. You'll have to have all of this work done before you could even have a fire drill. I can subcontract this out for you, get the job done right."

"Wouldn't that be a conflict of interest?" I said.

"Not for me, I'm just trying to help you people out. Without all this work being done you can't even have a fire drill."

"I'm just the messenger," I said. "If you write up what the violations are I'll present them back to the main office. They typically need to get three estimates before a job can be assigned."

"Yeah, well, good luck trying to get three estimates without my help. You know, people around here are very busy, and I don't think you will get anyone to come give you an estimate unless I grease the—"

"Well, of course we appreciate your help," I said, restraining myself, "but since the money here is taxpayers' money we have to follow a procedure that's in place."

"Well, sonny, you can follow a procedure or you can get the work done."

"Can you do me the favor of just writing up what the work is that needs to be done? Then I can get on it right away."

"Listen kid, this ain't the city. We are a volunteer organization. It's going to take me a week or two to get around to writing all this up. Remember the volunteer stuff comes after my regular work activities, so there is no priority to it."

"You do know that we need to get this fire code and drill situation squared away so that we can have a permanent certificate of occupancy."

"Oh, I am well aware of that, sonny boy," he said as he grabbed some grapes out of the bowl on the table. "I'm just not sure you are aware of the fact that you are going to need my help to get this done."

Sophia had come down from her room and walked into the kitchen. Her arm was still in a cast from the incident and she stopped in her tracks when she saw Chief Willy. She began a low growl and started to pick at the cast on her arm.

"Jesus Christ, put her back in her cage."

"Chief Willy, this is Sophia," I said, trying to ignore his comment.

"Well, Sophia looks like she been rode hard and put away wet," said the fire chief.

Taimi came around the corner behind Sophia, and stood in front of her to divert her attention.

"Sophia, let's go do your laundry and let Dr. Dan continue with the interview with the new resident," she said as she guided Sophia to the door leading to the basement. They walked past Chief Willy as he shook his head. Taimi let Sophia go in front of her down the stairs, looked back at me, and then closed the door behind her.

"New resident? What makes her think I might be as messed up as these folks?" wondered Chief Willy.

"Some people have a misperception of others," I said. "It's hard to account for their ignorance."

"You got one balled up place here, man," he said as he closed his notebook. "I'll write up the violations, but don't hold your breath. If I were you, I'd consider hiring me to do the work. I work on the incentive plan, capeesh?"

"Thank you, Chief. I'll pass that along to my superiors."

Chief Willy grabbed a few more grapes, turned his back and walked toward the front door. He opened it, walked out and down the steps, and left the door open. "Adios," he said, casually raising his right hand in the air.

I watched him waddle down the stairs and offered him the only gesture suitable to the circumstance: I extended the middle finger of each hand and let them sway back and forth until he was too small to see.

There were now pressures coming at me from every angle. I went to sleep every night with anxiety about the fire drill, the undealt-with separation from my wife, the dissertation, the mayor's bigotry, the townspeople, my overwhelming tuition bills, my falling-apart truck, my nonexistent sex life, my weight gain, and the loss of the friends I left behind when I took the job. My mom, dad, and sister had moved down to Florida years ago, so I was alone. Each day I'd try to put out as many of these fires in my head as I could, but I was exhausted and drained. Every morning I'd wake up to soaked sheets and soggy pillows from dread sweat. Exhausted before the day began, I'd down three, four, five cups of coffee just to jumpstart my brain. I was trapped in a life I'd deliberately chosen.

The only ray of sunshine came from one of the temporary workers who came through. David had the right disposition, a great way with the participants, and some enviable healthy habits. He told me he was part of the one-thousand-mile club. He ran twenty miles a week and each year broke a thousand miles. This appealed to me. I had absolutely no time to squeeze in a jog, but it was becoming a fad and something about it grabbed my interest. He told me to start off slow and take three months to build up to twenty miles a week. Do five for a couple of weeks, then ten for a few, then fifteen, and finally twenty. I decided I needed to jump in right away and ignored the recommendation. The first week I ran fifteen miles. Now in addition to everything else, I felt crippled. The aches and pains never left me, and I walked as if my underwear were made of sandpaper.

Mike

I parked in a space between the house van and two staff cars. Approaching the front door to the modest Cape-style home, I could hear the voice of a young man. "Jacob! Get away from that! Don't you dare pull that—"

A piercing, wailing house alarm engulfed the pleas of the young man, but other voices, yelling and screaming, became more distinct. Finally, a deep, booming, yet halting voice became clear.

"I . . . don't . . . like . . . this. I . . . don't . . . like . . . this! I . . . don't . . . like . . . this!"

It was Mike.

Mike was a giant: Seven feet and one inch tall, and viciously strong. I'd read his case. He had an IQ of forty-five and a severe anger management problem. Yesterday he'd thrown a couch, a full-size living room sofa, through the wall separating the living room from the first-floor bedroom in this respite home. He picked it up and threw it because someone had moved his toothbrush.

I was there to evaluate him for our group home.

I stood outside the front door debating whether I should go in when the front door exploded into the house. It was one thing to read about a giant, but another to see him on the other side of a screen door. In one move Mike yanked and flung the front door with his right hand so hard the entire edge of the door became imbedded into the wall behind it. With his left hand, he straight-armed the screen door I was standing in front of and, as if I had been a bug on its surface, pinned me to the side of the house. The screen door hit my nose and cheeks so hard that it made a permanent indentation.

Mike suffered from something called Sotos cerebral gigantism. In days gone by, the carnivals would have used someone like Mike in one of their freak shows. He would have been called a "pinhead" because this type of deformity makes his head come to a rounded point. Mike's size would amaze anyone, but what drew my attention even more was his voice. It was very low because his vocal cords were elongated. This, combined with his halting speech, made his appearance more cartoon-like than real. When he spoke, his words were deliberate and spaced apart. He was like the giant from Jack and the Beanstalk: Fee-fi-fo-fum is exactly how Mike talked—all the time.

Mike ran into the street with his hands over his ears, jumping up and down screaming in his unusual voice, "I don't like this! Stop . . . that . . . noise! I don't like this! Stop . . . that . . . noise! Stop it! Stop it! Stop it!"

Generally speaking, the residents from the institutions were more violent. They were used to fighting for food, defending themselves from physical and sexual assaults, and being aggressive toward staff. Mike was the strongest, if not the most violent, person considered for the new residence. If someone had been standing where Mike had thrown the couch, he or she would have been killed.

He had been taken out of his parents' house years earlier, then in the shuffle from Willowbrook, moved back home. It was overwhelming for his aging parents and he was moved again on an emergency basis into the respite home. He was staying in this home with three other temporary residents and staff trained to deal with psychiatrically impaired, exceptionally violent individuals. The respite homes provided a breather for the family or group home staff when someone was out of control. Typically, these respite homes are pure chaos. This one was no exception.

This was his second day of respite. He had stayed overnight and in the morning when he went to brush his teeth, someone had moved his toothbrush. The couch became airborne moments later. The modest Cape Cod-style home was nondescript and blended into the residential neighborhood. Nothing about it was unique or telltale, except for a slightly enlarged parking area for the staff. Other than this, you would never suspect who was inside.

In the street, yelling, the twenty-two-year-old giant looked to the entire world as if he were three. This was exactly the kind of attention the respite home didn't want in the neighborhood, so the group home manager ran to calm Mike down. The staff inside the home could not shut off the alarm, and Mike remained inconsolable. He continued his tirade until the fire engines showed up. This made things worse.

As the engines' sirens grew louder, Mike became more agitated. When they rounded the corner to the house, Mike began screaming, "NO! NO! NO! NO! NO!" and ran back into the house. I had peeled myself from behind the screen door and watched as the staff led the other residents out. Mike pushed them aside and went in. I followed and watched as he screamed at the strobe light and alarm. There was a huge hole in the wall below the central fire alarm where the couch had been thrown, and the alarm and strobe were housed behind a one-foot-square red grate in the wall up near the ceiling. Mike pounded the grate and screamed at it again until he saw the fireman in the doorway. Then he did something I didn't think was possible.

Mike saw the first fireman, pointed at him with his left hand and screamed, "No!" His thick fingers reached up and grabbed the red grate. With one yank he pulled it out of the wall, then, as if he were pulling toys out of a toy box, he started ripping wires and braces from the cavernous hole. He jerked the strobe light out of its holding and smashed it on the floor behind him.

The alarm was more difficult. As if he were delivering a breech baby, Mike reached in with both hands and finagled the alarm until he could rip it out of the wall. When he did, the wailing sound began to fade, and Mike stared at the contraption until it was silent. It was as though I were witnessing some primal conquest scene where the predator attacks, then watches the life pass out of its victim.

A slight smirk ran across Mike's face—a victory smile. It was over. I had been standing, undetected, until suddenly caught by Mike's eye.

"Who . . . are . . . you?" he said.

"I'm Dan. I came here to visit you," I said.

"I stopped it," Mike said.

"I see you did."

"I don't know you."

"No, that's right," I said. "But I wanted to get to know you, so I thought I would come visit."

I noticed that Mike was drooling. The continuous flow of dribble came right out of his mouth onto the alarm. There was no end to the river of saliva.

The volunteer fireman standing at the door didn't know what to do. He was trained to put out fires, not pacify drooling giants. When the group home manager apologized to him for the false alarm, he couldn't leave fast enough.

The staff and residents filed back in, and the group home manager, Jack, shook my hand. "You must be the shrink that came to take big-boy Mike. Sorry about this," he said.

Mike, Jack, and I were standing next to one another. I looked at Mike as I spoke to Jack. "Well, Mike here seems happy that he was able to stop the noise and the lights," I said.

"I stopped it," Mike repeated.

"Yes indeedeedoo you did," said Jack.

"Yes in . . . dee . . . dee *doo!*" said Mike as he clapped his hands and jumped up and down. "Yes in . . . dee . . . dee *doo!*"

Jack looked at me as Mike jumped. "He's all yours," said Jack.

"Right," I said. "Do you have the data on Mike?"

Mike was still jumping and saying, "Yes in . . . dee . . . dee . . . doo!" as we spoke.

"Sure," said Jack. "Incident reports, hospital reports, psychiatric reports, you name it, we've got it. I even got the tracking information from the university on his disorder."

Mike stopped jumping up and down as soon as he saw Jacob, the resident Jack had tried to stop from pulling the fire alarm. Mike swung around and dropped what was left of the alarm on the floor.

"I . . . don't . . . like . . . you, mister," Mike said to Jacob. "I'm . . . going . . . to . . . *kill* . . . you if you make that noise again."

Jacob was a very small man with Down syndrome. He seemed genuinely shaken by Mike's threat; scurrying back into his room, he slammed the door. Mike pointed at the door as if he had the power to open it by doing so, and called out to Jacob.

"I mean it mister . . . yes in . . . dee . . . dee *doo!* I'm going to *kill* you!" Mike said as he began to jump up and down again. "Yes in . . . dee . . . dee *doo!* I'm going to *kill* you!"

Jack spoke up right away. "Mike, we don't do that around here. Around here we don't threaten people. We don't say we are going to kill someone."

In a deeply apologetic voice, Mike responded. "I'm . . . *very* . . . sorry," he said, ". . . and it won't happen again."

"Thank you, Mike, for apologizing. That was very nice," said Jack.

"I know it was," said Mike. "Now can I have something to eat? Every time I say I'm sorry I get something to eat."

"Who gives you something to eat when you apologize?" I asked.

"My mommy and daddy do," said Mike.

"Your mommy and daddy do?" I repeated.

"Yes . . . in . . . dee . . . dee . . . doo, they do," Mike said as he began to jump up and down. "Yes . . . in . . . dee . . . dee . . . doo, they do."

Lilith

Lilith was one of the few from the institution placed in a sheltered workshop. Her stringy brown hair framed her slack-jawed face. Her jaw protruded further than her nose and her teeth, the few that were left crowding together on the top of her mouth. Her face looked like it had a thin layer of brown mold in patches along her cheeks and neck, and her thin shoulders flared down to an enormous waistline. Lilith was intellectually disabled, but also struggled with schizophrenia and a rare eating disorder called Prader-Willi syndrome, a condition that manifests through a food compulsion. All Lilith could think about was food. She dreamed of it, stole it, binged on it, and was obsessed with getting it. It wasn't any particular type of food she craved, like chocolate or bread. Rather, Lilith craved quantity. She could not stop herself from eating. She also had pica, the same condition as Albert, and on occasion ate nonfood objects with the same gusto. She had a particularly violent phobia of blood. Even a drop of it would cause her to throw her hands up in the air, screaming "Noooooo" at the very top of her lungs, and frantically, wildly flail her hands as if she was wiping fire off of them. This made it a priority for the staff to keep her away from incidents where someone bled. Her chart also noted she may have a unique musical ability via a condition known as Williams syndrome—something I'd never heard of.

What made Lilith's case particularly challenging was that she also had de Clérambault's syndrome, or erotomania. She had delusions about famous people, or people of status, being in love with her. This later became a problem when her attention turned to me. Apparently, years earlier she'd thought "Tricky Dick" Nixon was secretly in love with her—sending telepathic messages to her via the TV, a familiar delusion for erotomanics. Apparently, even a delusion has standards. It had stopped after Nixon's embarrassing resignation.

I met Lilith while consulting for an agency dealing with the "wild and mild," individuals with two separate diagnoses. The wild part meant they had a psychiatric diagnosis and the mild part meant they were mildly retarded. For some reason, I had become the obsessive object of her affection, and because of this I had to vary my schedule for visiting the center. I had typically gone on Wednesdays, but Lilith had figured out my schedule and stopped working at her job assembling first aid kits to fix herself up and put makeup on—for me. The program started at eight thirty a.m. and I stopped by between one and two p.m. Lilith stopped working at eight forty-five a.m. She was openly flirtatious and constantly grilled me about my love life.

"Hey, Dr. Dan. How about you be my boyfriend?" she would say while eating a banana, one of her approved snacks.

"Lilith, first let me remind you I am not actually a doctor yet, and while I appreciate your offer, I can't date someone I'm working with. It is actually against the law."

"You just afraid I don't got no experience in the sex department. Well I tell you, I got experience coming out of my butt!" she said. Then she would roar at her own joke. "Coming out of my butt! Get it! I got experience coming *into* my butt. Hey, Dr. Dan, I'll do this for you."

Lilith moved the banana in and out of her mouth. I had learned that walking away rather than addressing the situation worked best. Another staff person, Gloria, would counsel Lilith.

"Lilith, that isn't going to help you when you're on a job, now is it?" said Gloria.

"It might," said Lilith. "To get ahead you gotta give some head. Think about it!" she said as she pointed her finger in Gloria's face.

That was Lilith's favorite phrase. Whenever she knew it was time for her to stop talking she ended the sentence with the axiom, "Think about it." We often did.

I had staggered my schedule sufficiently to surprise Lilith so she wouldn't lose a day's worth of work waiting for me to show up. But the truth was, when I was there she wouldn't do anything else. Now that Lilith had become a candidate for the new home, my dealing with her became critical. I met with the staff, who teased me mercilessly about Lilith's affection toward me.

"I think the two of you would make a very lovely pair," said Carol, the vocational supervisor. "She could stay at home all day and eat everything in the house, and you could get two or three jobs to pay for it all."

"But I bet the sex would be unforgettable. Not good, mind you, but unforgettable," said Frank, a job coach.

"Your children would be these really smart, crazy kids who would eat the napkins at the Thanksgiving dinner table," said Fran, the work supervisor.

After the staff got this out of their system, we got down to strategies. The one we chose was to confront her directly. The basic idea was to tell her I was married (I didn't think sharing the fact I was separated from my wife would help the matter) and that in any case I wouldn't date someone I work with, and that I didn't want her to bother me with this anymore. We scripted it out, and decided it was the best strategy. We thought it would be best to deal with her in the program before she got to the group home. The downside was that Lilith had a history of self-injurious behavior. She would bite and chew at her hands and wrists. She would punch herself so hard in the head that on two occasions she had knocked herself out. We decided that I would tell her the next time I was in the facility, and that the staff would be on the alert for trouble.

The following Tuesday I showed up, and as usual, Lilith got up from her workstation and came over to talk to me. I looked around to make sure the staff members were ready, and then began.

"Lilith, I'm actually glad you came over to see me. There is something I want to talk to you about."

"How 'bout you take me in the closet, whew-yeah! You can do the nasty wit me in there. They call that the 'kissing closet' but we can call it the 'coming closet.' I can take you standin' up, you know." She wiggled her hips back and forth. "You can do that and not even get yourself dirty, un-huh," she said, making the motions again. "Think about it," she said, pointing her finger in my face.

"Actually, Lilith, I want to talk to you right here. Let's sit down at this table right here."

Lilith sat down and reached to hold my hand. I put her hand back on her side of the table and began. "Lilith, I need to tell you something . . ."

"If you don't like it standing up . . . it was just a suggestion . . . I'm flexible."

"I'm sure you are," I said as I heard the staff laugh in the background, "but what I have to say is that I can't date you. We can't have sex, and this is something that isn't going to change. I think you are working very hard to learn about what it takes to get a job, and you are working very well here. But I can't keep coming here if you are going to do this. If you keep making passes at me, if you keep thinking that we are going to have sex, then I won't be able to come here, or you won't be able to stay in the program. This is important, Lilith. Do you understand what I am saying?"

"Who is she?" she said in a steely, cold voice.

"Lilith, I am married, and I can't date you or have sex with you, period."

"No sex?"

"It's not going to happen, Lilith."

She took her index finger on her right hand and made a circle with her thumb and index finger of her left hand and moved her right index finger in and out of the hole she made. "None of this?"

"Exactly," I said, as I heard the staff laugh louder in the background.

Then she made a switch, sticking her right index finger into her mouth two or three times. "And none of this," she said, mumbling because of her finger.

"That's right."

"So we're broken up, right?"

"We were never together."

It happened in slow motion. It was like an avalanche of sadness fell over her, engulfing her. I could see her body sag and her face drain from the realization. I might as well have told her that her mother had died. This was the moment the staff had dreaded.

"I understand," she said with her head down. "It's because I'm not beautiful, right?" she said as she started to cry. "I . . . I'm not like the girls in magazines. That's what you want. I'm not beautiful, I know."

"Lilith, it's not because you're not beautiful."

"Then it's cause I'm fat. I got a fat ass. You know what John said? He said my ass was so fat they can see it on a weather satellite. I can't help that I want to eat all the time."

"It's not about that, Lilith."

"You're not married anymore, right? The staff said you're divorced. So who you gettin' it from?"

I hadn't counted on the rumor mill. "See, Lilith, that's just it. I have a personal life outside of here. It is mine—it's private. I can't date you, or have sex with you, and my wife and I have our private lives . . . I just can't have you, and me . . . we can't do this here."

A broad smile took hold on Lilith's face. I knew it wasn't a good sign.

"You are a bad boy! I'll be ready for you. Any time you want—you come right to the hospital, I'm in cottage thirteen, and we'll do it." She started to whisper, "You don't need no rubbers—my mother sterilized me when I was eighteen—I'm clean as a whistle!"

"Lilith! Stop! I can't date you here," I said, nearly yelling. "I can't have sex with you here. I can't have sex with you or date you at the hospital. We can't go out, we can't have sex. It can't happen. I don't want you to feel bad, but you can't keep coming on to me like this. It isn't the right thing. We're here to help you learn how to get a job and keep a job. If you did this kind of thing with a boss at work you would be fired. Believe me, I don't want you to feel bad, but I do want you to really understand what I am saying."

For the longest time Lilith just stared at me. She was thinking. She wasn't depressed as before, and she wasn't ignoring my words. Something else was happening.

"I'm too much woman for you, right?" she finally said. "You can't handle big momma, that's it, that's it. You're scared of me, that's why your wife left you, isn't it. You ain't got no action left in you"—she started moving her hips back and forth—"un-huh; you got no juice, Dr. Dan. Well I don't need a baloney bender. If you ain't got the meat I ain't yo' treat. Think about it!" she said, pointing at me.

Lilith got up and started to walk back to her workstation. For a moment, I thought everything would be okay.

"I don't need no limp-dicked wimp in my life," she said as she turned toward the refrigerator. She opened the door and, with both hands, flung it back so hard that it broke off its hinge, then she started grabbing any food she could get her hands on. She took a stick of butter and a lunch bag sandwich and stuffed them into her face. She swallowed the butter and grabbed for the refrigerator contents with both hands. Some grapes and a covered bowl of macaroni and cheese were devoured so quickly it seemed inhuman. A container of grated cheese was opened and eaten.

Within seconds she had tried to empty out the refrigerator, and the staff, although on alert, didn't have time to reach her before she got to the food. She forced food into her mouth without concern. Six of us couldn't pull her away, and she started to choke.

"Get Fire O'Grady down here!" one of the staff hollered.

Fire O'Grady was the psychiatric nurse. She had been in the field forever and had seen it all. Nothing fazed her. In her younger days, she had gained a countywide reputation and the nickname "Fire" for dealing with a junkie in the county hospital emergency room. The guy was high and had walked in with a beer bottle. When the nurses tried to take it away from him he smashed the bottom of it and grabbed one of the high school volunteers. He threatened to cut the young girl's face open with the broken glass if everyone didn't empty their pockets and give him their money. As people dug into their pockets, O'Grady came out of the bathroom behind him. The junkie had been screaming so loud he didn't hear her. Before he could do anything, O'Grady took the fire extinguisher off the wall and knocked him out cold. The nickname was born on that day and it stuck.

We tried to keep Lilith out of the refrigerator but we were no match for her obsession. She clawed her way in and held on to the racks of food. Her fingers were inside the rails of the racks and she flailed her arms, cutting herself and others with the racks. O'Grady was already on the way. She arrived with a hypodermic needle filled with Thorazine and stuck Lilith in her butt. Lilith was still choking, and with the staff on either side, O'Grady got behind Lilith and began the Heimlich maneuver. Food fountained out of Lilith's mouth as O'Grady gave several sharp jabs to her gut. Finally, Lilith heaved up some grapes and macaroni and fell to her knees. Her throat was clear. With O'Grady on the floor, still holding her from behind, Lilith looked over her shoulder and talked to O'Grady.

"Hey O'Grady, that was the most I got all week. You could have pumped that hand a little lower and it could have turned me on, you know. I'd be good to you if you want to meet me in the closet."

"You're not my type, Lilith. But anyway, I figure you'll be sound asleep in five minutes."

Lilith yawned. "Maybe three, O'Grady," she said as she shut her eyes and pointed her finger. "Think about it."

Casting

As other residents came into the home, there was some kind of outburst from Sophia. She had a cast on her arm from the day we met, to keep her from picking at the forty-two stitches. It often became a battering ram for newcomers. She may have assaulted other residents to establish a territorial claim and give a warning: she was not to be messed with. Her explosiveness was at the center of the Fearsome Foursome–as Sophia, Albert, Mike, and Lilith had been dubbed. Taimi was working around the clock and living in the staff apartment on the third floor. We had been interviewing for other staff, and the institute provided temporary workers until we could hire permanent people for direct service. I had hoped that some of the temporary staff might have stayed on, but a week with the Fearsome Foursome was enough to make the temporaries end their stay as soon as possible. When they saw the extremity, the volatility, and the sheer chaos, they left. Most didn't even come to pick up their paychecks. We had to mail them. If I'd had somewhere to go, I'd have gone right out the door with them. Although the home was grand, it had yet to become a place of safety. The regal building was clearly constructed as a sanctuary. Wooden crosses hung in every room, and in the back of the living room was a confessional. I couldn't tell if it had been moved there from another location, or if the nuns used it for absolving their transgressions.

There were days I never left the home. When I had a break, I went upstairs to study for my comprehensive exams. Finishing my PhD and running the home became not only the most important happenings in my life; they were the only affairs I attended to.

At Yeshiva University, I was a minority. None of my fellow classmates worked, and—with a last name like Tomasulo—they all knew who was the only non-Jewish student in the department. These novelties unnerved me, but by the end of my first semester I'd learned how to use the notoriety to ingratiate myself into the program. I realized that my cohorts didn't have real-world experiences with clients and I could use my knowledge to bring a fresh perspective to a class.

At the home, my need to get permanent staff onboard took precedence. Organizing the temporary staff never went well—often they were more of a liability than an asset. The effort of frequent phone and group interviews seemed nonstop. Getting together a talented staff became a full-time job itself.

Despite interviewing many candidates for the staff positions, we limped along without filling them for another two months. Dealing with Sophia's frequent rage episodes also caused concern. Her cast was coming off, and it seemed like the perfect time to try an intervention. However, I had no idea what that should entail. It was in the middle of all this that our new secretary showed up—the very last person you'd ever have imagined walking into a convent.

Gwennie

There was a fight or incident every day, and we needed to document these events in triplicate with detailed explanations, so we desperately needed a secretary. We had placed an ad in the *New York Times* and the *Daily News*, but as soon as a worthy candidate showed up for an interview, they would see Mike or Lilith and turn on their heels. Everyone seemed freaked out by the bizarre nature of the setting and the inhabitants. Everyone, that is, except Gwennie.

Gwennie was from London and came to America after a crash-and-burn romance with some famous (or thought-he-was-famous) punk rocker. She was drop-dead gorgeous, and not the kind of girl that you could ever imagine working in a place where there were crosses everywhere and a confessional. She came to the interview in a micro-mini skirt and with wildly teased hair. She wore a dozen bracelets, and the neckline of her blouse wasn't suggestive; it was more of a directional compass. She chewed gum and filed her alternating black-and-red nails as we spoke. I couldn't imagine how she would fit in—but she was the only one who stayed long enough for an interview.

"Gwennie. May I call you Gwennie?"

"Whotever floats your boat, govner."

"Gwennie, this is a job that requires you to do some typing and filing. Have you done this kind of work before?"

"Aw type eighty words a minute and, as you can see, I'm very proficient at filing," she said, not caring if I got the joke.

"What brings you here?"

She looked me dead in the eye. "Me boyfriend fucked me girlfriend, if you must know, so I fucked hers and decided it was time to make me way 'ere. I don't really give a rat's ass about anything and I need money so aw can rent a flat. The ad said the job started immediately, and that is about when I need some fucking money."

"Yes, I see," I said after I closed my mouth.

"So when do I start?"

"Well we have a procedure here for hiring someone, and right now we are looking at candidates, and—"

"And I am the only fucking candidate that's sitting here, right? Who the fuck do you think you are going to get to work with this bunch?" she said, nodding her head toward Mike, who had been standing in the hallway drooling.

"Okay, all right. I know you've got a point, but the secretary is also going to have to know everything about the New York State fire codes. We have to comply with all the fire codes to be granted our certificate of occupancy, and I need someone who can sort through and learn all that stuff and understand it."

She looked up from her nails. "Um not a twit!"

"I didn't think you were; I'm just saying that if I hire you, you have to show up every day and you've got to be on top of things."

"What's that supposed to mean? You want me to be on top of you, govner?"

I closed my eyes, slightly shook my head and smiled. "Can you start tomorrow?" I said, realizing my limited choices.

"I can start right after I finish my filing," she said, staring at the back of her hand.

Adding Gwennie to the staff helped and hindered in ways I couldn't have predicted. She was organized and efficient, yet continually oozed sexuality. I made the mistake of not explaining initially that the style of her clothes would need to change. I'd never been in a position where I had to explain to a young woman that she looked too provocative. She was a walking contradiction. In no time, she'd organized the office, scheduled medical and interview appointments, and tracked down the much-needed temporary staff to cover necessary shifts. But while she was handling all this, she wore clothes designed to show off her physical assets. Every day would bring a new hairdo, more bracelets, and more distraction. She was an amazing resource and a problem all at once: a major contributor and a major distraction. Albert chanted "Hi, hi, hi" every time he saw her and Mike drooled as if a fountain had been installed behind his tongue. Even Sophia and Lilith were entranced by her presence. Gwennie was the woman they wanted to be, and perhaps in Lilith's case, be with.

In the normal functioning of the home, the daily routine of preparing each meal, washing clothes, drying then folding the clothes, making beds, cleaning the bathrooms and kitchen, and watching TV, Gwennie was a one-woman parade. Taimi was matter-of-fact about it all, but the temporary staff, particularly the men, were more enthralled with her than with paying attention to their duties. Something had to be said.

But I wasn't immune to her erotic nature. Oh no. I had to train myself to not be seduced by the plunging neckline or micro-mini skirts. Fishing for an object excreted by Albert in the toilet bowl, managing a wayward giant, blocking an assault from a bloodied, naked woman, and trying not to activate an outbreak of violence by saying something interpreted as unkind to Lilith were easy tasks compared to telling Gwennie she was too suggestive in her attire.

Weeks after she was hired, we were about to bring in two more residents, Candy and Benny. They would bring with them their own unique circumstances, and this would mean the dynamics of the house would shift again. Gwennie had already proven herself indispensable, so I needed to have the conversation about how she dressed. We spoke one afternoon in the office as she was seated behind the desk and I stood in front.

"You've been amazing here, Gwennie," I began. "I don't really know how we got along without you."

"The last time aw got that kind of starter I was either fired from me job or dumped by me boyfriend."

"You're not being fired or dumped, but I do have a favor I need from you," I said, practicing my eye contact.

"Whot's that, govner?"

"Well," I began, searching for the right words. "I think you are very fashionable, and stylish, and have an amazing . . . way about you."

"But . . ."

"But, it might be hard to explain . . ."

She just looked at me dead-on.

"First, well, the jewelry. If you notice Taimi and I and the temporary staff don't wear any."

"You want to know where I score me jewelry?"

"Not exactly. We don't wear it because some of the participants can be violent—and the jewelry can be—well—something that could end up hurting them—or you—if there was a fight."

"Now aw understand why you people look so flat and plain."

"Yes, well, I was wondering if you might not wear so much—for safety's sake."

"Aw never thought about it—but it makes sense. I don't wont to be the cause of someone, especially me, getting hurt."

"Great, good, and there's one more thing."

"You don't like me shoes either?"

"No, in fact they are just fine—the shoes are fine—excellent."

"Then whot's next on the fashion hit list?"

"Your clothing is amazing . . ."

"But . . ."

"But it's a bit of a distraction," I said sheepishly.

"Aw see," she said, glancing down.

"It's distracting to our male residents, and quite frankly, to our male staff."

"Does that include you, govner?" Gwennie began laughing and started gently pulling on her dress top. "Well, that's a first. I never had a man tell me aw should be wearing more clothes."

"Well, yeah, just not so, you know, low," I said, pointing to the middle of my chest. "And maybe not so high." I gestured with my fingers pointing to the side of my thigh.

Gwennie laughed hard, almost uncontrollably, and covered her face. "They told me America was different, but this takes the cake," she said, unveiling her face. "But aw get it, and it's not a problem—it'll save me a half hour getting ready in the morning."

"Right, good, thanks," I said, relieved.

Gwennie stood up, knowing I was having a tough time with the conversation. "So aw can't wear this, then," she said, holding the edge of her micro skirt. "Too little to hide the mystery?"

It was my turn to laugh. "Thank you," I said, breaking my strained gaze to walk away.

"Would you like to see the one aw had picked out for tomorrow was going up to, govner?"

"No, thank you though," I said as I heard her laughing.

"It used to be a headband, but now it's one of me favorites."

"I'm sure it's lovely," I said as I walked out the door shaking my head. "I'm certain it is magnificent."

It was a brief oasis for us. As awkward as it was, it was great just to have a laugh. But the mood in the home was about to change: Candy and Benny would soon be moving in—and we were about to have our first fire drill.

Planning Our Escape

As our own struggles took place in the home and the community, there was still a great deal of fighting in New York at the Department of Mental Hygiene (DMH) and the Office of Mental Retardation (OMR). They had been arguing that a constitutional right to treatment was unrealistic because of the expense and the lack of evidence showing it was possible. It was a catch-22. Without enough examples of clients with severe intellectual disabilities in community residences, we could not draw statistically meaningful conclusions. Since it wasn't proven, the agencies argued they shouldn't try. Walden House and a handful of others like it, run by YAI, were the experiment. If we succeeded, community placement would be deemed possible. If we failed, it wouldn't—and the residents would go back to an institution. Somehow the fire drill became the unspoken yardstick for acceptability. If we could get our act together enough to organize everyone out of the house, it meant life in the community was at least a possibility. If we couldn't get out of the house in two minutes, nothing else would matter.

I wanted to attempt a fire drill before all of the participants had moved in. I thought it would be a good idea to train and rehearse with just a few of us rather than the entire group. Because I'd seen Mike's reaction to the fire alarm in his home, I strategically arranged to have our initial drill while he was at a doctor's appointment in the city. Hoping to stack the deck in our favor, I whittled down the fearsome foursome to three. It was brilliant—and it could not have gone worse.

Four of us were responsible for getting Sophia, Albert, and Lilith out of the house. Gwennie, Taimi, David, and I had developed what we thought was a reasonably good plan. Taimi would get Albert, Gwennie would wait near the front door, David would steer Sophia, and I would have Lilith. It looked excellent on paper. Daytime in the house was an effort at trying to establish a routine. We were typically up by seven, dressed and downstairs for breakfast by about seven twenty. We'd all make breakfast together, eat, and clean up. Then everyone would make their bed and clean their room, and house chores were assigned. This may sound easy, but keeping Sophia from attacking someone and Albert from eating something unfit for human consumption were daily challenges. Lilith and Mike had the potential to become loose cannons at any moment. So being on edge was our norm. After breakfast and cleaning the kitchen, we would clean the bathrooms and vacuum the floors. The plan was to get the residents into a daily routine first, then expand our skills as opportunities for the participants grew. The hope was to get people into sheltered workshops or assisted employment as soon as possible after the fire drill requirement was passed. For our first fire-escape effort, I told Gwennie to surprise us sometime between one and two in the afternoon, after we finished lunch. We were scattered about the house when we heard her cockney inspired accent.

"Ding, ding, ding, alright blokes, let's get ourselves out of here! Make believe the bloomin' place is on fire!"

I clicked the stopwatch in my hand. Lilith was in the living room watching TV and I approached her. "Lilith, we have to go outside for a few minutes," I said in my firm, yet polite voice. "Let's go outside and then you can come right back in."

"Gawd damn it!" she protested. "I can't sit down for one minute without you people bothering me!"

I put my hand on her shoulder and she flailed it away. "Lemme be alone for a gawd damn minute! You're always rushing me!"

Albert was in the bathroom and Taimi, according to state law, couldn't walk in on a male resident while he was in the bathroom. She knocked on the door. "Come on, Albert—we have to go downstairs for a minute."

Nothing. She knocked again.

"Albert, come on out."

Sophia was in the kitchen near the sink looking out the window and rocking slightly. David knew better than to touch her, so he opened his arms and stood alongside her. Gwennie called again.

"Ding, ding, ding, alright blokes, let's shake a leg!"

"What the hell is wrong with you people!" yelled Lilith. "Leave me alone!" She made random swats in my general direction.

Sophia grunted when she heard Lilith, looked at David, and went back to looking out the window. Taimi knocked louder on the door. "Albert, we have to go downstairs. Come on out."

"Hi, hi, hi," she heard from behind the door.

I pleaded with Lilith to help me out and she grumbled while she pushed herself out of the chair. "You people work me to the bone!" she complained. "I don't get a gawd damn minute to myself in this place."

Tick, tick, tick.

Albert came to the door with his pants around his ankles.

"Hi, hi, hi."

"No, no, Albert. I'm sorry, go back and pull your pants up!" said Taimi, closing the door so he'd have privacy. "Just hurry up and I'll wait."

Lilith got up and walked directly into the kitchen. "I'm hungry!" she announced.

"Lilith, you just had lunch—we have to go outside for just a minute," I said, following her.

Lilith flailed her arms and Sophia grunted as she saw Lilith coming in. I locked eyes with David, realizing a potential face-off between the two of them. He and I made a back-to-back barrier shielding each of the two women from getting near each other.

"What's the time?" asked David.

"Eternity—I don't know," I said.

"Ding, ding, ding, govner. We're going to need a bleedin' calendar to measure this!" said Gwennie.

When Albert finally came out of the bathroom, he walked right past Taimi to his bedroom. Apparently, he didn't like being disrupted during his bathroom ritual. He walked into his room and shut his door. Part of the respect we had been trying to cultivate was not to barge in on participants if their door was shut.

"Albert, I am sorry I interrupted you in the bathroom, but it is important. Can you open the door please?" Taimi asked.

David and I, in an unspoken agreement, opted to make keeping Lilith and Sophia from going at each other a priority, rather than the fire drill. The four of us danced our dance of terror as we kept Lilith away from the food, Sophia away from Lilith, and David and I from touching either of them.

After what seemed like a month, we made our way down to the foyer. Gwennie opened the front door and we ushered everyone out onto the porch on a colder-than-usual May afternoon. Even with Mike out of the picture, my brilliant plan took twenty-six minutes and thirty-seven seconds—and that was with four staff and only three residents.

We were screwed.

Candy

They'd left her for dead.

Candy was beaten after a gang rape and discarded like a used tissue. Two policemen found her naked and motionless in the woods behind her high school the morning after. Her unblinking eyes seemed frozen, her neck had been badly cut, and she showed no reaction when they called her name. She was in a program for students with intellectual disabilities and at the time of the attack was twenty years old.

Although her body survived, her psyche was dead. The police called for a psychiatric ambulance. Her body was like a large sack of sand and difficult to move. The ambulance took her to the emergency room, where the doctors had seen this type of thing before. They knew she had been assaulted, and examined her with the purpose of collecting evidence. Afterward, she was taken to the psychiatric ward and held in an observation room. Candy gave no indication that she knew where she was or what had happened. She stayed in the hospital, in this condition, for three months.

Initially, since she was not a threat to herself or anyone else, she was not given any medication. She didn't feed herself, so they gave her fluids and nutrition intravenously. When it was time for Candy to come home, her parents brought her to her room. They tried to establish a normal routine, but it was impossible. How do you live with someone who isn't really there? Candy was catatonic, beyond the reach of human contact.

No other professionals were willing to work with her, and Candy was eventually placed in Willowbrook. She was moved around to other institutions, and eventually her parents took her back home and put her on the list for me to evaluate. After another month at home, Candy was brought into my group home office in nearly the same condition as she had been in months prior. Her parents walked her down to my room and explained the details of what had happened. Candy sat motionless and stared off toward nothing in particular. To demonstrate her condition, her father made a sudden loud noise by slapping his hand on my closet door. It was sudden enough and loud enough to make me blink and raise my heart rate. Candy didn't flinch.

I asked her parents to leave the room. As I spoke to Candy, my heart sank; I realized that none of my words or caring could affect her. She was as lost to the world as if she were in a coma, but someone in a coma didn't sit up and stare through you.

After the third or fourth meeting alone with Candy, I invited her parents back and expressed my discomfort. I explained to them that my understanding and experience in these matters was limited, and as much as I wanted to help Candy, I could not in good conscience sit across from their daughter asking endless unanswered questions. I recommended they take her to a training program where she might be stimulated by the activities and by others with what was then called mental retardation. Perhaps being around activity and people would be helpful.

Candy's parents were frightened by this prospect. They had no desire to let their daughter out of their sight for any extended period. They made it clear that if I were unwilling to continue the "therapy," they would take her back home, leave her in her room, feed her, bathe her and dress her, and wait for the day she would recognize them again.

This also seemed unacceptable to me, so I negotiated with them a three-month deadline on my work with her. The agreement was that if no improvement took place within a month, I would seek services for Candy elsewhere. They agreed, and I set myself up with a clinical supervisor: my journey to find Candy had begun. But this was uncharted territory in 1979. Psychologists had little knowledge about, interest in, or tools to work with people with intellectual disabilities—much less those who have been traumatized and catatonic. Candy's condition and circumstances were far beyond anything I'd ever encountered. No one had any real insight on how to work with her. Psychologists and psychiatrists were knee-deep in the phenomenon Dr. Stephen Reiss had labeled overshadowing. No one was interested in looking at secondary diagnoses, conditions, or treatments. If the person was classified by the then-in-use diagnosis of mentally retarded, then no further diagnosis or treatment was sought.

This never made sense to me. It was the equivalent of saying that someone had a heart condition—so why bother treating her broken leg?

In addition to the supervisor, I consulted a variety of colleagues about Candy's condition. I read the literature and spent time looking at case studies of such trauma with children, believing this might hold a clue as to how to approach her. Somewhere in the middle of these resources came the suggestion of using art therapy. I provided Candy with a drawing board and paper and hundreds of crayons. The first several times I had to put a crayon in her hand, but she wouldn't do more than hold it. Finally, after I moved her hand to make marks on the paper, she began drawing concentric circles. I had placed a brown crayon in her hand, so the choice was not hers, but the circles were endless. During the first session this happened, she continued endlessly and only stopped when I put my hand on hers.

The transition from my putting a crayon in her hand to Candy choosing her own color was excruciatingly slow. Three times a week, I tried to get her to pick her own crayon, but it was only when I placed one in her hand that she would begin the circling movement. I finally decided to put two crayons of very different colors into her hand. She chose one by letting the other drop. This seemed less of a choice than simply a way to find something to draw with.

Three weeks had gone by, and except for hundreds of circles being drawn, "therapy" was going nowhere.

My training in art therapy was limited, but I hoped to find some way for her to express something, anything, about herself. I decided to try to give her some direction and drew a picture of myself, a miserable line drawing with the only distinguishing characteristic being my beard. I hoped none of my colleagues would see this because this drawing wasn't my attempt to mimic the type of sketch she could render; this was flat out the best I could do. I made the outline in brown and the beard in black and colored my blue shirt and black pants in as well. When I was done, I asked her to draw a picture of herself. I handed her the three crayons I had used and she dropped the black and blue and began making concentric circles *around* the figure I had drawn. It was the first concrete acknowledgement that Candy knew there was something else in the world other than her. None of her circles crossed any of my lines.

Candy began drawing on the paper we shared during the sessions. I drew my effort at representing myself with my name next to the figure, and eventually Candy drew a crude likeness of herself with a scribbled "Candy" alongside it. She responded to my outstretched hand to shake hello, but when I clasped her fingers she either left her hand motionless or withdrew it. Her eyes never met mine. It wasn't much, but it was a beginning.

I knew she would be the outlier in a home of outliers. She would be the one most different from the rest. However, I also knew no one else would be willing to work with her. Since we were an experimental home, inclusion of difficult cases—not exclusion—should be the goal. With a host of doubts and reservations, I took Candy into Walden House. My hope was that, somehow, we'd find a way to reach and teach her. But just the opposite happened: it would be her character strength of perseverance and grit that would astonish me and make me want to know more. Some twenty-five years after working with her, I'd receive honors for being the first psychologist to offer a form of group treatment for people with intellectual disabilities who have been traumatized. It would be Candy who would teach me how someone could recover after all hope and dignity were lost.

Benny

At thirty-eight years old, Benny lived at home and drove a car. He was mildly intellectually disabled and would become one of our highest-functioning residents. As a baby, he contracted an infection that spread to his brain through his sinuses. He suffered brain damage and, as a result, spoke with such a heavy nasal quality that his speech was nearly unintelligible. His parents doted on him, but after his father died Benny, then in his early 30s, decompensated and had trouble doing, well, anything. At his father's wake, Benny was inconsolable. He would see his father lying in the coffin and cry, hit his hands against his head, and run out of the funeral parlor. Over the three days of the wake the scene was repeated—and his mother asked the family physician to sedate him for the funeral. At the burial Benny was relaxed but still clearly upset. He cornered the priest and asked some pointed questions.

"Where mah fah-dah?" he asked.

After some confusion and interpretation, the priest explained. "Well, Benny, your father is in heaven now."

"I want to see him."

As the story goes the priest did his best to explain where heaven was, what goes on there, and the fact that his dad was in God's hands.

"Ah wan to see him," Benny insisted.

Apparently, this was where something got lost in translation. "You will see him one day," said the priest trying to comfort Benny. "Your dad is in heaven and when you die you'll go to heaven and you'll see him then."

Benny apparently simply said "Okay," and left the funeral parlor. No one missed him for quite a while. He had gone directly from the funeral parlor and stood in the street trying to get hit by a car. His love for his father was so great he was willing to do the unthinkable: to get to heaven to see his father, he was going to kill himself. While he didn't get hit, this would be the beginning of Benny trying to hurt himself. Months went by, and Benny got better and worse. His mother explained that he said he was hearing voices. Voices that told him various ways to kill himself.

I started seeing Benny the day after he stood naked waiting for the New York City-bound train to run him over near the Poughkeepsie train station. A Good Samaritan pushed him away seconds before the train would have killed him. As part of the arrangement with New York state, some of the residents had to come from the community. Since Benny's father had passed away and his mother was elderly, Benny was one of the candidates. During our interview, I learned to interpret Benny's speech and understand more about his thoughts.

"Hi Benny; do you know why you are here?"

"Uh huh."

"Tell me how come."

"I wa-wa seema fah-duh."

"I'm sorry Benny, can you repeat that?"

"I wawa seema fah-duh."

"Fah-duh?"

"Uh-huh."

"I don't know what fah-duh means."

"I wawa seema fah-duh. Seema fah-duh."

"Did you think your father was coming to the train station?"

"No. I take the train to go to heaven."

"You thought that if you stood in front of a train you would get killed."

". . . and then I see my fah-dah."

The most intriguing part of working with people with severe cognitive and emotional disabilities is that, after a while, you start to understand their logic. It actually made sense to me that if Benny wanted to see his dead father in heaven, he would want to kill himself to get there. But what didn't make sense was the fact that he did it naked. I was ready to chalk that one up to some crazy psychotic thing, but Benny had a better answer.

"Benny," I began, "I understand why you would want to stand in front of a train to get killed so you could see your father in heaven, but I don't know why you wouldn't want to wear clothes. Can you tell me why you took your clothes off?"

"You don't need no clothes in heaven," he said.

The truth was that Benny was hearing voices all the time. They told him what to do, and he listened. The year before the train incident, he had driven his car off an embankment and into a pond because the voices told him the engine in his car was too hot. Six months earlier he tried to stab his mother with a steak knife because he had seen her crying and wanted her to be with his father in heaven so she would be happier. He told the police that his father said he missed her—and if Benny killed her, his father would be happy and proud of him.

Taking in Candy and Benny changed the dynamics in the home. Sophia, Albert, Mike and Lilith had taken all our attention just to keep them civil. Taimi, Gwennie and I forged a bond based out of deep mutual respect and trust. Gwennie organized everything and Taimi had a sixth sense about intervening before something would explode. She'd notice Sophia getting agitated, or Albert eyeing a tasty pen cap, and swoop in to save me from having to monitor him in the bathroom for the next few days. Mike was, for the most part, a gentle giant, and as long as we beat Lilith to the front door before she made an obscene remark to the postman, we were managing—but just barely. But now we had Benny, who brought with him the threat of command auditory hallucinations and suicide, and Candy, who lived in a world of silent emptiness. The three of us had each other's backs, but the daily potential of an unimaginable crisis left us feeling like an ill-equipped bomb squad. Yet somehow there was meaning and satisfaction in what we were doing. It was as though some unexplained force in the universe had conspired to bring us together.

Taimi

Taimi was unique in many ways and was proving to be invaluable. She was a tough, streetwise kid whose mother had helped her get a job at Walden House. She looked tough, with the kind of no-frills, take-no-prisoners attitude that was as refreshing as it was in-your-face. She was only about five feet tall and twenty or so pounds overweight. You never had to guess at where you stood with Taimi; she was unfiltered—and as upfront as anyone I'd ever met. She didn't own a dress, so jeans and a sweatshirt were her daily uniform. Although she had no desire to waste her money on fashion, she was the first to comment on anything stylish in the newspapers or on TV. She was always clean, but never wore perfume, lipstick, or eye makeup, or fixed her hair. She had the perpetual look of just having rolled out of bed. If Gwennie was yin, Taimi was our yang.

She may have been a walking contradiction, but there was no one who could better tap into the deep pain and pathology of the residents and tune into their needs. She had great instincts about people and had the unique gifts of empathy, compassion, and directness. Her raw intelligence was evident by her knowledge of facts, research, and political understanding. I may have had some experience and academic credentials, but Taimi had real skill and talent, and she always had her heart and head in the right place. Outside of a few of my professors at the university, she knew more about psychiatry than any of my fellow graduate students. I was technically her boss, but she was the one who knew which way the wind was blowing. I think Taimi admired me because I was training to be a psychologist but devoting my energy to people who would never be self-referrals for a private practice.

Taimi had a sixth sense about everybody. Although she was rough and tumble on the outside, inside she seemed to have both emotional radar and indefatigable energy. She knew when people were off. She was tuned into their balance and a word, look, or wink could avert disaster. I was also never able to get up before her. It didn't matter if it was six a.m. or five a.m.; she always seemed to be already at work—puttering, cleaning, catching up on paperwork, washing the refrigerator, setting the table. She kept her private life to herself, and I never heard her talk about a boyfriend or girlfriend (or anyone for that matter) outside of the home—except her mom. It wasn't the usual banter about her mom's pitfalls and shortcomings you'd hear from a young woman in her twenties. She spoke about her mom in a way that indicated she was proud of her. Her parents had been together for more than thirty years and, according to Taimi, were still very much in love, "whatever *that* is," and had a great relationship. Apparently, Taimi's plan was to live at home forever, but in a flash of inspiration she simply decided it was time, and with her mom's help, Walden House allowed her to accomplish two firsts with one stone: moving out and getting a job.

Taimi liked to sketch, and once I found her pad filled with charcoal drawings of the residents. She saw beyond their disabilities and limitations to capture their potential—their possibilities. They were stunning portrayals. Her drawings revealed the essence and promise of each resident. When I realized the extent of her artistic ability, I asked if she would help me with material I needed for my dissertation. I wanted sketches for research I was doing on developmental aspects of memory. I wanted to show children and adults with intellectual disabilities pairs of objects interacting together, and then later show them one of the images to see if they recalled the other. I needed specific line drawings of objects interacting in simple usual ways, like a fork piercing a piece of meat. Then a series of images with objects interacting in slightly odd ways, like a football resting in a frying pan. Finally, I asked Taimi to draw objects interacting in extremely odd ways, like a fish smoking a pipe. I explained that the theory was that the more bizarre the interaction, the better the memory for both older children and higher-functioning intellectually disabled adults. Younger children and lower-functioning people with intellectual disabilities would do better recalling simpler, more functional interactions between objects. She grasped the idea behind this immediately and we speculated about how this difference in memory ability might be useful in different types of training for the people we were working with from Willowbrook. She seemed, at times, as excited about doing the research as I was. Taimi was one of the first people I met with artistic and scientific ability combined, and her intellect and artistic abilities were a natural extension of her personality: simple, articulate, and right on target.

She seemed to genuinely love and care for each resident, but had a special affinity for Sophia. I think she connected with Sophia's rage. One night we were in the house alone downstairs after all the residents were in bed. Taimi asked if she could make a call from the office and, of course, I said it was fine. I closed the door to give her privacy and went into the kitchen on the other side of the house—but could hear her voice escalate; she was arguing with someone. I heard her screaming and slam the phone down five or six times. When I opened the door, I could see she'd cut her hand and broken the phone's handset. She looked as if she was ready to kill someone. She unplugged the phone and took a handkerchief out of her back pocket to cover the cut on her hand.

"You'll have a new phone first thing in the morning," was all she said, and she walked past me, upstairs, and the incident was never mentioned again. The next morning the phone was replaced, and I watched her and Gwennie help Sophia apply lipstick for the first time without a trace or discussion of the rage from the night before. Here were two of the most unlikely coworkers with the loving goal of helping Sophia do something she had never done before. It was one of the most tender moments I can remember from Walden House.

Even now, decades later, Taimi's talents still impress me. Eventually I'd go on to work at both at the University of Pennsylvania with Martin Seligman and design and teach courses in Columbia's Department of Counseling and Clinical Psychology. In these and other roles, I'd be responsible for training, facilitating, and supervising all types of therapists. Taimi would be the model I'd use to compare their progress and potential. If seasoned or budding therapists didn't have Taimi's values at the core of their being, this was what we worked on. Taimi taught me that techniques and philosophy are no substitute or adequate preparation for helping others heal. If students or trainees didn't have what Taimi had, our first discussion was about what motivates them. If money, prestige, or status were their only incentive, I'd usually direct them to other professors, trainers, and supervisors. Taimi was then, and remains now, the gold standard.

Harold

Finding staff to work at the home continued to be difficult. At the end of four months, Taimi, Gwennie and I were more or less doing everything ourselves. When I took the job at the group home, I thought it was something a non-handy guy could do. But I was finding that the tools I brought—my hammer, as it was—weren't big enough, strong enough, or the right kind. I needed more master craftsmen who brought unique tools, like Taimi, if the house was ever going to become a home. That's when Harold showed up. He would be our grandmaster—with surprising skills—and he had something we desperately needed: power tools.

Several new staff had come to work, but few lasted longer than two weeks. Even with David helping as often as he could, we were overwhelmed. Sophia's and Mike's outbursts were at the top of the list of reasons people left, but Albert's feces showing up in unexpected places (including closets, dresser drawers, and the medicine chest) and Lilith propositioning every guy who entered the home were other reasons people moved on. We used temp workers from various other human service agencies, but word had gotten out that we weren't an easy gig, so other staff were less willing to take shifts. When either Taimi or I took the rare day off, we always checked in with each other. Neither of us had any real downtime.

The most difficult part became planning, buying, and preparing food. It had become all-consuming. Gwennie, it seemed, had never cooked a meal in her life, and Taimi could only tell us what food to buy, which, not surprisingly, was only the food she liked. Cap'n Crunch and Lucky Charms were her faves, which meant they became ours, so things like vegetables, fruits, and orange juice never made the list. As for me, if an aptitude test existed for culinary skill, my score would have been lower even than that for my talent for anything mechanical. It was time to hire a cook.

But it wasn't like I didn't try. I'd interviewed a half-dozen men and one woman for the position. Two of the men showed up drunk for the interview, two clearly didn't have the skills, and one I asked to come prepare a meal so we could sample his talent, but he never showed. The other guy prepared a meal even Albert wouldn't eat.

The woman was, by far, the most competent. She had a great résumé and references, and cooked a beautiful chicken dinner. But she couldn't get by with the salary we were offering, and my financial hands were tied. In desperation, I called the Office of Vocational Rehabilitation. This state office helps people with disabilities or other difficulties get jobs in the community.

"Not OVR," said Taimi. "They'll only send us people who are on parole."

"I'm sure they won't send someone on parole with the kind of program we have," I assured her.

OVR sent Harold over for an interview. He was a very muscular black man, maybe in his thirties. His face looked like the sculptor didn't have time to finish it. It lacked definition, wasn't symmetrical, and had scars that looked like burned wooden matches were pressed into his skin. His eyes were only slightly puffed, but they seemed like they had at some point been twice their size. When he handed me papers, his right hand looked like it had been carved from the bark of an oak tree. He casually mentioned he'd spent the last four years in prison, but gave no details of the crime.

"My parole office said you was hiring, that you need a cook," he began as I looked at the papers.

"Harold, do you know what kind of a place this is? What we do here?" I asked, leery of his four years in prison.

"Some kind of halfway house. Don't know halfway between what and what, but it don't matter. I can cook, you need a cook, we both get what we want," he said, looking directly at me.

"The people who live here, Harold, are disturbed, and they have some disturbing behaviors. You would be here for every dinner, plus breakfast on the weekend. You'd be spending a lot of time with some very disturbed folks."

The sentence had barely finished coming out of my mouth when a fly came near Harold's head. His left arm moved so fast to snatch it that for a moment I wasn't even sure it had happened.

"I lived in prison for four years. I know disturbed people. I need to work and keep out of prison. I'm halfway myself. Ain't nothing much you're gonna throw at me I can't handle."

I couldn't argue with that and decided Harold was worth a try. He was sober and showed up, which made him our top candidate. I reached across the desk and shook his hand. "We're all halfway between something and something else," I said. "Everyone has to pull his or her weight and help one another. When can you make us a sample meal?"

"I can cook for y'all tonight."

"I don't know what we've got in the fridge," I apologized, "but I'll put you on the clock right now. Just sign some forms so we can pay you. If the participants like the meal, you're hired."

"I can cook and I can sign my name," he said.

"That puts you in the top half of this group," I quipped.

Harold signed his name, promised he would be back at four, and shook my hand as he stood up. "I won't disappoint you," he said. "I'll show myself out."

Harold walked out the front door and closed it behind him. I could see him bounce down the steps; he stopped just before he reached the bottom. He turned his left arm out as if he were going to stretch, and then, with a slight upward boost, he released the fly.

* * *

A routine had formed. Although we were still having trouble getting staff, Taimi, Gwennie, and I were able to keep the peace for the most part, and the participants seemed to be enjoying, or at least getting used to, our new home. Taimi and I got up together, made breakfast, and helped Jake, Mike and Lilith get ready for their programs. When Gwennie came in, she helped Taimi get Albert, Sophia, Candy, and Benny to do chores around the house.

Dinnertime allowed us to be together, but it was chaotic. We all scrambled to get dinner on the table, and then had to manage as people ate and left. Some, like Albert, ate so fast we were hardly seated before he had finished. Others, like Candy, needed an hour before she would even venture a mouthful.

Harold had kept his promise. He came in about four-thirty and started looking through the refrigerator and pantry. I was in our kitchen, and noticed that he was rearranging food in both places. He was making it his kitchen.

As the six o'clock dinnertime came near, the first real whiff of a home-cooked meal filled the house. The smell, and the warmth of the kitchen on a cold February day, drew us like flies to honey.

Albert was particularly entranced. I imagined he'd never encountered such an all-encompassing aroma, and when he realized Harold was the magician making it happen, Albert moved himself close by Harold and began to rock and smile.

"Albert likes you," I said to Harold.

"I see that," Harold said softly. "Why don't you all sit down, it'll be easier for me to serve you."

His voice had an authority to it, but without a trace of harshness. He was simply clear and direct. We sat down.

Taimi, Gwennie, Sophia, Albert, Mike, Lilith, Candy, Benny, Tom—the new staff person—and I sat down. We were all a bit like children waiting for Christmas dinner, and we watched as Harold began the food parade. He placed two large bowls of salad on the table along with two bottles of dressing.

"We didn't have any of this in the house," said Taimi.

"Can't have a good meal without a good salad. I brought some of my favorites," said Harold as he turned toward me. "And don't worry, Dr. Dan, this is my gift to you for tonight. You don't have to worry about paying for the salad."

"Thank you, Harold, and I wasn't worried at all. We don't have any money to pay you with," I said with a smile.

Two pies and several bowls of steamed broccoli and green beans followed. Taimi and Gwennie began dishing it out, and Harold went back to pulling more stuff out of the oven.

"This is incredible!" said Taimi.

"Unbelievable," offered Gwennie.

"Not bad," mumbled Tom.

Everyone except Candy was eating and obviously enjoying the food. Candy, still catatonic, sat motionless in front of her plate.

"Harold, in case it isn't obvious, you are our new and favorite cook. This is incredible," I said as I took another bite. "Did we have all of this? We love it!"

"Just tomato cheese pie, some greens, and stuffed peppers, nothin' fancy," said Harold.

"Well, govner, everybody loves it," said Gwennie.

"Everybody except Candy. She must not like it," said Harold as he replenished the salad.

"Candy's catatonic from post-traumatic stress disorder, she—" began Tom.

"Tom, no labels," I interrupted.

"I don't care what country she is from, she still got to eat," said Harold.

"Catatonia isn't a country, you idio—" began Tom.

"Hey!" yelled Taimi as she pointed her finger at Tom.

"Sorry," said Tom.

"I know what catatonia is, son," said Harold as he began washing one of the pans. "Just trying to lighten the load."

"Candy needs more time to eat," said Harold. "That's all."

"She got too many choices in front of her. Let me fix a plate," suggested Harold.

"Everybody's a shrink," muttered Tom.

"Saw it in 'Nam more than I cared to," said Harold. "We did it this way. Take the choice out of the equation."

Harold put a small portion of stuffed pepper on a plate and replaced the full dish in front of Candy. He folded her hand around the fork, and then pierced it into the piece. "Like this, honey."

Candy stayed motionless, fork in the food. Harold walked back to the stove. "Rest of you go 'bout your business, she get to it when she ready."

Tom shook his head. Taimi and Gwennie looked at me for a cue.

"Well, I am ready for seconds," I said. "Albert, you want some more?"

Albert shook his head yes. Sophia pointed to the pie.

"Sophia wants some too," said Taimi.

Harold fussed at the stove while Taimi and Gwennie dished out extras. Candy wasn't moving, and Tom, annoyed by the whole scene, took his plate and silverware to the sink.

"I've got better things to do than to wait for nothing to happen," complained Tom. He put his dish in the sink and began to walk away.

Harold, now drying the pan, spoke, but didn't look at Tom. "Son, I'm the cook, not the maid. Rinse it, then put it in the dishwasher like I imagine everyone else has got to do."

"I don't have to take orders from you!" Tom bristled.

"We all do our own dishes around here, Tom," I advised. "You don't want to be a bad role model for others, do you?"

Tom wiped the dish, dumped it into the dishwasher, and left. As he stormed out of the kitchen, Candy ate the piece of food on her fork.

"Candy! You little stinker!" Taimi yelped. "Do you want more?"

Harold was already bringing over another piece.

"Questions just make things more difficult," said Harold. "Here you go, honey." Harold repeated what he had done earlier with Candy. He lovingly folded her hand around the fork and gently pushed the prongs into the bit of stuffed pepper.

"Just go about your business," he said casually. "She'll let us know when she's done."

* * *

After a few weeks, Harold had the house humming. The meals were astounding. Harold had provided us with a structure that drew us together. No one was late for dinner.

"So where do you go when you're done here and not thrilling us with your culinary talent?" I asked Harold one night as he was wiping down the counters, preparing to leave.

"I drive over to Pete's downtown and have a beer, maybe two, then back to my room."

"Your room?"

"Yeah, I have a studio over the candy shop on Broad Street," he said as he wrung out the dishtowel. "It ain't much, but I can afford it, and that's what counts."

"I've never been in Pete's," I said.

"Well, it ain't much either, but it's where the locals hang out. I like to learn about the local scene. Find out what the rules are, and who makes them," he said as we helped each other lift the garbage bag out of the pail. "That's the first rule of prison, Dr. Dan."

Out the window, we both saw the young boy in the yard next door. He was in the far corner, facing away from us, moving his right arm in a jerky motion.

"What the hell is that boy doing?" asked Harold. "I see him over there a couple of times a week doing the same thing; can't figure it."

"Me either," I sympathized. "But I think that might be the fire chief's son."

"The girls have been talking about Chief Willy," said Harold. "I'm looking forward to seeing this guy."

"You'll probably meet him sooner than later," I said as I tied off the top of the garbage bag. Then we both took another look out the window at the boy.

I was right. Weeks later, Harold would reveal to me his first encounter with Chief Willy

* * *

As Harold told it, he sat down at the bar and ordered a beer. He kept to himself, his eyes mostly focused on the TV: Walter Cronkite and the evening news.

The man at the other end of the bar was sufficiently inebriated. Harold shook his head and watched the man as he pestered young women nearby.

Between Harold and the man was a woman alone at the bar. The drunk slobbered up to her.

"What's a good-looking trick like you sitting all alone for?"

"I'm not a trick and I'm not alone," she said with disgust.

"You won't be alone anymore if you saddle up with me," he spluttered out.

"You're sooo pathetic . . ." she began.

Her boyfriend was back. He stood between them.

"Is there a problem?" said her boyfriend.

"Aw, jeez, kid, you're blocking my view."

"I'm going to block more than that if you don't back off," he said, staring.

"You don't know who you're talking to. Get out of my way," the drunk said dismissively. He pushed the young man back, shoving his shoulders. The boyfriend immediately slapped the guy's face and issued a warning.

"Don't make me wipe the floor with you."

The drunk, enraged, began swinging wildly. He landed only glancing blows and the young man backed away.

"Come on babe, let's get out of here," he said as he grabbed her hand.

The drunk made a botched attempt to grab her other arm, and her boyfriend slapped him in the face with the back of his hand for trying. He pointed his finger in the man's face and whispered. "I'll fuck you up so bad you'll piss blood for a week. Stay away from us," he said, and pushed the palm of his hand up into the drunk's nose.

The man stumbled and caught himself on the bar. When he looked up there was no one between him and Harold. "What the hell are you looking at, you black bastard!" he said, holding his bloody nose and slurring his words. "Who let the eggplant in here?"

Harold tossed a few dollars on the bar and pushed his chair back. The drunk came charging toward him. "I said," he paused as he hiccupped, "what are you looking at?"

The drunk took a few roundhouse swings, but Harold left his hands at his side, and dodged each punch. Finally, the guy yelled at him. "Stay still!"

"Okay," said Harold.

The drunk swung hard, but Harold blocked the punch expertly with his left arm, and then deflected every other punch the same way. He never raised his right hand. Finally, the man swung, missed, and hit Harold's glass on the bar. It broke and he began to bleed.

"Damn it! Shit, damn it!" he screamed as blood splattered onto the floor.

Harold turned and walked out the door. He was already at his car and didn't quite hear the bartender as he came around to help.

"Chief Willy, are you okay?"

Jeffery

Jeffery wasn't right. He was the eleven-year-old son of the fire chief, Willy, who lived next door, and although I wasn't a seasoned clinician I could tell there was something not okay with his isolation. I could tell there was something off about him. You didn't need a degree to see he had some type of attention deficit along with his propensity for isolation. He was always running around his yard falling and hurting himself. I knew I would have to deal with his father because we needed to pass the fire codes, and I'd heard that Willy was a pretty good drinker, and I knew that attention deficit hyperactivity disorder (ADHD) was more likely to occur in families with alcoholism, but Jeffery looked like the ADHD poster child. He seemed distracted and accident-prone and was always cut and bruised. Some of the bruises didn't look like they were from falls. They could have been caused by his skinny arms being squeezed too tightly by his father, or his mother's wedding ring cutting open his chin, but he was so disaster-prone it was hard to tell.

There were some tricky politics involved with seeing problems with Jeffery. Do I let his father know? If I did, if I said: "I think your child has a condition that is treatable," how would he respond? "Oh, thank you," wasn't on the top of my best guess list. But something was clearly wrong and somehow not letting his parents know seemed wrong. Many years later, after I'd developed my skills as a clinician, I'd learn that even when people want information about their ailment or their child's, they often need to have it given to them in ways that would allow them to be motivated to change. Otherwise, it's a war. People will argue about what you tell them, dismiss it, or simply never come back. But at this stage of my career, I had no idea what to do and took the path of least resistance: I did nothing.

Jeffery was also cruel to animals. From the kitchen window of the convent, I could see him kicking a stray cat or dog, or punching them after luring them with a piece of meat. I'd heard a rumor that the summer before we moved in, Jeffery caught a good-sized box turtle and buried it upside down in a hole a foot deep. He'd soaked the poor thing in gasoline, lit it on fire, and watched the creature burn until the fire went out, then threw dirt on it and buried what was left. But in the morning, Jeffery found the grave opened and the turtle gone. The rumor was he lived in fear of the turtle's revenge.

My first encounter with Jeffery was on an early afternoon. He was sitting, legs spread open, in the middle of the sidewalk between the convent and his home. He was completely engrossed in a task I could not see. When I went outside to put the garbage out, I walked over and watched as he used a razor to sever a spider's legs.

"Guess they won't be calling him a daddy long legs anymore," I quipped.

Jeffery didn't say anything. He looked up at me with a deadpan face, which shone with a type of satisfaction I could not fathom. He went back to the task at hand and after I watched him slice off the next leg, I walked away. His vacancy terrified me. It was only a few days later I'd learn more about what helped create it.

I could hear his mother yelling. I remembered her from the town meetings. She was the one always leading the fight against the group home. She said there was no reason to bring crazy people into the town; that's why she paid taxes—to keep emotionally unstable people locked up. Her yelling was muffled by the closed windows and doors, but her blare came from the second-floor window nearest the convent: Jeffery's room. Suddenly the bedroom window opened and the screaming became louder and clearer. I could hear Jeffery and his mother going at it.

"I am sick and tired of washing the piss stains out of your sheets every goddamn night," I heard her scream.

"No! No! No! No! No!" Jeffery shrieked as his mother pushed the sheets out the window.

She stood at the open window waving the yellow-stained sheets. "You want to wet your bed like a little baby? Do you? You want to piss in your pajamas every night?" she said to Jeffery. "Then let's show everybody what a little baby you are. Here everybody. This is what baby Jeffery does at night. Baby Jeffery! Baby Jeffery!" she bellowed. "Baby Jeffery! Baby Jeffery!"

"No! No! No! No! No!" he protested again, trying to grab the sheets.

His mother held him back with one hand and waved the sheets with the other.

"Baby Jeffery! Baby Jeffery! Hey everybody! Baby Jeffery!"

"Give me your wet pissy pajamas you baby!" I heard her yell as she turned back into the room. "I'm going to take those piss-pants right off you right now," she roared. I could hear but not see the struggle.

"No! No! No! No! No!" I could hear the boy say. "No! No! No! No! No!"

There was a struggle, then what sounded like two hard slaps against flesh. There was nothing for a moment, then I could hear Jeffery cry.

Armed with flags of humiliation, Jeffery's mother waved the sheet and blue and white pajama pants out the window.

"Baby Jeffery, everybody! Baby Jeffery lives here!"

This from a woman who complained the residents of the group home might be emotionally unstable.

Jake

"Jake's mother died."

These were the first words Frank spoke to me as I answered the phone. We had worked together years earlier in the sheltered workshop in New Jersey and Frank was Jake's job coach at the center I ran. I hadn't spoken to Frank since taking the new job. He went on to explain that Jake had spent three days alone with his mother's body on the living room floor. It was only when a neighbor came over to investigate that he found Jake sitting on the couch, traumatized by his mother's death. It appeared as if he had sat motionless for those three days. Frank explained that there were no provisions made for Jake, and that he was in a respite home in New York State because that's where the closest relative lived. It was a temporary placement until he was institutionalized or placed in a group home. He wanted to know if I could pull some strings and get him into the new group home. Frank knew I liked Jake because of his unique abilities: He was an autistic savant.

But Jake was also a hard person to look at. He had an acute case of acne that had gone untreated for many years, and kids in high school called him "crater face." His breath was bad, and he had a habit of standing too close to people. It was common for him to come within six inches of someone's face when he spoke, and the first time he did this to me I recoiled involuntarily. He also had a stare, an unnerving, vacant gawk that went through you. Although not completely shaven, his hair was buzzed to the scalp, which made looking at and being close to him a challenge.

The closely shaven head, unoccupied stare, and derogatory "crater face" name kids called him gave way to the epithet "Moonie," a disparaging term from the 1970s that referred to followers of Sun Myung Moon and the Unification Church.

But Jake's horrid hygiene was at all times in stark contrast to what he was wearing. He was of average height and build, but always impeccably dressed. He wore neatly pressed pants and a dark gray or brown cashmere sweater pulled over a Lands' End shirt—even in the summer. His silver watch with a leather strap continually displayed the correct time, and a silver pinky ring ornamented his right hand. Everything was neat and clean, but witnessing his acne and having to endure his ferociously bad breath always made me want to retch. Sometimes, when Jake wanted to make a point, his volume went up slightly and his stare shifted leftward. The gaze would remain fixed until he finished his point and walked away.

When I first met Jake, about five years earlier, he had already memorized the Manhattan phone book—all of it. This was before *Rain Man* popularized the notion that people like Jake existed. You could read a number to him and he would tell you the name and address of the person connected to it. If you read the address, he would give you the name and number. If you provided him with the name, let's say Sophia Smith, he would give you an answer that told you precisely how many Sophia Smiths were in the phone book, then proceed to recite the addresses and numbers.

As if that weren't enough, his command of the Yellow Pages was even more intriguing. If you read a number to him, he would let you know if the number was set in boldface type, and if the business had an advertisement in the book. If it did, he would tell you what page it was on and deliver the ad to you from memory.

Two years earlier when I'd worked with him, Jake was employed Thursdays and Fridays in the sheltered workshop for people with intellectual disabilities, and he worked Mondays, Tuesdays, and Wednesdays at an assembly plant putting together transistor radios. He was the only Caucasian male working in the factory, and was, by far, their most loyal employee. He had not missed a day of work or been late in more than three years.

The sheltered workshop staff and the factory workers knew him to carry large amounts of cash in small bills. It was not uncommon for him to pull out a couple of hundred dollars in twenties, looking for change to buy a soda. The source of his money was never questioned, and remained a mystery until the week after I tested him.

The state required IQ tests every three years to validate intellectual disabilities. As part of graduate school psychology training, we had to test people with different aptitudes. Jake's abilities were about as different as they came. Since I wasn't charging a fee, the state gave me permission to do the testing with the provision that one of my professors, a licensed psychologist, would oversee the exam results. What I didn't realize was that I would be asking the questions, but it was Jake who would be testing me.

As the director of the sheltered workshop where Jake was a participant, I had a small office where I could carry out the exam. He was one of about forty people with intellectual disabilities in a program that provided simple contract jobs, such as stuffing envelopes, or packaging Styrofoam cups into a box, or any number of other inane jobs that typical industry workers would become too bored with to complete. The workshop provided daily structure and work—essential elements in the habilitation of people with chronic mental illness or intellectual disabilities.

One of the more amazing things about Jake was that when he met you, he solicited all the information he could about your personal life: birthday, anniversary date, employment start dates, everything. When I told him my birthday was July 20, 1951, he said it had been a Tuesday and this year it was going to be on a Saturday. He also knew that on my eighteenth birthday, Neil Armstrong, whose birthday he said was August 5, 1930, walked on the moon. He seemed to know this information intuitively, spontaneously, and it was all correct.

I was seated behind a table preparing the materials for the IQ test I was about to give. Jake had been told to meet me at the room at two p.m. He walked in without knocking at exactly two p.m. "Hello, Dr. Dan."

"Yes, hello Jake. It probably would have been a good idea to knock on the door," I suggested.

Jake turned around and knocked on the back of the still-open door ten or twelve times like he was tapping in a small carpet nail. He didn't do this to be facetious—he was just following my direction.

"August 19 is next Thursday, and you and your wife will be married six years on that day. I hope you have a very nice anniversary," he said without smiling.

I was used to Jake's unsolicited announcements, but this one caught me off guard. If he hadn't said it, I would not have remembered. "Thank you, Jake."

"You are welcome."

I invited Jake to sit across from me at the desk. He sat down and stared just slightly past me.

"Jake, I am going to ask you some questions and I would like you to give me the best answers you can, okay?"

"Okay," he responded.

"Let's start with an easy one," I began. "How many legs does a dog have?"

Jake gazed off, upward, to the left. It was as though he were imagining a dog and mentally counting the legs. He stayed fixed in this position for about twenty seconds.

"Jake, do you have an answer?" I finally queried.

His eyes darted back and forth, as if scanning the ceiling for a picture of a dog. "Ahh . . ." he hesitated, "ahh . . . two."

"Two?" I asked the man who had memorized the Manhattan phone book.

"Ahh . . . two, Dr. Dan," he said as his voice began to go up. "A dog has two legs."

He kept scanning the ceiling for the dog. I was shocked and busied myself with finding out what to do when the examinee misses the first question. Jake continued.

"A dog has two legs, Dr. Dan," he said, staring at the ceiling. "Two in the front . . . and two in the back."

I had no idea how to score this and made a note to check with my professor, then went to the next item. "Let's move on to the next question, okay, Jake?"

"Sure, Dr. Dan," he said, staring at my forehead.

"What are the four seasons of the year?" I said, hoping for a quick response.

"Fall, winter, and spring," he said.

"That's good, Jake," I said to encourage him. "What's another season?"

"Another season?" he asked.

"Yes. I need you to give me a different season. One that you have not mentioned."

"Oregano."

"Oregano?" I said, dumbfounded.

His voice began to rise. "My mother seasons our pizza with oregano," he explained.

"Yes, I am sure she does, Jake," I said, trying to keep my wits about me. "But I need another season like the ones you said before."

"Before?" he said, looking up at the ceiling.

"I asked you what the seasons of the year are and you said, fall, winter, and spring, remember?"

"Yes I do, Dr. Dan."

"Good. I need one more season like fall, winter, or spring."

"I don't know any more of those seasons," he explained.

"Are you sure?"

"Fall, winter, and spring are all I know."

"Okay," I said, deciding not to push it, "so which one is your favorite?"

"Summer."

But it was when we tested his memory that you could see the true brilliance and awe of Jake's condition. "Jake," I said, "I am going to say some numbers and when I say them I would like you to say them back to me. For example, if I say three, two, seven, what would you say?"

"Three, two, seven," he said with his usual stare.

The sequence of numbers built, and he flawlessly answered each question. He did this to the limits of the exam, and, intrigued, I asked him to remember twenty digits. He did this perfectly: then thirty, then forty. I am convinced I would still be sitting there reading him numbers if I had not decided to go to the next section of the test. His capacity for memory seemed truly without limit. But asked to reverse a sequence of numbers, Jake responded in a way I would not have predicted.

"Jake, I am going to read some numbers to you. But this time when I say them I want you to say them backward. Okay?"

"Yes."

"For example, if I say three, seven, nine, what would you say?"

Jake had been sitting across from me. He put both hands straight down on the sides of the seat, evenly pushed back his chair, stood up and turned around.

"Three, seven, nine," he said with his back to me.

"Jake," I said.

"Yes?" he answered, still facing away.

"Can you face me?"

"Yes," he said as he turned back around.

"I need you to say the numbers in reverse."

Jake turned around again.

"Three, seven, nine," he repeated.

"Thank you Jake. I—"

"You are welcome, Dr. Dan," he said with his back to me.

"Jake, can you face me?"

"Yes," he said as he turned around again.

"Have a seat, Jake."

Jake pulled out the chair, sat down, and in dozens of micro-thrusts he inched his chair up until he was as close to the desk as possible.

"I need you to face me but say the *numbers* backward. Do you understand?"

"Yes," he said.

Jake reached down and clutched the seat of the chair again, but this time leaned forward over the desk while he strained his neck over his left shoulder.

"Three, seven, nine," he said.

I stared at his contorted body and realized what I was up against. "Thank you, Jake," I said. "We are done with this part of the test."

"Dr. Dan," Jake said, still contorted.

"Yes, Jake."

"How long do I have to stay this way?"

"You can go back to the way you were," I offered.

Jake stood up and faced away from me.

"No, I am sorry, I meant you can turn around and sit back down here with me and face me. We are finished with those questions. Please sit down again," I said.

We continued the exam with him answering flawlessly until we got to a question about what the first meal of the day was called. Jake began looking at his favorite spot on the ceiling for the answer.

"Can you tell me what the first meal of the day is?" I asked.

"Yes I can," he said as his eyes drifted upward.

I waited, but nothing came forth.

"Can you say it out loud to me, Jake?"

"Yes I can," he repeated.

Nothing.

"I would like you to tell me what you know about the first meal of the day," I pushed.

"The first meal of the day is the meal that breaks the fast from the night before," he told me as his eyes darted back and forth.

"Yes, that's very good. Do you know what we call that meal?"

"Yes I do."

Nothing, again.

"Can you say it, Jake? Can you say out loud to me the first meal of the day that we use to break the fast from the night before?"

Nothing.

"How about things people eat for the first meal of the day?" I said, hoping we could get something score-able.

"Olives," he answered.

"Olives?" I queried.

"Yes."

"Olives alone?" I asked in search of an omelet.

"Olives, cheese, and beans."

"Olives, cheese, and beans?" I asked.

"Yes."

"Does your family eat olives, cheese and beans for the first meal?"

"No, of course not," he said without inflection.

"Then why would you say people eat olives, cheese, and beans for the first meal of the day?"

"Because the people next door to us do."

"They eat olives, cheese, and beans?"

"Yes."

"The people next door to you eat olives, cheese, and beans for their first meal of the day?"

"They are from the Middle East and people there eat differently than we do. They eat olives, cheese, and beans first thing."

"Jake, what do you call the first meal of the day *you* eat?"

"Lunch."

"Lunch? You don't eat anything before lunch?" I said incredulously.

"No."

"You don't eat a first meal of the day?"

"My first meal is lunch."

I stared at Jake, trying to think of the next thing to say. "Thank you, Jake," I said. "We are done with this part of the test."

We continued testing with the same extreme results, but it was the section on similarities that got my attention. "Jake, can you tell me how an orange and a banana are alike?" I asked as we began the section.

"You can't eat the skins because they will make you sick," he offered.

"Any other way?" I asked, not knowing if his last answer would be score-able.

"Yes, there is."

I waited, but nothing came out of his mouth.

"Jake, can you tell me how else an orange and a banana are alike?" I probed.

"Yes I can."

Nothing again. I was having déjà vu.

"Can you say it, Jake? Can you say out loud to me how an orange and banana are alike?"

"You can eat them for breakfast."

The test caused me to doubt my own intelligence, particularly about my career choice, but I scored it as best I could. The pattern of his scores certainly reflected the calamitous difference in his abilities. He had as many perfect scores as he did zeros.

I was also supposed to measure his adaptive behavior—functional aspects of his ability to do things like dress and feed himself, as well as his ability to engage in social activities. As it happened, I tested Jake on a Friday, and on Wednesday the following week I was called about a problem he was having at the factory where he put the radios together.

"Let me see if I am getting this straight," I said on the phone with Frank. "Jake has been working on the same assembly line for three years and he is their star employee—right?"

"Right."

"But now no one will work with him—and they are angry and disgusted with him—and nobody can tell you why."

"They are telling me just that they have to fire Jake and that no one will work with him."

"Did they say why not?" I asked.

"All they said was that all of his coworkers refused to work with him and he was fired."

"What am I supposed to do?"

"Go see what the problem is!"

"Isn't that *your* job?"

"No. My job is to authorize *you* to find out what the problem is. Jake gives me the creeps, man. He is better off with someone like you."

"Okay," I said reluctantly.

I found my way to the industrial area and the warehouse. Although it was in a rundown section of town, it was relatively neat and clean. I had called Jake's home, but no one answered the phone. I drove over to the workshop, where I found him sitting outside.

"Jake . . ."

"Hi, Dr. Dan."

"Jake, what happened?"

"I can't work here anymore."

"Why not?"

"They don't like me, Dr. Dan. They don't like me," he said as his voice started to rise and his eyes drifted off. "They don't like me and I can't work here anymore and I don't have anywhere else to go until tonight, Wednesday, at eight o'clock in the evening at Saint Lucia's church."

"What is at Saint Lucia's church?" I wondered aloud.

"Bingo."

"I didn't know you played bingo."

"Yes, I do. I play bingo with my mother on Wednesday nights."

"Why won't they let you work, Jake?"

"Because I have a cold."

"They won't work with you because you have a cold?"

"Yes, Dr. Dan," he said as he raised his voice and forced his eyes up into his head.

"Let's go inside, Jake."

"Okay," he said as he moved inside the vestibule.

Jake's boss, Raphael, was a very kind, short and heavy Hispanic man. I had met him once before, and he seemed to be the kind of man who was fair and reasonable, but always harried. He liked Jake right from the beginning, and tolerated his odd ways and poor hygiene because Jake would never let Raphael down. He always did his job, was always on time, and never got in any trouble.

"Raphael, what happened?" I said as I greeted him.

"Dees men will not work with him anymore—they say he is making them sick."

"How is that?"

"Here, I will show you. Come talk to dees men. They will tell you."

I followed Jake through the workshop and there were a dozen or so assembly lines for different kinds of radios. Each line had eight to ten workers, and each person added their component to the frame of the portable radio, and then passed it to the next person on line.

Raphael took me over to Jake's place in the line.

In Spanish, he must have explained who I was, because as soon as he did the six men toward the end of a ten-man line began making faces and wiggling their fingers and hands, speaking very rapidly. It was clear they were upset and disgusted as they spoke. The two men closest to me picked up pieces of the radios they were assembling, held them in their hands while expressing their revulsion, then threw the radio back down. They spoke over the top of one another, and the general reaction was the same.

"What are they saying?" I finally asked.

"Dey say Jake has a cold on Monday and wiped his nose in his hands—he blew his nose right into his bare hands, then kept working. Dey said all of them start to notice and there was real, how you say, boogers, and stringy snot all over the radios. When they tried to tell Jake, he don't understand, and he wouldn't stop working, so the radios just piled up. No one would touch them and Jake won't stop working. I tried to tell him what was wrong, but he is, you know, a very strange person, and he would not stop. Finally, I had to stop the assembly line and Jake stood there waiting two hours until lunchtime, not saying a word. I told him when he went to eat lunch that he had to go home, and then I told him he could not work here anymore. I don't know what else to do."

"I understand. Did he say anything when you told him why the men were upset?"

"Nothing."

"Well, that sounds like Jake. Thank the men for me, and can I have an office to talk to him in?"

"Of course."

I walked back with Raphael to the foyer, and Jake was standing right where we left him. Raphael directed us into a small storage room, and we sat down on a couple of boxes.

"Jake, do you know why the men were upset?"

"I had a cold, Dr. Dan, they don't want to work with me because I had a cold. It was ... was ..."

Jake's face distorted. He brought both his hands up to his face and sneezed twice very violently into his bare hands. He rubbed them slightly and looked right at me.

"God bless you, Jake."

"I hope that God blesses you too, Dr. Dan."

"Thank you Jake," I offered. "Why don't I get you a handkerchief?"

He reached into his left rear pocket and produced a perfectly pressed, unused, white-as-snow handkerchief. "I have one right here, Dr. Dan," he said as he held it out for me to see.

Eyes wide with disbelief, I cocked my head and asked the obligatory question:

"Why don't you use it, Jake?"

"It will get dirty."

"I understand, Jake. Is there anything wrong with it getting dirty?"

"My mother would have to clean it, Dr. Dan."

"What would be wrong with that?" I asked.

"If I get it dirty, my mother would have to clean it."

"Yes, that is true. Is there something wrong with that, Jake?"

"And I don't want to make work for my mother, Dr. Dan. She's almost sixty-two, she'll be sixty-two in another seventeen days, and if she works too hard, she'll die, Dr. Dan, she will die," he said, raising his voice and eyes. "And I don't want my mother to die. Where would I go, Dr. Dan, where would I go if my mother died?"

"Jake?"

"Yes, Dr. Dan."

"I don't want your mother to die either, so you know what I'm going to do?"

"No, I don't."

"I'm going to buy you a box of tissues, Jake, and I would like you to use them to blow your nose and sneeze into, okay?"

"Okay, Dr. Dan."

"And Jake?"

"Yes."

"I think it is very nice the way you think about your mother."

"Thank you. I love my mother."

I also explained to Jake that he had to wash his hands at every break time. The issue was settled and when I explained it all to Raphael, he understood and rehired Jake. I gave Raphael twenty dollars and told him to use it for lunch and soft drinks for the men on Jake's line. He called me later in the day to tell me that once the men saw the tissue box and had their bonus lunch, everything was back to normal.

I was intrigued by Jake's bingo playing and showed up a little before the eight p.m. start time. As I arrived at the church, Jake was walking in—the box of tissues I'd given him earlier under his left arm, his mother holding his right arm. I said hello to him, and he told his mother who I was. She smiled and said hello, and they walked past me into the church hall. The moment they came through the door you would have thought a celebrity had arrived. A sea of silver-haired elderly ladies yelled out his name and waved, and several of them rubbed his left arm three times. I later learned this was a ritual many did to bring them luck.

His mother bought three cards, paid her three dollars and walked over to her friends. The man selling the cards greeted Jake and had a stack of sixty-four cards waiting on the side. Jake pulled out three twenty-dollar bills and four singles and they were all happy to see him. All the time he was in line, women were greeting him and stroking his left arm three times. I bought my one card and followed him.

Jake had a reserved table. He made an eight-by-eight square with the cards, then went off to talk to his many friends. I drifted around behind him, smiling, but feeling completely out of place. Except for Jake, I was likely thirty or more years younger than anyone I could spot in the room.

Following the announcement that the game was about to begin, everyone but Jake scrambled for a chair. I found a vacant one in the corner near the back of the room, and noticed that Jake had left the main hall to get a soda out of the machine. He bought a Coke, then stayed in the back as the numbers were called. I considered getting up and going after him, telling him it was time to sit down, but thought better of it and attended to the numbers on my card, scanning them each time a number was called. Jake never sat down. Immediately upon finishing his Coke, he bought an orange soda and began to drink it. I reasoned that his not playing the first game was part of a superstition. I was wrong.

After many numbers had been called, an intense, loud, high-pitched voice pierced the room from out in the hallway: "Bingo!" It was Jake.

"Fourth card from the left under the 'I,' the numbers seventeen, thirty-eight, forty-one, and sixty," he said in his monotone, emotionless way.

A gaggle of the gray brigade scurried over to check his cards. They conferred with the man who called the numbers.

Jake was a winner.

He collected his money—$230—amid grumbles, false smiles, and people who were generally in awe, me included. Then he handed the money to his mother, the archetype of motherhood: small, frail, gray, proud.

Jake won three times that night and took in $480. As I left, I said goodbye to Jake and his mother. They were off to the diner with friends for dessert to be bought with his winnings.

In that two-hour bingo game, Jake earned more than double my weekly salary.

* * *

"Of course, Frank," I said into the receiver after he told me the story of Jake's mother's death. "I've got some friends down at the state office. I'll do everything I can to get Jake into the home."

Signs of Sophia

The pain of the separation from my wife was eclipsed by the sense of being untethered in life. I dove so deeply into my work and school that I covered the gut reaction of loss with the idea I was doing something noble and important with my life. But largely, it ended up being a way to escape the feelings of confusion and disappointment. I was confused because I had my life packed into a tidy little plan, the contents of which were spilled out into the stream of life. Some elements, like school and work, stayed afloat, while others, like friends and family, sank as I drifted downstream. I was disappointed in myself, my marriage, and my friends. They disappeared when we separated and were not there when I reached out—so I stopped reaching. Maybe I should have tried harder, but I just didn't have it in me. The cord I cut from my wife severed me from a life I thought I was crafting. My mom, dad, and sister had moved away years before and were not there for support. The night I left for the A-1 motel, everything I had built in relationships ended with a thud. I never saw my wife again, nor any of the friends I thought were close. I could work 24/7 and it would give me the illusion that I was needed and important and had purpose. I'd stumbled into working with people with intellectual disabilities not because it was a calling, but because I wasn't fit for anything else—it was all I could do. When my marriage capsized I simply clung to the only thing that was afloat—work and school. Now that all the residents were in the home, I became determined to do something more than just manage the chaos. But managing madness takes time, and none of us had a clear idea of what was possible. We were all castaways of one sort or another and were finding purpose, meaning, or something at Walden House we could wrap ourselves in as an identity. As a team, we were fully invested. We had become committed to a cause—not so much because we believed in it, but because we were all rebels of some kind: rebels without a clue.

By the end of the first four months, Sophia had drawn blood from, or spilled hers on, everyone except Mike. She didn't take kindly to new participants when they moved in. Either she believed the entire residence belonged to her, or she needed to establish her territory. In either case, when Sophia went off, someone got hurt. Everyone operated on high alert when she entered a room.

In the 1960s, Sophia simply would have been called deaf and dumb. Today we'd say she was audiologically challenged and intellectually disabled. She couldn't talk because although she wasn't fully deaf, we learned that she couldn't hear properly, and her cognitive limitation kept her from processing information accurately. She did best when words were paired with visual cues. If someone was smiling when they spoke to her, she seemed to understand that their words had positive intention. Her psychiatric condition caused her to be triggered by both internal delusions as well as by events in the real world. This made it impossible to predict exactly what would set her off, but she did have a loose pattern.

Sophia averaged better than one massacre a week, and we were required to write up all of the gruesome details in an incident report, necessary when someone drew blood (their own or others') or needed medical attention. In addition to Taimi and me, several other staff members had witnessed the carnage brought on by Sophia. Between her violent episodes and Mike's threatening presence, temporary staff became glimpses more than presences. Taimi and I began referring to them as "guest staff."

In each report, no matter who filled it out, there was a common denominator: right before Sophia hit someone or hurt herself, she grunted. The grunts didn't seem to be directed toward anyone, but in the twenty-one incident reports we'd gathered, she'd grunted eighteen times. What, if anything, did they mean? We concluded that Sophia was trying to communicate. She would grunt, then haul off and claw at someone's face or scratch them with her nails, hit them with her cast, or bite herself until she broke the skin. She became vicious when she got angry, but it was hard to determine what exactly activated her. The data showed no pattern to her victims; she was an equal opportunity abuser. The only trait that could be a signal was the grunt. She would make a sound, escalate her protest, and finally let loose.

In treating aberrant behaviors, the first thing to look for is patterns in the incidents. Is there an antecedent? Does it happen at the same time of day? Does it happen at home rather than work? It is toward men? Toward women? In other words, does the madness have a method?

The best way to understand patterns is to look for pain, whether physical or emotional. If the person is in physical pain, then the violent behavior is a reaction to the intensity of the pain. In this case, you look for a medical or physical solution. Medicine, surgery, or simply a warm bath might do better than any fancy behavior program. Even a toothache could be the culprit. Yet if the trigger is emotional, you have to find out what precedes the behavior and what the frustration is. Could her effort to talk make Sophia mad enough to attack? It was a question worth exploring.

I watched her for another week, taking notes with this idea in mind. It seemed for all the world that she was trying to say something; and that her frustration seemed to come from not being able to get her message across. Benny was her favorite victim. She knocked him unconscious for the first time about a week after he moved in.

He hadn't noticed Sophia was sitting in an overstuffed chair watching Road Runner cartoons. Although she sat only about twelve feet from the set when Benny entered the living room, he walked directly over to the TV, put both hands on the top, and leaned over the cabinet to watch the show. His body blocked the entire TV from Sophia. She grunted once, twice, and stood up on the third count. I heard the second grunt from the kitchen too late to prevent the catastrophe. Sophia had picked up a folding table near her chair, swung it with all her force, walloped Benny to the ground, and whacked him unconscious. Taimi and I, along with a guest staff person, got there just in time to see her sit back down to watch Wile E. Coyote foiled again.

Beep-beep.

I asked my friends in the field about her unusual grunt-and-strike pattern. One was a trusted consultant I'd used at the sheltered workshop who explained client problems in a way that made me understand. Dr. McGreggor soothed me with my decisions with his comforting brogue and infectious laugh. When I had thoughts of joining the Navy to help pay for graduate school, he was unambiguous: "Danny, me boy, the Navy will own you for four years to pay for your remaining two. Ay, not the most creative answer to your problem. Give it some time. You'll come up with something."

Months later, when I told him I was going to take the inmates out of Willowbrook, his ruddy face and stout body roared with laughter. "Ay, for Christ's sake, that's what we call an overcorrection. Hurry up and see if the Navy would still be willin.' Tell 'em you'll be obliged to do eight years for them if they get you out of the Willowbrook gig."

We both laughed, but then he added, "I'll give it to ya, that's effin' creative, but you're the man for the job. You got the temperament for it," he said. "If they don't eat you alive, you'll be a damn fine one to do it." McGregor helped me think through the possibilities about Sophia's behavior. Two psychiatrist friends offered some other thoughts, but they fell back on their training: Sophia was incurable.

Diagnoses and theories ranged from temporal lobe epilepsy to intermittent explosive disorder, but none of them sounded right to me. Sophia was as violent as they came, but there was something else. I remembered how happy she became when Taimi returned to the room that first day. Amid the blood and chaos, Sophia smiled at Taimi—she was happy to see her. Even at the core of her insanity was an appreciation for another human being. I decided to consult with Taimi as we washed the carrots and potatoes, preparing for dinner. Preparing food comforted me—not that I was any good at it. Most of whatever I cooked could be used as a doorstop, but it was the mindful preparation, and the eternal hope I could make something edible, that I enjoyed. Although I rarely produced anything I would call delicious, fixing dinner was a private pleasure for me.

"Taimi, you've been working with Sophia for a couple of months. What do you think's going on with her?"

"Sophia needs a mother," she offered, rinsing the carrots.

"Isn't that the truth? What about her grunt and attack thing? What do you think's going on there? Some psychiatrists I know think she may have temporal lobe epilepsy, and . . ."

"Psychiatrists are assholes." She paused to check herself. "You're a psychologist, right?"

I raised an eyebrow, but nodded.

"You tell me, do you know any psychiatrist who would even think about doing anything with these people besides fuck them up with medication? Their only solution is turning people into zombies. Do me a favor, will you? Don't ask them for an opinion, because you know what? They'll give it to you and for the most part they don't have a flaming idea in their head about what to do. They'll give you a diagnosis, something fancy: 'schizoid personality type with borderline intellectual functioning, dysthymia with psychotic features,' or my personal favorite, 'severely retarded with psychiatric disorder NOS,' and I'm sure you know what that means, not otherwise specified, so they don't even have a fucking clue about what it is. And it doesn't matter, because no matter what the diagnosis, the treatment is the same. Give them enough medication so they don't bother anyone. Give them enough Thorazine to kill a moose and move on to the next brilliant diagnosis."

I thought about arguing with her. I really did know a few good psychiatrists, but she was right about how medicines were being misused to treat people with intellectual disabilities. "That's exactly why I'm here asking you. I know they didn't give us anything to go on, and I'm interested in what you think."

"I knew I liked you. You'll go far with that kind of attitude." She chopped the broccoli florets. "What do you want to know?"

"What do you think's going on with Sophia? What do you think the grunt and kill thing is all about?" Taimi glanced off to the side; I could tell she was considering whether to tell me something.

"All right," she said. "I *do* think I know what's going on with Sophia, but you've got to promise you won't laugh."

"Taimi, did you see my blood-soaked shirt and tie on the first day? Do you think I'm going to laugh at someone who, for all practical purposes, saved my life?"

"Good point, but I'm warning you," she picked up a carrot and pointed it at me, "I'm very fucking sensitive, and I will make your life hell if you laugh."

"I got it. By the way, I've never been threatened with a carrot."

Taimi hesitated for a second, and then looked me straight in the eye, pointing the carrot at me. "She's trying to talk."

She waited to see my reaction. I nodded; she shrugged and said it again.

"She's trying to talk. That's what I think's going on. I think she wants to say something. And maybe in Sophia language she is saying something, but she grunts it out, and when people don't magically understand what she's saying, she gets pissed off and takes them out. Don't you get pissed when someone doesn't listen to what you say, or someone ignores you? That's what's happening with Sophia. She tries to talk and, when people don't listen, she gets pissed."

I continued to nod. "That's the most insightful thing anyone's said about Sophia."

"Imagine those goons who held her down and raped her. She probably thought she was calling for help and no one came. All she was left with was rage. That's why she doesn't trust you. You're just another male staff person who's going to fuck her. She's got no reason to trust you; that's why she threw the dresser at you and hurt herself. I bet she learned to fight as much as she could, and then hurt herself enough to get medical attention. It was the only way she knew to stop someone and get control."

I had learned more in three minutes with Taimi than I had in five years of graduate school. "How did you get all this? I mean, how do you know her so well? This is brilliant!"

"Yeah, well, I guess all we have to do is teach a twenty-eight-year-old crazy, retarded girl to speak and we're home free."

"That's right! That's the answer!" I slapped the linoleum counter. "If we teach her to communicate, she might use words rather than violence to express her needs. Brilliant!"

"You *really* must have smoked a lot of dope in the sixties. Were you one of those flower child peace, love, and happiness dudes? If you really think we can get her to talk, *you* are the one with brain damage, Dr. Dan."

"Not talk with words, Taimi. Sign language. We can teach Sophia sign language."

I was on fire with the idea. I scraped the carrots and the potatoes and went on and on about how we could do it. I knew a little sign language and so did Taimi. We showed each other what we remembered of the alphabet in American Sign Language, and tested each other on the words we knew. Twisting our fingers to make letters and words, we both could feel the excitement of possibilities. In the four months I'd been there dealing with problems and catastrophes and issues galore, this was the first sign of possibility. Teaching Sophia sign language was—literally—a sign of hope.

* * *

Sophia loved orange juice. In the morning, she often took a poured glass from the staff, drank it down in one graceless gulp, and held out the empty glass, grunting. We learned quickly to limit the amount of juice we kept in the pitcher, so after her third grunt we could show her the empty pitcher. Sophia seemed to understand this concept—only after four incident reports. Each disaster came on the heels of a temporary staff person telling Sophia she could not have more, resulting in the permanent departure of yet another employee. We got by with a drive-through workforce.

Since the grunt, the juice, and the incidents were all wrapped up together, I figured I'd teach Sophia the sign for juice. The sign is simple: You stick your thumb up to your mouth and squeeze your fist a couple of times. It's easy, unless, as I learned, you're used to grunting for what you want.

The plan seemed uncomplicated: while Sophia sat across the dining room table from me, I would keep a tray of tiny cups filled with a thimbleful of juice on the chair next to me, hidden from her sight. I planned to use a behavior modification technique called shaping: Sophia would get a bit of juice each time she approximated the sign for juice. I had budgeted twenty minutes and twenty thimblefuls of juice to teach her the sign. It looked good on paper.

The dining room table was wide enough so that if Sophia wanted to smack me she would have to jump out of her chair, giving me time to duck, run, or block the incoming. It was three p.m. when Taimi brought Sophia in smiling and sat down next to her. I had been able to hide the cups on the chair, out of sight.

"Hi, Sophia. You look happy today. You like being with Taimi?"

Sophia nodded and looked to her left as she smiled again at Taimi.

"Taimi will sit next to you and I have something for you that I think you'll like. Would you like some orange juice?"

She nodded and grunted, still smiling at me.

"Good, 'cause I have some extra juice here."

I took the small cup—the kind they might use for mouthwash in fancy restaurant bathrooms—and handed it, half-filled, to Sophia. She took the tiny cup with her left hand, poured it into her mouth, held it out for me, and grunted. So far, so good.

I pointed to the cup, said the word *juice*, then reached for her right hand with both of mine and tried to squeeze her fist twice while saying *juice*. I wanted her to make the connection between squeezing her fist and her request. I had planned to give her another cup as soon as I grasped her fist.

It was exactly the wrong thing to do.

As I leaned forward to take her hand, she yanked back her left arm. She jerked it back so hard her elbow hit Taimi's nose.

"Shit!" Taimi yelled as she covered her bleeding nose with both hands.

"No, Sophia!" I screamed.

Sophia, grunting and yelling, beat Taimi about the head. I scrambled over the dining room table, and between the two of us, we got Sophia under control.

As Taimi and I held Sophia down on the dining room floor, Taimi spoke through her blood-soaked hand. "Nice, nice, very, very nice, Dr. Dan."

"Taimi, I'm so sorry. I'm so, so sorry."

I held Sophia down by her shoulders with both of my hands. Taimi used one hand on Sophia's stomach and held her bloody nose with the other. "Any more bright ideas, oh, wise one?"

"My God! What do you think happened here? Why did she go after you and not me?"

"Because I betrayed her, you lunkhead."

"What do you mean?"

"I betrayed her. I told her Dr. Dan had a surprise for her, so she was happy. As soon as you grabbed her hand she thought you were going to rape her. I bet she got set up all the time in Willowbrook."

"Holy shit. I never thought about that . . ."

"Obviously," Taimi said, checking her nose.

"I'm so sorry."

"We covered this ground already."

My enthusiasm for the idea had eclipsed my thinking through the situation. It wouldn't be the last time I'd blunder ahead not thinking through the contingencies and consequences, but it tempered my "ready, fire, aim" approach considerably.

"I am *so* sorry. Let me take you to the hospital," I asked, talking breathlessly over our ongoing struggles with Sophia.

"I don't need to go to the hospital, but there is something I need from you right now."

"Anything. Whatever it is, you got it."

"Don't fuck with me now, you promise?" She looked at me through her bloodied fingers.

"Promise."

"A raise."

"You got it. I promise to get you a raise. You deserve it."

"Damn straight I do."

"All we have to do is get past the fire drill requirement, and I promise you a raise." This had been bureaucratic nightmare number one for me and I couldn't fight more than one battle at a time.

"What's the big fucking deal with the fire drill?" she grumbled.

"To get a certificate of occupancy, we have to prove we can get everyone out of the home in two minutes."

"Impossible." She held a napkin from the dining room table to her face as she tilted her head and adjusted her blouse.

"It better not be. If we don't get a CO, the town can legitimately, legally throw us out, and that's the end of the group home. Then everyone goes back to where they came from. They go back to whatever might be left of Willowbrook, or back to their institutions, or back to the streets."

Taimi's nosebleed had gotten worse. She talked directly to Sophia.

"Sophia, we're going to let go of you. Dr. Dan wasn't going to hurt you; he was trying to help you. I'm sorry we scared you. Okay?"

Underneath Taimi, Sophia smiled and nodded.

* * *

At our next meeting, almost a week later, Taimi escorted Sophia into the dining room and left. I had the tiny cup of juice waiting for Sophia. She drank it down, and with my left hand I offered her another cup, but pulled it back slowly. With my right hand I stuck my thumb up in the air and squeezed my fist and said *juice*. She looked through me and reached for the cup. I pointed to her hand, and made the same gesture again with mine. She reached again for the juice, and this time I gave it to her. She smiled, drank it, and held the cup out for more. I didn't give her another, but rather used my right hand to make the sign for juice. She had no interest in my hand, but I persisted. I stuck my thumb up in the air saying, "juice, juice," then quickly tapped her right thumb as I said it again, careful this time not to hold her hand. She didn't respond, but gave the slightest grunt. Startled, I drew back, cowering when she made the sound, and immediately gave her another cup.

The question was, of course, who was conditioning whom?

I was concerned she would lose interest. The amount in each cup needed to be enticing, yet negligible enough to keep playing the game.

I began again by making my usual sign, but this time when I touched her thumb, she stuck it up on her own. Yes! My face beamed. I hollered, "juice!" and brought out three more cups. Sophia sucked down each in rapid succession.

After tossing down the third cup, she held it out to me with her left hand. I patted her right thumb with my index and middle finger, and she looked at me for half a second, but stuck her left hand out with a cup for me to refill. I tapped her thumb again, and again she looked at me vacantly, as if we were just beginning. Finally, I turned my fingers around so they faced up, and tapped underneath her thumb. This time she held her whole fist up with her thumb ever so slightly extended. Good enough for me. I pointed to her thumb and said "juice, juice," while handing her the next cup. The moment she drank it, I tapped under her thumb again. This time she responded quickly with her thumb flashing upward. I quickly said "juice" again, and gave her another.

Without delay I tapped under her thumb, and for a second time she gave the thumbs up. This time she took the cup with her left hand and, in that instant, stuck her right thumb up in the air. I smiled, pointed to her thumb, said *juice*, and gave her another cup. She did it again, and I repeated ad nauseam.

I'd begun the session with twenty cups of juice, and they were rapidly dwindling. Down to the last six, I realized that Sophia felt truly empowered, enjoying her newfound communication skill, but that shortly I would run out of motivation. I had put so much attention into engaging her, I hadn't planned the ending.

As the last few cups evaporated, I thought back to the day I learned to water ski. Some friends who owned a boat took me up to Greenwood Lake in New York, determined to teach me. For more than an hour they gave me all the directions: bend your knees, don't pull up, keep the skis straight, push against the water. In my baggy cut-off jeans, I tried over and over and over until I felt exhausted and desperate to quit. We gave it one last try. Somehow, all the learning came together and I popped up on the water while my friends cheered me on. I was barely able to contain myself. I skied around the lake, making cuts in the water, going back and forth across the wake as my friends continued the celebration. When my fatigue finally caught up with me, I realized that we'd never discussed how to stop once I was up.

The boat was pulling me. It never occurred to me to just let go, and I thought the only way my success could end was with disaster. We made a wide turn near the southern end of the lake when a small, waterlogged branch caught my left ski and ripped it out from under me. This flung me into the air and the towline jerked out of my grip. It wasn't exactly a somersault, but I twisted around several times and landed in such a way that my worn and baggy cutoffs were ripped away by the impact. As I treaded water, my shorts floated to the surface and my friends laughed uncontrollably as they cruised past.

My stomach tightened as I handed Sophia the last cup. I had a familiar thought. The only way my success could end was with disaster. Time to hold on to my shorts.

Normalization

A direct teaching intervention finally worked. Now engaged with the act of learning something constructive, both Sophia and I felt a sense of being empowered. This made everything—all the craziness and pain and trauma and confusion—worthwhile. Since our first sign language class hadn't ended well, I felt desperate to find a way not to crash land this session. While my mind scrambled to figure out how to keep this from becoming a catastrophe, the front doorbell rang. It was a lovely sound: the first eight notes of the Westminster Chimes.

It is 1971. I am sitting in front of my parents' RCA TV watching the last season of the Beverly Hillbillies.

The Beverly Hillbillies was a popular TV sitcom of my childhood—the story of a family from the Ozark Mountains who found oil on their property and became fabulously wealthy. They moved to Beverly Hills with their newfound riches and lived in a huge mansion. They had a running gag in the show where the doorbell, the Westminster Chimes, would ring and the family scrambled around frantically looking for the source of the sound. The sound would be followed by a knock at the front door, which always bewildered them.

When we moved in to the convent I noticed Sophia had a similar reaction to our chime. Her whole life was spent in the institution and she didn't know what a front bell was when she heard it ring. It meant nothing to her. I found it charming that we had our version of "The Beverly Hillbillies."

The first few times the bells went off, Taimi went to the door to answer it. Sophia often tagged along, and was genuinely surprised to see someone standing there when the door opened. After a while she knew the chimes meant we should wait by the front door. This was one of the few events in life she found amusing.

The chimes rang; Sophia smiled, drank the last of her juice, and pushed away from the table—disaster averted.

It was only the mailman with a package that needed a signature. Taimi signed for it as Sophia looked on. While Sophia went to the door, I put one full cup on the table. When she returned, I showed her the one cup was all that was left. She stuck her thumb up in the air and drank it down. Sophia was learning to speak.

The temporary staff had arrived while I taught Sophia and it was one of the unusual times when the home was quiet. We were out of orange juice and a few other items and Taimi offered to walk downtown, about three blocks away, to pick up what we needed. I suggested the two of us go and take Sophia. It would be our first outing.

Taimi liked the idea and explained it to Sophia: "Sophia, do you want to take a walk with Dr. Dan and me to get some more juice? We'll walk to the store, buy some, and come back."

Taimi and I realized this was a completely foreign concept. The idea that there would be a place to buy food, that it would have to be paid for with money, and that there would be many people she wouldn't know was completely outside of Sophia's life experience.

Sophia agreed. It was early spring and light jackets would do. We explained to the temporary staff what we were doing and that we would return within half an hour. We told them we would walk rather than taking the van. We put our jackets on and set off on our journey.

Sophia's gait was stiff but stable. We walked slowly and only held her hand at street crossings. Sophia seemed to enjoy the walk. She occasionally stopped to pick up a piece of litter from the street, inspect it, and put it back—a pack of Lucky Strikes cigarettes, a bottle of Coca-Cola she tried to drink out of, and a gob of gum even she knew wasn't good to eat. She returned each of these to the place they'd been found.

The small grocery store had a fruit stand outside and Sophia went right for it. Taimi stopped Sophia, held both her hands, and looked right at her: "Sophia, I need your help," she began. "I need you to keep your hands to yourself and only hold the things I give you to hold, okay?" Sophia smiled and nodded her head. Taimi seemed to have a direct connection.

Once we were in the store, Taimi immediately picked up two cans of soup. She handed them both to Sophia. "If her hands are full it will make it more difficult for her to pick up something else," she explained. Then Taimi handed two boxes of cereal to me. "This is what Wolfensberger called normalization, Dr. Dan," she said, with one of her patented sly smiles.

Normalization was one of the main concepts behind deinstitutionalization and had been put forth by Wolf Wolfensberger, a leader in the field. The idea is simple. People with intellectual disabilities should have the same access to housing, employment, schooling, exercise, recreation, and, the big one, freedom of choice. Disabled people no longer needed to be "protected," like in Willowbrook. They get the same shot at life as the rest of us—the same "dignity of risk." To make Sophia's actions the "normal" thing, Taimi handed me some things to carry as well.

By the time we got to the checkout line, we had ten things and used their express lane. We all placed the goods on the conveyer belt. Sophia was engrossed in the project. She hadn't noticed she'd become the focus of stares, whispered comments, and giggling from some teenagers. Sophia stood between Taimi and me in the checkout line, guarding the payload with her eyes while the conveyor belt moved the goods forward.

Believing the food was being taken away, Sophia let out one of her signature grunts and grabbed at the soup cans. Taimi and I both realized that she had never seen a conveyor belt before and Taimi clutched both of Sophia's hands and pulled them in front of her. Taimi shook her head and smiled, and said one word to her: "Watch."

The cashier was a young high school student and her sweetness made a potentially explosive situation dissolve. She rang up the soup cans and handed them back to Sophia. "Here you go," she said, looking back toward us. "A lot of kids get freaked by this." Taimi helped Sophia put the cans back on the belt as the cashier rang up everything else. When it got to the end, the cashier handed it to Sophia again, and again the soup cans made the trip down the belt. The woman behind us gave us a forced smile. She had no idea what to make of it. But Taimi and I knew the significance. For the first time we'd ever seen her do it, Sophia threw her head back and let out a high-pitched squeal of delight. She was laughing.

We packed the items into three bags so each of us could carry one—normalization. We began the walk up the slight hill toward the home when the inconceivable happened.

It began to drizzle, then turned into a light rain. We could see the house a block and a half away and Taimi and I lamented about not bringing umbrellas. Sophia stopped suddenly and put down her bag. In a second she had her blouse off and was naked from the waist up. As Taimi and I scrambled to stop her she continued trying to take off her pants. There was no grunt, no struggle.

"No, no, no, no!" yelled Taimi, quickly covering Sophia and pulling her blouse back on. I made a lame effort to shield the scene, but a few cars honked and someone whistled as they drove by. I let Taimi manage the physical contact, very much aware what this scene might look like with a man trying to subdue her. Plus, I had already learned my lesson on day one. I was useless other than being like one of the clowns at the rodeo, so I tried to cover and distract.

"What's happening? What's happening?" was all I could say. As Taimi frantically got the blouse back on, she convinced Sophia to pick up her bag.

"She's been in the institution her whole life and thought it was shower time. She's never felt the rain."

Ice Cream and Candy

I'd been working with Candy regularly. While Candy improved, which was to say that she wasn't always zombie-like, she would take part in regular activities, and her emotionless expression occasionally softened. But she was less engaged and less connected than others, and I decided to call in her parents to decide on our next step.

"I'm sorry to say that my work with Candy has not produced the kind of results we all would have hoped for," I began.

"But you have seen some changes," said her father. "We've even seen some when she comes home. She comes down to eat dinner when we call her, and it looks like she is enjoying watching TV."

"Well, we think she is enjoying the TV," said her mother. "It's so hard to know."

"I'm sure there have been changes; it's just that I am not sure what we can hope for," I said. "I don't know about her chances for recovery from a trauma like this. I am not sure what our goal is with Candy at this point."

"I'll tell you what the goal is," said her father. "The goal is for us to have our daughter back and for those lousy bastards to go to jail for the rest of their miserable lives. *That's* the goal, Dr. Dan, plain and simple, and I know you told me you ain't a doctor yet—it's just easier to call you that."

"Of course," I said in my best professional demeanor. "I understand."

"No, you don't. Nobody could understand this," said her mother. "How could this happen? How could this happen at her school? I blame myself. I never should have let her go to that school!"

"This isn't your fault, honey," said her father. "This is no one's fault except whoever did this. Candy has to remember, those people have to pay," he said, directing his comments toward me.

"You're right, of course. I don't understand what you are going through, but I do understand how much you love your daughter," I said. "But after all this time I don't have any clue as to how Candy is feeling.

"She has responded more, that's true," I continued. "But I don't know if she will be able to express what she is feeling, or if she will be able to recall the events of that day. I just don't know."

"Those bastards dragged our little girl into the woods, raped her, and left her there to die, and my wife thinks she is responsible for that. I don't care if this takes the rest of her life, I want Candy to get better and for her to remember who did this to her."

"I know this is difficult," I said. "Why don't we go another few weeks and see how things are, then?"

I felt more like I was avoiding the situation than dealing with it. At the very best I was buying some time to figure out what to do.

Nothing dramatic happened for our next several sessions. Candy had been having trouble sleeping since she'd moved in and had been on a variety of different medicines to help. I consulted with the psychiatrist medicating Candy and we agreed it would be a good idea to experiment with cutting back on the medicine. She had been on an assortment of tranquilizers, antidepressants and sleeping pills, and the psychiatrist, Dr. Joan Habbib, was willing to reduce some of the tranquilizers. No one was prepared for what happened when she did.

The third day following the cutback, Candy started talking, almost nonstop, in the session. It wasn't gibberish, but it seemed to be a nonstop stream of consciousness that was little affected by what I asked or said.

"How was your week, Candy?" I said.

"It was fine. I had a fine week. It was good!" said Candy excitedly. "My mother took me for ice cream on the weekend, yeah, ice cream last week. It was good, chocolate chip she bought me. It's my favorite, chocolate chip; she got it for me after dinner. It was after dinner; she made meatloaf. I hate meatloaf that's why she got me the ice cream: meatloaf and potatoes. I like the potatoes. Mashed potatoes. They are my favorite. I like them so much. My father likes the meatloaf, but I like the mashed potatoes. With gravy. You *have* to have the gravy or else they're no good."

I was stunned. No one could have predicted this. Candy had been in the most vegetative state I'd ever seen, other than a coma, and was now electrified. I tried to ask some questions.

"Candy, it is so good to hear you talking! Would it be okay if I asked you some questions?" I said.

"Sure, I like questions. I *like* questions. My mom asks me questions all the time. She wants to know about school. *Yeah*, about school. She wants to know who hurt me. She asks me all the time, all the time: What happened to you Candy, she says?"

"What do you tell her, Candy?" I asked.

"I tell her I can't tell her," Candy said. "I wish she would stop asking me. I can't tell her who hurt me."

Candy stopped mid-sentence and gazed away. For the briefest moment she looked as if she had become catatonic again. Then, as quickly as she had drifted off, she started talking, but this time she whispered. "I like the big chips," she said as her eyes refocused on mine. "The big chips are my favorite. Chocolate chip ice cream is *good*."

"Candy," I said, "do you remember what happened that day?"

"No more ice cream for me!" she said sharply. "I could never eat ice cream again!"

"Why is that, Candy? Why could you never eat ice cream again?" I asked.

"Chocolate chip," she said. "I could never have chocolate chip ice cream again."

"Why couldn't you have chocolate chip ice cream again?"

"*Because!*" Candy said in a loud whisper as she raised her eyebrows.

"Because why, Candy?" I answered in turn.

"*Because*," she said, "they would cut my neck open with a *knife*! With a knife! They cut me just a little bit to show me. It would hurt a lot if they cut my neck open. I would bleed all over and die."

"They told you they would cut your neck if you told what happened?" I offered.

"You couldn't eat ice cream if they cut your neck open. It would come right out!" she said excitedly. "You would put it in your mouth, but it would come right out your neck," Candy said as she started laughing. "That's funny: ice cream coming out of your neck, heh-heh, that's funny. You would have ice cream all over you. *Yeah*, all over you, ice cream, *chocolate chip* ice cream."

The Enemies

There is social upheaval everywhere in America—resistance to the advances of the civil rights movement of the sixties; the landmark supreme court case *Regents of the University of California v. Bakke* arguing that affirmative action was unfair if it led to "reverse discrimination"; the seeming plateau of women's rights work as the Equal Rights Amendment fails to achieve ratification, and women's wages remain below their male counterparts'. Traumatized and rejected, many Vietnam vets drifted into homelessness, drug use, and obscurity. As Bruce Springsteen warned, there was "trouble in the heartland."

When the home first opened, seven years had passed since Geraldo Rivera first showed the videos. As the legal process limped along to move people out of Willowbrook and to the least restrictive environment in the communities, the people left inside were no better off. They still wore rags as clothes and defecated in broken toilets, and the vile stench that had been a trademark of the Willowbrook buildings was only occasionally masked by a stinging whiff of bleach. The inmates of Willowbrook remained unprotected, unaware of the world going on around them in 1979. They didn't care that Cambodia had fallen or that the Ayatollah Khomeini took over Iran. When you can't read a newspaper and don't have a car, you don't think about things like waiting in line for a tank of gas or that Mother Theresa has just won the Nobel Prize. You spend your time and energy guarding your food and your life.

At Walden House, life was different. We tried to talk about the events of the day, watch the news, and listen to the music on the radio.

When the Village People gave the world their song "YMCA," the participants loved it. The song is about a man down on his luck and being encouraged to go to the community resource, the YMCA, to live. Did the participants relate? They got animated when the song came on the radio and made interesting random gestures with their arms when the letters were announced. They had no idea that the letters Y-M-C-A were the goal of the arm signals used by the Village People they'd seen on TV. When the song came on it looked as if there were an ensemble-style seizure taking place. When Taimi bought Sony's wild new gadget known as the Walkman, she brought it into the home to the delight and amazement of all. Everyone wanted time with it, and we bought one for the home as the ultimate reinforcer. Participants worked hard to earn time to listen to their favorite songs. We could always tell when someone was listening to "YMCA" by the episodic flailing of arms.

Another type of music also made its way into the home. When Springsteen released *Darkness on the Edge of Town*, we played it on the home record player day and night. When "Badlands" came on, it somehow synchronized us. We all felt connected. Not just the house and the staff, but it seemed like the whole country, at least for these few precious moments, moved, hummed, and mouthed to the music as well. Did the participants relate? As Bruce would preach: "We'll keep pushin' till it's understood, and these badlands start treating us good."

Since the first fire drill was a disaster, I'd decided to do the first semi-official one. Gwennie planned the whole thing and worked with the contractors. It wouldn't count because it was an internal test evacuation—but there would be an actual alarm. The firehouse was simply told we were testing our equipment over the next half hour and not to come. Again with Mike out of the house on a prearranged schedule, I pulled it, pressed the stopwatch, and each of us—Taimi, Gwennie, Harold, Phil (another temporary staff person), and I— snapped into position.

On cue the participants snapped into theirs. Harold was in the kitchen with Sophia and Benny. The moment the alarm went off, Sophia grunted, then smacked Benny in the head with a coffee cup, which gave him a black eye. Then spit at him. She ran down to the basement while Harold tried to comfort Benny. But all Benny could do was mumble and cry, hold his head and shake it.

Gwennie went to get Sophia, and Taimi followed Albert, who had run up to his room alternately holding his ears and biting his left hand. I was with Candy, who became paralyzed and then wet her pants. But it was Lilith who surprised us all. She ran into the kitchen again like the first time, but then went right for the pantry and wouldn't leave—instead, she started ripping into boxes and gorging herself.

Jake was our lone hero, the model evacuee. He was counting his bingo money and left it on the bed, walked downstairs past all the confusion and stood outside the house with Phil, following his instructions.

How long did it take us? Who knows. The situation deteriorated rapidly and I abandoned the drill. Phil brought Jake back in, we retrieved Benny from the basement, stopped Lilith from gorging herself, and calmed Albert down. Taimi helped Candy get changed. As for Sophia—I simply began filling out yet another incident report.

The town meeting the night before also had not gone well. It had been raining for days and everyone was crowded into the town hall with their umbrellas, raincoats, and boots. The business of installing new parking meters, changing the garbage day pickups, zoning permit arguments, and the ongoing problems of deliberately set fires in vacant lots and garbage cans all over town took nearly two hours. It was hard to stay awake as I stood in the back of the room. Finally, under the opening of "new business," a question came from the floor. A woman holding a baby stood up.

"Mr. Mayor, I live two doors down from that group home and I've seen some of the people in there. One of them is a giant and I don't think any of them can speak. There is a black man coming in and out of that house at all hours of the night and someone, I won't say who, told me that he was just released from prison. What are you going to do about this?"

Before Mayor Billings could answer, a man on the other side of the room stood up. "I'm retiring next year and I want to put my house up for sale, but I'm not going to until you toss those people out of here. How did they get the right to come in here in the first place?"

I raised my hand.

Mayor Billings saw me, and ignored me just as quickly. "I can assure you everything in my power is being done to rid us of these misfits. I live here too and I don't want our beautiful town ruined by a bunch of retards living high on our hard-earned tax dollars."

"May I speak?" I yelled from the back of the room.

Mayor Billings banged his gavel.

"No, young man, you may not. The hour is late and the good people are tired, so I am not going to open a discussion at this time. I will put this first on our agenda next meeting."

A tall, thin man in the front row who had been taking notes raised his hand.

"Carl, you are going to have the final comment for tonight's meeting," said the mayor. "And I am doing that out of deep respect for your column in our local newspaper."

"Mr. Mayor, now you know I live right across the street from the group home and that I also have a niece who has Down syndrome. I haven't seen anything untoward at the group home, and I know for a fact that my niece isn't dangerous. Are you saying all people with an intellectual disability are dangerous?"

I was heartened. Finally, someone with a sensitive thought.

"Carl, no one with the kind of love and support in your family could ever have a mean bone in their body. But these people are from

Willowbrook and are little more than caged animals. The state wants to experiment with moving them into the community and I say let them experiment someplace other than our fine town."

The mayor banged the gavel.

"I move that we adjourn for the evening and pick this discussion back up at our next meeting when we've all had a good night's sleep. Do I have a second?"

Someone on the town council seconded the mayor's motion. He banged the gavel again.

"We are adjourned."

Food Fight

No one was late for Harold's dinner. Ever. Albert was in the kitchen the moment Harold lit the stove. Sophia, Benny, and Lilith arrived moments later. Mike would sit at the dining room table waiting to be served and was reminded daily to help set the table. He did so willingly, and without reluctance. But someone, usually Taimi, had to tell him every day. Jake escorted Candy into the kitchen at precisely 5:45, the assigned table-setting time, and helped her get with her chores. Once they were finished, he got her seated. Jake helping Candy was a natural role. He was good at it. He anticipated her needs. But it was never anything anyone had asked him to do.

We lived at the kitchen and dining room table. Not in the living room, as the name might suggest, or on the porch, or in the foyer or the office or the basement, or the backyard. We washed the tomatoes and helped each other slice cheese and make coffee. Sophia had taken remarkably well to the idea of earning chips for her signs and as she reached her first ten, we began teaching others some of the simple signs. Thank you, yes, no, please, sorry, help, love, good, bad, upset, happy, sad, mad, and you're welcome. When you think about it, if we all could communicate this core of our reactions in the world it might indeed be a better place.

We opened boxes, threw out the garbage, and cleaned our plates with an unspoken peace, a serenity that comes from preparing food and sharing it with others—a trust that grows from the earth through the seed of each vegetable. It is love being created and consumed and enjoyed. We were part of something we created, and then took in so we could create again. None of us knew exactly what that was. But we showed up, prepared, and ate. We were family—kind of.

Taimi and the staff person du jour would organize the troops. I was usually the last one to arrive. They always had my place ready.

Gwennie was officially done working at five, and we didn't sit down to eat until six. But somehow she was in the kitchen each day helping Harold and orchestrating the participants. We'd had a few talks about her dressing more appropriately—that her neckline and miniskirt hemlines should be more than a foot apart. To her credit, she tried. But there was no hiding her natural attributes. If she was within Mike's field of vision, a puddle of drool formed on the floor. Once, Taimi caught me in an extended glance. "Down, boy," was all she had to say. All I could do was laugh. I was busted.

I imagined Gwennie was hanging around to get a free meal. This was fine with me; we needed all the help we could get. But it wasn't food she was interested in.

"You seem to keep yourself in pretty good shape there, govner," I heard her say to Harold as they stood next to each other chopping fresh green beans and lettuce.

"Old habits die hard," he said.

"Well, you look like you've had this habit for quite a while," she said, running her finger over his bicep.

"I used to make a living with my body, so staying in shape was just a job."

"Ah could say the same thing, govner, but I don't have a bleedin' rock where me arm muscle should be."

Harold laughed. "There wasn't much else to do in prison, and I wanted to be ready, you know, just in case."

"Just in case? Just in case of what?"

Harold put the knife down and looked at Gwennie. A broad grin came over his face. "If boss-man will let you out early tomorrow, why don't you come with me downtown. I'm taking Candy, Mike, Jake, and Lilith shopping at three, and I could use some help."

Gwennie turned to me and smiled. I smiled and nodded back. It never occurred to me that sending a parolee and a groupie might not be the right thing to do. In my mind, they were the best and most qualified and conscientious people I knew.

* * *

Harold and the entourage went in the home's van. I knew better than to tag along.

"I'll gas 'er up, too," said Harold as I handed him the keys.

"Just use the Gulf station on the corner," I said. "We have a credit account with them, so you can sign for it." As they drove off for the largest group trip downtown we'd taken, I hoped there would be no incidents. It was about an hour later when I learned what had actually happened.

Here's what they told me: Harold pulled into the station with Gwennie in the front seat, Candy and Lilith in the middle, and Mike and Jake in the back. The gas station attendant came around to Harold's open window.

"Fill it up regular," said Harold.

The man stared at the crew inside the van. His jaw dropped.

Harold looked at the man and jerked his right thumb over his shoulder. "It's my family," he said, wiggling his thumb side to side.

Gwennie burst out laughing, then Harold did. "Sorry, man," said Harold to the attendant. "We from the group home, we got an account with y'all."

The attendant nodded and went off to fill the van with gas.

"You certainly took that bloke by surprise!" said Gwennie as she recovered.

"Got to keep it light, or things get heavy real fast."

"Got that right, govner."

At the store, Harold, Gwennie, Candy, Mike, Jake, and Lilith grabbed a cart and among stares, pointed fingers and mutterings, they walked into the local supermarket and down the fruit and vegetable aisle. Harold took out his list.

"We need two dozen ears of corn, four heads of lettuce, six tomatoes, two bags of oranges, two pounds of string beans, a bag of whole carrots, two large eggplants, a watermelon—I like watermelon," said Jake as he recited the list from memory.

"You got all this list in your head?" said Harold.

"I do," said Jake unemotionally.

"You got the whole bleedin' thing in your head, but you only saw it for a second!" said Gwennie.

"I'm sorry," answered Jake. "Did I do something wrong?"

Both Harold and Gwennie assured him he hadn't, so Jake continued.

"We also need a box of strawberries and grapes and three lemons and fresh spinach."

"Damn, how do you do that?" said Harold.

"You said a bad word, Harold. Dr. Dan isn't going to like that."

"You are right, Mike. That was my fault. Will you forgive me?"

"Of course, Harold."

"For if you forgive men their trespasses, your heavenly Father will also forgive you," said Jake. "That's from Matthew, chapter six, verses fourteen and fifteen."

Lilith had stayed back from the group and was over plucking grapes as fast as she could and stuffing them in her mouth. Gwennie saw her and took her by the arm back to the cart. With her mouth completely full, Lilith apologized. "Whyddoday weave these things right out if they don't want you to eat them?"

"It's hard to explain, Lilith, but we can't eat everything we see."

"Why not?" asked Lilith.

Jake recited the list from memory as the shoppers went down each aisle. Mike reached all the things needed on the top shelves, while Lilith and Candy found comfort in straightening the items in the cart. Gwennie compared prices.

"We don't need to be buying soup for twenty-six cents when we can get the same kind of soup for nineteen cents," she said, looking at cans.

"We don't need to buy soup at all. I make my own soup, for about three cents a quart," said Harold.

"So you got arms like Samson, and the mind of Julia Child."

"Aunt Jemima, more than likely."

Gwennie laughed. "Suppose we all got a different frame of reference."

They got in line, and the overflowing cart finally reached the cashier. Mike, Jake, Lilith, and Gwennie were in front, unloading the goods. Candy had been pushing the cart and was holding on to the handle. Harold was behind her. That was when the fight broke out.

"You gonna eat all that, son?" said the man standing behind Harold.

Gwennie heard what sounded like a put-down and looked up to see a very well-dressed black man standing behind Harold. As Harold turned around he cocked his fist. Every vein in that stone of a bicep became inflated: a bulging purple road map of pain.

His arm arced so quickly the speed alone was shocking. The man in the suit blocked the would-be death blow, and in seconds a dozen fists flew in a barrage of impossible-to-stop punches. But neither man hit his mark.

"NO!" screamed Gwennie.

Candy stood frozen and Jake scurried away with a stiff bilateral shuffle where his left hand and left foot, then right hand and right foot, moved together instead of in a normal alternation.

"You better stop it, mister!" Mike screamed.

Just as suddenly as it started Harold and the other man laughed and hugged each other. Gwennie chased after Jake. Lilith started eating the grapes.

"My main man. Harold, you dog, man, you still got it," said the man in the suit.

Harold put his arm around the man and waved his right hand in the air. "Ladies and gentlemen, the heavyweight champion of the world, Mister Floyd Patterson!"

The people in the store gathered around Floyd. Pens and paper seemed to appear out of nowhere. He smiled, nodded and signed whatever they had. Some people had him sign stuff in their cart: a box of cereal, a box of tissues. Two boys standing behind Floyd started boxing the air. The cashier reached across the checkout with her pen and a piece of register tape.

"Will you sign this for my son, Mr. Patterson?"

"I certainly will," said Floyd.

Jake returned with Gwennie and stopped Lilith from eating the grapes. Mike was jumping up and down at the excitement. But Candy had become a statue. Harold put his hands on top of hers.

"Candy, this man is a friend of mine and we were just playing. He is a friend of mine and I would like to introduce you to him, so you can be a friend too."

She softened immediately. "A friend?"

"This is Mr. Floyd Patterson. He is the heavyweight champion of the world, and the most gracious gentlemen you'll ever meet," said Harold.

"*Was* the heavyweight champion of the world."

"You still the champion in my world," Harold said as he helped Candy find Floyd's hand.

Gwennie would later tell me it was the only time she saw Harold on the verge of tears.

* * *

The commotion died down, the food was rung up, and the unlikely group moved to the parking lot toward the van. The walk was narrated.

"Floyd Patterson. You won the Olympic gold medal in 1952, the youngest person to win the world heavyweight championship at twenty-one years old," said Jake in his monotone manner.

"I have a fan," said Floyd.

"The only person to regain the title," added Jake.

"That's true," answered Floyd.

"Fifty-five wins, eight losses, one draw. Forty wins by knockout. You lost your last fight to a man named Muhammad Ali on September 20, 1972. Muhammad Ali was also a gold medal winner at the Olympics, but his name was Cassius Clay back then."

The group had reached the van and put the bags in the back. Everyone was helping.

"Jake has the gift of memory," said Harold.

"Heard what happened," said Floyd.

"I'm out now. It's all good. I get to cook for these fine people," said Harold.

"You were almost as fine a cook as you were a boxer," said Floyd.

"I had to learn to cook, 'cause all you would feed me was those damn knuckle sandwiches."

"Harold, you said another bad word!" bellowed Mike, "but I've forgiven you already."

Harold, Floyd, and Gwennie laughed as Floyd and Harold hugged, then Floyd extended his hand to Gwennie.

"I got to be getting along. It was a pleasure," said Floyd.

"I believe you're the first champion of the world I've ever touched," said Gwennie.

Floyd smiled and turned to shake Jake's hand.

"Before Muhammad Ali you lost to Jerry Quarry," said Jake.

"He remembers what I'm trying to forget."

As Floyd walked away, the crew piled into the van and Harold pulled out of the parking spot.

"What did you see?" asked Gwennie.

For a moment, Harold didn't respond.

"Worked construction when I wasn't trying to be a boxer. It was raining so they let us out early," he said as he drove. "Came home to find my brother doin' my wife. He knew I'd kill him, so he grabbed my wife's .22 pistol and shot me three times. Right here." Harold pointed to his heart. "I beat the hell out of them. Would have killed them both if I didn't pass out," he said, looking straight at the road.

"Christ," said Gwennie.

"Didn't care about nothin'. Didn't get a lawyer, just let it happen, figured my life was over anyway."

"Wasn't it self-defense, or temporary insanity, or some bullshit the lawyers make up?"

"I forgive you, Gwennie," said Mike from the back of the van.

"Nothing mattered. I didn't care what they did to me. A wife, a brother, a career, and a reputation gone in two minutes. Being shot was a blessing. I would have killed both of them, and I would have died in prison," said Harold. "Now I got a chance to help those more in need than me."

Gwennie put her hand on Harold's as they pulled into the driveway. Everyone grabbed a bag. I opened the front door to greet them.

"So," I said, "How was downtown?"

Gifts

The group tumbled into the house and revealed their adventure to me. Each took their turn, like excited children back from the amusement park, to share his or her view. They talked, I asked questions, but something else was happening with our group.

The bags were all placed on the kitchen table or counter and Harold and Gwennie began taking the contents out of each. As each bag was emptied, Jake straightened it out on the table and folded it back into its flattened design. With the precision of an origami expert he creased each line of the bag and folded the top lip so the bottom edge of the bag would fold into itself. Each bag was stacked on the previous one: A work of art.

Candy, with some direction from Gwennie, placed the dry goods in the pantry. She would match new boxes with existing ones to find their rightful place. Mike noticed Candy couldn't reach the upper shelves and moved over to help.

"Let me put that up there for you, missy," said Mike.

Candy handed boxes to him, one after another, and Mike tucked them away. The paper towels, the tissue boxes, the toilet paper went on the very top shelves. When Mike put them up, Candy looked up to watch him.

"I can't even see them," she said, giggling. "You are so tall!"

Mike pushed the last of the paper towels so they would stay on the shelf, then saw the jagged cut line on Candy's neck. "What happened to your neck?" he asked.

Candy was handing Mike the tissue boxes. "That's where David and John and Tommy cut me so I wouldn't tell anybody," she said, handing Mike a box of generic tissues.

"Oh," said Mike. "Does it hurt?"

"No," was all she said.

It was the first time Candy had uttered the names of her attackers. I immediately scribbled down the names.

The house had a rhythm and order to it that grew out of preparing for dinner. Somehow, by the end of the day it was sitting around the dinner table that allowed the sense of family to warm our lives. We looked forward to the food Harold so thoughtfully prepared, but even more, we anticipated seeing and catching up with each other at the end of the day. We had become a family.

Sophia had been with me and began putting away the fruits and vegetables when everyone else came in. She was at the refrigerator and Benny, who usually avoided her, handed Sophia a head of lettuce and two tomatoes. Sophia reflexively brought her hand to her mouth like she was blowing a poorly aimed kiss, her effort at the sign for thank you. Benny returned the sign for you're welcome by bringing a salute with his right hand cupped in front of his face. Not a single drop of blood was shed.

But the fire drill problem hung over us. Gwennie was tackling the endless regulations of the fire code and the dreaded visit from Chief Willy was about to happen.

* * *

As the knock came at the door I walked over to let Chief Willy in. I hadn't noticed that Gwennie had been watching from the other side of the kitchen. As I opened the door, I heard Gwennie's voice and turned to see her. As usual she was dressed more like the town hooker than a group home secretary. "Aw have an idea," she said, using a voice I hadn't heard her use before.

Willy turned on his heel, walked right past me, and I could swear he started to drool as bad as Mike. He nearly jumped across the room to shake her hand. His right hand was heavily bandaged.

"Hey darlin', I'm the fire chief. Willy's the name. Some fires I put out, and some I start."

"I bet you do," said Gwennie as she looked him up and down.

I was listening to cheap dialogue from some college porn movie. "Gwennie is the secretary here," I said.

"Darlin', why have they got such a fine woman like you wrapped up in a place for retards?" he said, still holding her hand.

"They are actually quite harmless, and the work is easy. I can save my energy for . . . other things," she said suggestively. "Willy," she began, "or would you like me to call you chief?"

"I don't care if you call me Chief or Willy; it's fine, I'm fine," he stammered.

"How about Chief Willy?"

"Great. Great. Fine."

"Chief Willy, I am going to need this hand of mine for a while, but you can hold on to it later if you want to. Lovely bandage."

"Ha ha!" he stammered out. "Of course you can have, you know— your hand. This is nothin,'" he said, holding up his bound-up hand.

"Aw would like to get me pen an' as you walk around, tell us what ain't right and I'll write it down—save your fingers for better things—then we can move this little problem along. You think that's a good idea, Chief Willy?"

"That's the best idea I heard all day."

Gwennie and I exchanged looks. She went out of the room to get her pen.

"Man, would I like to put a smile on that woman's face. You dog, you—you been keeping her for yourself, is that it?"

I shrugged my shoulders. When Gwennie returned, I could tell she had sprayed some perfume on. She flashed me a coy smile when she came into the kitchen and I stood back and watched her at work.

"Tell me, govner," she said, directing her comments to Willy, "where do we begin?"

"Well, darlin', the first thing we have to do is change these outlets here to ground fault outlets—you know what they are?"

"I believe I do. If you get zapped by something plugged into them they can interrupt the voltage and shut off so you don't light up like a Christmas tree and explode."

"Smart girl. I like that," he said as Gwennie glanced at me and rolled her eyes.

"Then we will have to rip out the wall back here for a zero-clearance wallboard that you would need for the gas stove."

"A zero-clearance wallboard?" Gwennie asked.

"Yeah honey, it's a term we use in the business . . ."

"Oh, I'm familiar with it, it's what they call a Wonderboard and is used because it has a zero flashpoint. You couldn't light that board on fire if you wanted to, am I right Chief Willy?"

"That you are, darlin'. How'd such a pretty thing like you get to be so smart for a woman?"

"Me brother works in construction, and when I feel like I have to bash someone's head in, I work with him swinging a hammer."

Willy laughed. "Well then, you know that it's a big job we have to do here."

"And Chief Willy—you say this is necessary for us to be in compliance with the fire code, yes?"

"Absolutely."

"The state fire code?"

"Yeah, honey, it's a very complicated legal document."

"The NYS code number 718 provision of fire safety requirements for multifamily residential units?"

Willy and I both just stared at her.

"Or would it be the 516 document on partial hospitalization facilities?"

"It's, it's . . . the 718," said Willy.

"Oh good, I was hoping it was. Because that document clearly states that zero clearance isn't required for gas and electric stoves, only wood and coal burning. Ah bet we saved a fortune on things right there, don't you think, Chief Willy?"

It would have been hard to determine if it was Willy or I who was more shocked.

"I'd, I'd have to double check that, darlin,'" stuttered Willy.

"So, it seems that we need ground-fault interrupters for the countertop in the kitchen, but that we don't need the zero-clearance wallboard."

"You'll have to run a 220 line in here and you'll need two smoke detectors that are hardwired to the police station."

"Ah thought the 220 lines were only if you knew you were going to put in an electric stove, Chief Willy. Did I get that wrong?"

"I, I believe you're right, missy. I must be dazzled and confused by your beauty," he said, trying to recover.

"I bet that's what you say to all the women you tease."

Willy laughed.

"And Chief Willy, did you say we needed two smoke detectors here in the kitchen?"

"That one I am one hundred percent right about."

"Actually, Chief, I think you are trying to be very nice to us and give us a break—and as much as we appreciate it I think we want to stick with the letter of the law here."

"You're confusing me, darlin'."

"Well I am sure you know that with a kitchen of this size, four hundred and twenty square feet, that we need one smoke and one heat detector, and I know those heat detectors are expensive, and that you want to help save me, I mean us, some money, but I think we have to go with the state law on this one."

"You saw right through me," he said nervously. "But you will need a type A fire extinguisher."

"Now will that be in addition to the ABC multi-efficient type that is required by state code?"

"Did I say A? I meant ABC of course," he said, rubbing his forehead. "I do have to look at the furnace too, is that in the basement?"

"It surely is Chief Willy; do you want to go see it?"

"Only if you promise that you'll bring your pen and pad."

"I'll tag along too," I said out of pure anxiety for Gwennie.

"That's all right, Dr. Dan, I can handle this just fine."

"I just thought I would come along," I said, giving her a look.

"Now doc, I am sure you got better things to do than hang out in the basement with this lovely lady and me."

Gwennie moved right over to the basement door and opened it and Willy followed like an obedient puppy. As he followed he turned to look at me, squinted his eyes, smirked, made a palm-upward fist with his right hand and pulled it toward him twice: the international men's signal for getting laid.

I was frantic. Gwennie could certainly take care of herself, but Chief Willy was a loose cannon. The door to the basement closed and my mind scrambled to come up with ideas for what to do. Suddenly Lilith walked into the kitchen. I hadn't heard her getting dropped off at the front door by the workshop van. Instantly, intuitively, I knew the only way to deal with a loose cannon is with a looser one.

"Lilith I, er, I'm not sure where Gwennie is. Could you check and see if she is downstairs for me?" I said, putting my half-assed plan into place.

"Why the hell is it always me," she said while swinging her hands. "I do everything around this gawd damned place—you bastards work me to the bone. I don't think you get it. I ain't your slave, you know.

You think that just because I got a bad brain that you can do whatever the fuck you want to do with me. Now if we're talking about the dirty deed and like that, you *can* do whatever you want to do to me, but I ain't your slave, buddy boy. Think about it!" She spouted her patented phrase and pointed at me.

"I am sorry, Lilith. Gwennie was supposed to be showing the fire chief around. Chief Willy, he's a big man and he puts out fires," I said, baiting the hook.

"That bitch wants him all to herself, don't she? I'll find her, I'll find him. Don't you worry, damn-near-doctor Dan."

"What was that?" I asked.

"What?"

"What did you call me?"

"Damn-near-doctor Dan. That's what Taimi and Gwennie call you when you ain't around," she tattled. "They talk about your divorce and who you might be talking to when you make those payphone calls."

"That's funny, Lilith," I said, trying to hide my curiosity. "What else do they say?"

"Don't be asking me no questions," she said as she put her hands up to her ears. "I ain't even supposed to know this all. I'm going looking for Gwennie."

Lilith ran over to the cellar door and stampeded into the basement. I could hear her voice fade as she made her way down the stairs. I followed her.

"What you two doing down here?" she bellowed. "Any hanky panky? Cause I want in on it. Oh my gawd, you must be Chief Willy. Man, I want to do the horizontal mambo wit chew. Man, you a big one—ol' Lilith can take you though. Let's get to it. You don't want that skinny bitch. You a bad boy wanting this hunk of chunk for yourself. Un-huh boy, you better step aside cause big momma Lilith is coming in for the kill. Hey, Chief Willy, where do you want to take me? Over here by the washer—or maybe back here by the . . . oh . . . my . . . this is a beautiful piano. How 'bout I play a love song for you, Chief Willy?"

I was pleased that my plan of disrupting them had worked. Her voice was continuing to grow faint as she walked back into the basement, yet I could still hear her clearly. Chief Willy, disturbed at the interruption, took a step back when he saw Lilith. I never expected to hear what happened next.

"Damn, you're fat! The taxpayers have been feeding you good!" he said with disdain.

I had reached the basement and there was silence for a moment. I hadn't factored in Chief Willy's talent for being hurtful, and Lilith was visibly shaken by the words.

Years earlier, the night before the Macy's Thanksgiving Day Parade, I'd gone into the city to watch them blow up the balloons. It is quite an exciting time, and there are usually large crowds that come to watch. Little by little, you see these enormous figures come to life and take form. I remembered thinking to myself that they have to go through the same process in reverse, but that no one comes out to watch the great forms deflate.

That was what I was watching happen to Lilith. The life force was being drained from her, and, having seen this before at the workshop, I was worried that a full-blown meltdown was coming.

She pulled back the bench and sat at the piano. Her bent, grubby fingertips grazed over the top of the keys without pressing down, producing a rhythmic ticking of her fingernails passing over the separate keys. She moved her fingers back and forth several times, enough for the three of us to make eye contact with one another, each happy that she didn't just start banging on the piano as we expected. Then, as suddenly as Lilith could burst into a Tourette's-like rage of curses and verbal assaults, her hands morphed into delicate, flexible tentacles that stretched across the keyboard. Her eyes closed and she began to sway her head ever so gently. Note for note, she played Chopin's *Sonata no. 3 in B Minor: I*, perfectly performed with all the right notes and inflections.

We were mesmerized. Was this part of her Williams syndrome? We had never seen this from her before; she'd never mentioned it. It was as though she were channeling Chopin, not just playing his music. As suddenly as she began she stopped and turned to us. "You want to do me now, Chief Willy?" she said in her most caustic, crudest voice.

Willy's mouth dropped open.

Lilith aimed her patented finger sword up toward Willy's nose. "I bet you want to know what else I can do with these fingers," she said as she got up from the piano. "Think about it."

* * *

Harold had come back from shopping downtown with Mike and Jake and was bringing food into the kitchen. Mike had taken his bags into the pantry and placed the extras, the paper towels and the tissue boxes, on the top shelves. Jake carefully folded each bag once he took the food out.

"I still can't believe you can remember everything that was on my food list," said Harold to Jake. "You never had to look at it once."

"I remember everything, don't you?" said Jake in a monotone.

"Nah, Jake, in fact I'm still trying to forget some things."

"Like being in jail?"

"Like being in jail."

"Why did you go to jail?"

Mike was reaching up to put the paper plates on the top shelf, then placed a box of wooden matches on the middle shelf. "Jake, jail is where they put bad people because they are bad," offered Mike. "I'm never going to jail because the minute I am bad, I apologize."

Jake looked over at Mike, then back at Harold. "Did you apologize?" asked Jake.

"Well, kinda," said Harold. "I did my time and wish it didn't happen."

Mike had finished unloading his bags and was carrying them out of the pantry. Jake turned toward Mike and held out his arms to receive the bags. Mike gave them to him.

"You boys are working real good together. I like that you are helping each other," said Harold.

"We have to," said Mike. "If we're not nice to one another we go back to Willowbrook."

"Is Willowbrook a jail?" asked Jake.

"I don't know, but I don't like it, so that's why I'm nice, mister."

Jake turned to Harold. "Were you in Willowbrook?" asked Jake.

Harold burst out laughing, which started Mike laughing. Jake seemed confused for a moment, but Mike and Harold couldn't stop and eventually they both became so weak with laughter that they had trouble keeping themselves upright. Jake seemed uncertain about what to do, but then began staring at the ceiling and broke out into a high giggle. He was laughing, but it was a new experience for him.

"I don't know what we are doing!" said Jake in his high-pitched voice. "What are we doing?"

"We're laughing, Jake," said Harold, trying to recover. "We're laughing like there's no tomorrow."

* * *

Lilith had just finished her recital when I heard Harold, Jake, and Mike come in. Chief Willy had become flustered by Lilith, and was in the process of making a hasty exit. In his rush, he banged his bandaged hand. "Godamnit!" he screamed as he shook his hand. The bandage began to turn a dark red from his blood.

Lilith saw the bloodstain and screamed, "Noooooo!" at the top of her lungs. She began wiping her arms and hands as if her life depended on it, flailing them wildly, bolting up the stairs screaming.

Chief Willy nursed his wound and mumbled as he walked past me up the stairs. "I don't know what this world is coming to," he said, beginning his climb. "This whole place is crazy."

Harold came toward the open cellar door. As he moved toward it Lilith came screaming through, then he and Chief Willy came face to face. Harold noticed the name tag, and remembered the night at Pete's. "Well, well, well. So, *you're* Chief Willy," said Harold, with a grin on his face.

Chief Willy was stunned to see Harold, but finished coming up the stairs and pointed his finger in Harold's face. "You ain't done with me!" he bellowed as he pointed his bandaged hand.

Harold swung the door open wide to allow Willy to pass. "Don't worry, I'll let you know when I am," said Harold as he laughed. Then he poked his head down the stairs to ask a question.

"Who was playing Chopin?"

Hot Dogs

My personal life was in chaos. The stress of the impending divorce, trying to write my dissertation, and dealing with the staffing issues, the fire drills, and the day-to-day problems with the participants had begun to affect me. I wasn't doing well. I'd stopped my daily running routine and lost my network of friends. The group home was more than seventy-five miles from where I used to live, and I'd lost contact with nearly everyone I had known. My life had become work and school. Living at the group home meant I had no social life. Except for Harold's magnificent meals, I was eating poorly and getting no exercise and little sleep. I started looking for an apartment so I could rebuild my life.

All of my efforts went into planning the next fire drill. We started rehearsing getting people out of the house, one by one, as quickly as we could. Taimi would practice with Albert while they were upstairs making his bed.

"Hey, Albert," Taimi said. "What if there was a fire drill right now? Ding-ding-ding. Let's practice what we would do!"

She grabbed his hand and took him down the stairs and out the front door. Each of us randomly began helping the participants exit the house individually. Harold worked with Mike and Jake, Taimi worked with Albert and Sophia, Gwennie took Lilith and Benny, and I ushered Candy out whenever I could.

The drills had to be arranged with the fire department, and the timing began from the moment the alarm was activated until it was shut off by one of their members. Chief Willy was there with one of his cronies for the first one and just shut it off after ten minutes. The two of them chuckled, and just walked away. They never said a word to us.

The ding-ding-ding drills, as we called them, were actually going quite well—splendidly, in fact. One on one, there was calm and ease to the process. We were easily able to escort people out onto the front lawn and explained that we would wait until the alarm had gone off. No one challenged the drills.

With the inspection out of the way, or at least behind us, I thought we'd have a shot at getting out in time. We rehearsed and strategized, planning the event so we could maximize our collective egress. I'd become single-minded about it all. For nearly two weeks, all we did was obsess about getting out of the house in less than two minutes.

On the day we were ready, Chief Willy and a new crony came over. Gwennie met them at the door.

"Wot a lucky day for us," Gwennie said as she opened the door. "I don't know how the town is able to spare two of their bravest for us, but come on in."

"Darlin', you know me, and this is Felix," Chief Willy said as he shook, and stroked, Gwennie's hand. "He pretty much does what I tell him to do, and I told him to come see the most beautiful woman in the world working with a bunch of idiots."

Gwennie peeled her hand away from Chief Willy to shake Felix's. "Working with you boys today is my pleasure," she said. "Don't be so hard on yourselves."

Gwennie retrieved her hand from Felix's and with a gentle sweep of her arm invited them into the foyer. They looked at each other, uncertain if they'd been insulted.

We moved into my office and the plan was set. Chief Willy and Felix would watch from my office, which was off the foyer. I would pull the alarm right outside my door, and the moment we were outside they would shut it off, which would record the time. We were ready to go.

Mike came out of the kitchen and walked into the foyer as we were finishing our discussion. He opened the foyer coat closet and began rummaging around on the bottom.

"I can't find my shoes!" he said as he rifled through the closet.

With Mike so close to the door, it occurred to me it was the right time to pull the alarm. "Well, let's get this show on the road," I said, moving the conversation along. "If it is all the same with you, I'm ready to go."

Gwennie turned to Chief Willy. "All right with you, govner?"

Willy gestured toward the foyer, giving it his blessing.

Mike was on his knees, looking through the closet and talking to himself.

"Where are my shoes? I can't find my shoes!"

I pulled the alarm. Gwennie began her stopwatch.

The piercing alarm was no ding-ding-ding; it was a blaring, yelping blast. The strobe light began, and the house was instantly vibrating, pulsating with a mind-numbing, belching siren.

"I don't like that!" said Mike from inside the closet.

Staff and participants were getting ready to respond, but they never got the chance.

In one seamless motion, Mike turned from the closet and pulled the entire alarm and strobe out of the wall. The four of us watched in awe. It was a one-handed yank that liberated the beast from its dwelling. With one long snatch, Mike jerked the wires and the contraption out and onto the floor. The alarm was so brief no one had enough time to react. Mike gave the fixture a little shake just to be sure, and then dropped it on the floor. He turned right around to look for his shoes in the closet.

"Here they are!" he said with glee.

Mike picked up his shoes, shut the closet door, and went back into the kitchen. Chief Willy and Felix started to laugh, stepped over the mess in the foyer and left. Taimi, Harold, Gwennie, and two new staff I'd brought in to help gathered around. Gwennie held up her stopwatch.

"Twenty-eight seconds," she said.

I covered my face with my hands. "I'm sorry. I completely forgot to tell you," I said through my hands. "Mike has an issue with fire alarms."

"Ya think?" said Taimi.

"I learned this the first day I met him and I forgot to tell you. I was just trying to deal with it in my own way. I'm sorry."

"You forgot?" said Harold incredulously.

"Aw did a lot of drugs, and for a while forgot me first name. But I think if I saw a giant dismantle the Palmer industrial-grade fire alarm with one hand I might be remembering it," Gwennie said.

"I am so sorry," I said, covering my face now with just one hand.

Taimi walked back toward the kitchen. "Expert, shmexpert," she said as she turned.

"I'll be getting you a dustpan," said Gwennie.

"You forgot?" said Harold. "Damn." He went back into the kitchen.

Gwennie handed me the dustpan and went upstairs, calling as she went. "False alarm, everyone. Nothing to worry about. Just a little misunderstanding. Everything's all right," she said as she walked.

I started sweeping up the mess. I could feel my bottom lip begin to quiver and my eyes swell.

"Carry on, people. Carry on." Her voice faded as she continued up the stairs.

Tears fell into the white, chalky plaster dust. I wiped my eyes with my sleeve and knew I'd reached my breaking point. It was time to make an appointment with my mentor, Dr. Abrams.

* * *

I wanted to be like him when I grew up. He was a giant in his field. He was a towering intellectual, having published more than a dozen books and over one hundred articles on developmental psychology. He was well-known, well-published and well-liked. Yes. When I grew up, I wanted to be like him.

I started dressing like him. I had a beard and was already disheveled and absentminded, so I completed the cloning by wearing vests I'd bought for fifty cents at the Goodwill thrift shop. I rounded my shoulders, and learned how to shuffle. If only I wore thick black-rimmed glasses, people might have mistaken me for his son.

I really wanted to be like him, but of course there were a few things in the way. First, I would never be as smart as he was. He read everything, worked with everyone, and knew more about developmental psychology than anyone I could imagine. They assigned me to him not because he was an expert in intellectual disabilities, but because if anyone knew something about it, it would be him. I felt privileged and slightly awestruck.

I'd had classes and research seminars with him. He was truly brilliant. When it came time to get my dissertation proposal in front of him, I was aware that my skill and his standards were not in alignment. I struggled to put together the proposal, but the truth was the separation from my wife, the difficulty with the residents and the mayor, and my living arrangements all took their toll. I put together a proposal, but had no confidence in it.

The university was housed in Greenwich Village and his office was on the fourth floor. He had the largest office in the department, about fifteen by twenty feet, with a large window that opened out to the New York cityscape.

Floor-to-ceiling shelves completely engulfed the room, filled with books, journals, and stacks of papers. The desk, a palm-wood beauty he had built in Bali during a research trip, was unique, yet with classic lines. His chair was his father's. His dad was a psychologist who had actually met Freud.

To enter Dr. Abrams' room was to enter the kingdom of the intellect. Information, culled wisdom, was at his fingertips. There were cartons of books, always books, on the floor. The cartons were stacked and none were ever removed. Instead, more were continually brought in.

The plants hung from ceiling hooks. They crowded each other for outside light, each plant vying for position, the leaves all desperately reaching for the city sun and finding just enough to thrive. They were spider plants, or what he called *mali madres*, "bad mothers," because they threw their baby sprouts out of the pot. It was an interesting plant for a man who was one of the world's best-known developmental psychologists.

The desk was covered with paper stacked to varying heights. He was always shuffling papers, or looking in the drawers, or in the boxes behind the desk. There were pens and glass paperweights on top of some of the piles, and random paper clips placed like scattered stars. There was order in the randomness of their placement.

But the crowning object in the menagerie was a fishbowl with a lone goldfish, Socrates, who was too large to do more than wiggle in the water. Socrates, or some ancestor of his, was ever-present. Students from twenty years earlier would refer to this fish icon on Dr. Abrams' desk. No one asked if it was the same fish.

I was often late to class, or my study group, or getting home, or getting to work, but I was never late for an appointment with Dr. Abrams. No, he was someone I treated with the respect of the train schedule. I was on time and prepared. The man deserved at least that from me.

I knocked but had learned from my years with him that he didn't answer. The unspoken contract was, of course, that if he invited you to be there at a certain time that he would be ready to receive you. The ritual was the same: knock, then enter.

"Hello."

He motioned toward the chair facing his desk in the center of the room. I sat down. "Hello, Socrates," I said to his constant companion. To Dr. Abrams, I said, "Thank you for letting me see you today. I'm sorry I'm late with the proposal, but I . . ."

Two large boxes were on the floor, and Dr. Abrams was pulling books out and selecting shelf space for them. He interrupted my excuse with a gentle wave of his hand and a shake of his head.

"There's just a lot going on," I said, cutting to the chase.

"Like what?"

"I left my wife and was living in a shithole," I said, catching myself. "Sorry, Professor."

"Yes," he said absentmindedly. "Left wife—living in shithole."

"I don't know what I'm doing with these profoundly disturbed people. And the fucking alcoholic next door was snoring and then he died and so I moved into the group home . . . sorry."

"Yes," he said, wandering around the room looking for a place to rest his book. "Profoundly disturbed people, fucking alcoholic snores and dies, and you now live where you work."

"I'm not sleeping, I can't hold on to staff, I've got a nonverbal violent woman with an IQ of thirty-six, a freaking giant, a man with pica, synesthesia, and encopresis, a woman with Prader-Willi and with intermittent explosive disorder, a Down syndrome man whom I can't understand, at all, and a woman who was catatonic."

I'd gotten so agitated that the papers I brought with me fell to the floor. I stood up. A paper fell out of my hand near the fishbowl.

"Sorry, Socrates. And my staff? The best person has never gone to school and is better with every one of the participants than I am . . . and the cook is an ex-con who knows more about life than I ever will, and my secretary has this insanely gorgeous body, and she knows it!"

He blew some dust off of one of his books.

"Boy does she know it, and she wears a top with a plunging neckline. That isn't suggestive"—I draw a line with my finger down the center of my chest toward my navel—"it's a directional compass."

I settled myself into my chair and rearranged my papers. "And I'm distracted."

He was still putting books away.

"Violent woman, giant, pica. Synesthesia, encopresis," he said, and then paused. "Interesting, Prader-Willi, intermittent explosive, catatonic, Down Syndrome, savant." He paused again—"interesting. No staff, great staff, ex-con, directional compass—" He stopped and smiled. "Very interesting. Distracted, yes?"

"Yeah, this is my life, and if I don't get my degree I can't get a university job, or a license. I can't get this all done," I said, throwing up my hands and letting the papers fall to the floor again. "I'm out of control. I don't know what to do! And the fire code requires everyone out of the house in two minutes! It's impossible!" I could feel my bottom lip starting to quiver. I was determined not to fall apart any further. I've ruined my life. Craziness is all around me. I can't take care of everyone and myself."

It was no use. I held my hand to my face. I had lost it.

"I can't handle the paperwork and bureaucracy. I can't do it all."

He came over to me and stood alongside. He put his left hand on my right shoulder and took a deep breath. "Give up."

I stopped crying and pulled my hands away from my face. "What?"

"I recommend you give up."

He patted me on the shoulder twice, and then went back to his books. "Give up?"

"Yes, of course. Nothing is working out how you planned, your personal life is chaotic, and you're overwhelmed with responsibilities, and have no idea what is going to happen, yes?"

"That's true."

"So give up."

"What about my dissertation?"

The professor waved his hand dismissively. "Let it go. What do you need that for? All it is going to do is prepare you for a career with disturbed people, more headaches, disappointments and obstacles. I say let it go," he said as he continued going through boxes on the floor.

"Just like that?"

"Just like that."

"Just give up?"

"Just give up," he said, studying one of the books in the box. "Just give up and do nothing. Maybe get a hot dog pushcart in the city. Sell hot dogs on the street. It is a good living, you are your own boss, and you are independent. I see you as a hot dog vendor."

"You think I should sell hot dogs?"

"Yes, the good ones."

I didn't know what to say.

"Of course, you will have to get a permit to have a business, a pushcart business, from the city," he said casually, "and insurance, for when someone sues you because the hot dogs were not cooked well enough."

I nodded.

"And you will need to display a certificate of inspection approval from the Board of Health. They are picky and difficult, but you can deal with them."

I was listening, but I couldn't quite believe what I was hearing.

"And, people will criticize you and your good hot dogs. And hoodlums will steal your fine food, and try to rob you at night when you come home with cash."

I may as well have been on drugs or in a coma. I nodded like I was one of those dolls with the bobbing head in the back of a car.

"You will be frightened about walking home, but you can hire bodyguards. And be sure to get up early so no one steals your good spot on the street. Are you a good fist-fighter?"

Finally, I understood. "Thank you," I said.

He continued to put his books away.

"Yes. I recommend you give up, and prepare for a life of ease."

I stood up and tapped Socrates's fishbowl. "I'll let myself out."

Dr. Abrams pointed at me with his pinky. "Remember what Freud said."

"What's that?"

"When God closes a window . . ."

I listened intently; I knew his father had been with Freud, so I thought a little bit of history was coming my way. "Yes?" I answered.

". . . he opens a group home."

I laughed. "I don't think Freud said that!"

"He would have if he had known your situation. Leave your draft on the desk."

"Right!" I plucked the dissertation draft from my papers and put it on his desk.

I bought a hot dog from the first vendor I saw. I told him I wanted one the way he makes it for the Buddhists.

"How's that?" he asked.

"Make me one with everything," I said, laughing to myself.

He smiled and shook his head, and then handed me his masterpiece. When I gave him the money I told him to keep the change. That's when it was my turn to be the straight man.

He rubbed the coins in his hand. "Thanks," he said, "but real change comes from within."

* * *

I came back to the program with renewed energy and enthusiasm. We were going to nail this fire drill.

For six weeks, we worked like a well-oiled machine. The violent incidents had lessened in frequency because we had taught the group sign language. People were cooperative with each other, and the slightest bit of hope emerged. We needed it.

My proposal had been approved. Dr. Abrams had one or two suggestions, but he was in favor of me doing research on people with intellectual disabilities. He'd given me the proposal back with his comments and a note scribbled at the top:

Give this a try before purchasing a cart.

We practiced the drill over and over. The new staff members were taught how to help people exit the first day they were there. We were all fans of Peter Sellers and his character, Inspector Clouseau. Just as Clouseau's faithful servant, Kato, could surprise Clouseau at any time to keep him on his toes, we decided any one of us could initiate a fire drill any time of the day or night with the yelling of "ding-ding-ding."

It was working. Time after time we gathered up and moved out of the house. We averaged ten times a week. In half of them, we finished in less than two minutes.

I took on the challenge of working with Mike. When the alarm was replaced I kept the old one and had the installer tell me how to wire it up so I could use it to train the big man. He showed me and Mike and I had several "desensitization" sessions. I certainly didn't want it in his charts that I was desensitizing him to the alarm.

I worked with Mike in the dining room on the first floor. I explained everything to him before we began.

"Mike, this is the fire alarm that you removed from the wall."

"I don't like that noise!"

"Yes, I know, and I am going to teach you a very fast way to stop hearing it."

"Okay."

"I am going to make this alarm go off . . ."

"I don't like that noise!"

"Yes, I know. I am going to make the alarm go off and the very second you hear it I want you to leave it alone . . ."

"But I don't like that noise!"

"Yes, right, but instead of destroying it, which you are very good at . . ."

"Thank you."

"Yes, but instead of destroying it we are going to leave it alone and get as far away from it as we can."

"As far away from it as we can?"

"Yes, can you do that?"

"I don't know."

"Would you be willing to try?"

"Okay."

I got Mike ready, then touched the two wires from the alarm to the battery. The chirp blast from the beast probably didn't last a half second.

Mike swiped the alarm off the table with one shot.

"I don't like that noise!"

I could hear Taimi and Gwennie laughing in the kitchen.

"That's why," I said as I picked it up off the floor, "that's why we are going to leave it."

"Leave it?"

"We are going to get as far away from it as we can. Do you know why?"

"Because I don't like that noise!"

"Yes, and every time you destroy one of these we just get another one that you don't like. But if you learn to get as far away from it as possible, you can always be sure you won't have to hear it."

"Okay."

"So the minute you hear this you get up and go outside."

"As far away from it as I can," he said.

"Yes! Very good, are you ready?"

"Okay."

"Here we go," I said as I touched the wires.

The chirp was shrill and Mike stood straight up and left the dining room. I actually hadn't thought he'd respond so quickly and he was already out of the room and in the foyer. I followed him and made a surprised face at Taimi and Gwennie as I went to the front door.

Mike was already crossing the street. There was little traffic but he was shuffle running and cars were stopped. Taimi and Gwennie came behind me laughing as I ran after him.

"As far away as you can," Taimi yelled as I ran after him. "Go as far away as you can."

I was laughing and running at the same time. Every step of his was equal to four of mine. As I ran, two words kept echoing in my mind: "Expert, shmexpert, expert, shmexpert, expert, shmexpert . . ."

* * *

It was easier than I thought to redirect Mike. I explained that the end of the property was as far as he could go, and for a month the entire home practiced. We were perfect. In forty-six official tries, we were out in less than two minutes in forty-one of them. We were ready.

On the day of the drill Chief Willy and Felix returned. This was our third effort, and we could all feel it. We were going to do it. We got into position as before, and Gwennie crossed her fingers and pulled the alarm.

Mike was with Lilith and they went out first. It was the first time I'd seen him hold her hand. "Come on missy, we have to get as far away to the end of the grass as we can."

One by one the participants streamed from all parts of the home with Harold and Taimi and Gwennie and a new staff person moving them right along. The clock was ticking. At the one minute, thirty second point, it was only Benny who was taking his sweet time. He kept looking around and stalling. When he bent over to fix his shoelace, which wasn't loose, Gwennie hooked him under the arm and provided him with a direct escort. He stubbornly trundled his way down the front steps. The moment Gwennie hit the grass she held up the stopwatch and clicked it. "One minute and forty-eight seconds!"

We all began spontaneously jumping up and down, high-fiving. We'd done it! We'd pulled together to do the impossible. But it was Harold who realized something was wrong.

I remember seeing his face and his walk and his determination as he bounded back up the stairs. The alarm was still blaring. Chief Willy hadn't shut it off.

I ended up right behind Harold. He was less than an inch from Willy's nose.

"Shut that fucking thing off."

Chief Willy smiled and took out a special key from his keychain. Willy inserted the key into the monitor and turned it once halfway. The alarm stopped. Outside the celebration was still going on.

"That was *very* close," said the chief to Harold and me. "You only missed that by thirty seconds."

"Bullshit!" Harold screamed into Willy's face.

"Now, Felix and I, our hearts go out to you. We both witnessed how hard you tried in your failed effort, and we will duly note that in our report."

I saw Harold's fist tighten, and stood between him and the fire chief.

"It's not worth it," I said with my heart pounding in my ears. "You'll go back to prison, and they'll go back to the institution, and these two guys and the town will feel justified for throwing us out. Please–please."

I watched a calm come over Harold that was as welcome as it was scary.

"Boy, I guess I was all wrong about you, Chief Willy. I guess you weren't done with me and this home after all."

"That's right, boy. You had no idea who you were tangling with."

Harold put his arm around me and grinned. "Ya know, I just don't feel like cooking tonight. What's say you let me treat this group to pizza and celebrate?"

"Sure," I said, finally taking a breath.

"What you got to celebrate?" Willy said with a smirk and a nod toward Felix.

"I always celebrate when I'm inspired."

"Inspired? What are you inspired about?" asked the chief.

"Something I learned about inspiration from a man I have a lot of respect for," Harold said with the slightest smile.

"What was that?" asked Felix.

"Inside of a ring or out, ain't nothing wrong with going down. It's staying down that's wrong." Harold put his arm around me and walked me out the front door.

"You done good, everybody," he said, holding up his arms. "Let's all get in the van—it's pizza time!"

The group started clapping and hooting and making their way toward the van, high fives and jubilant fists shaking in the air. From behind us Felix called out.

"Hey, who said that?"

I turned back toward them as Harold looked on.

"Ali," I said, as Harold started to smile. "Muhammad Ali."

Where There's Smoke . . .

Albert was agitated. He woke up moaning. Which meant so did I. It was 4:05 a.m. He was sitting up in bed, rocking and biting his left hand. It was the most distressed I had ever seen him. He slapped himself, hard, with his right hand. This whack of his hand against his head was such a crisp smack that the sound was as uncomfortable to hear as it was to watch him hit himself. I'd learned techniques for subduing such self-injurious behavior, but my instinct was to leap toward his automaton-like smacking with both my hands. Instead, I grabbed one of his pillows and cushioned the blows with it.

"Albert! Stop, stop, stop! You have to stop! What's the matter?"

Taimi was right behind me. "Jesus Christ, Albert! What are you doing?" she said as she grabbed his arm with a towel.

We were trained in such incidents to use towels to hold arms and legs rather than our own hands. The theory was that the towels would give us more control, with less pressure and in a more humane way. It would also keep us from losing grip due to the sweat from our own anxiety. The theory turned out to come in handy.

But Albert was not to be calmed. He hit, or tried to hit himself as hard as he could. None of this made sense.

"What the fuck is happening?" asked Taimi.

"I dunno, he must be panicked about something!"

Albert broke free from both of us. He was trying to escape from us, or so it seemed. He had no interest in hurting us as he wriggled himself free, and he bolted out the door. Taimi still had the towel around his arm, but he shook it loose, and I couldn't get a grip on him. My hands were sweating like it was 110 degrees.

Albert jockeyed down the steps and ran through the foyer. I was petrified he would run into the street. But instead he headed straight toward the kitchen. I was about fifteen feet behind him and Taimi about five feet behind me. Albert was biting hard on his left hand, and with the point of his elbow he pushed open the door to the kitchen. The second he did, I detected the first whiff of smoke.

"Shit!" I yelled.

"What?" asked Taimi.

"It's smoke! He smelled smoke!"

There was a fire in the pantry and the back door was opened. Albert was in the middle of the kitchen biting his hand and smacking his head and wailing in a high-pitched, frantic voice.

"Go back upstairs and get everybody out of here!" I screamed to Taimi.

She turned on a dime and I grabbed the fire extinguisher. When I looked in the pantry, there were four fires—two on the middle shelves to the right, and two on the lower shelves in front of me. These fires had been set.

I had never used a fire extinguisher before and my anxiety made this a bad time to learn. I fumbled with the pin and Albert moved right up to the flames.

"NO! Albert! NO!" I panicked at seeing Albert near the flames and dropped the fire extinguisher. The kitchen only had a heat detector, as the reasoning was that a smoke detector in the kitchen would go off with every piece of burnt toast. The pantry was now engulfed with flames and I worked at getting Albert back out to the foyer.

"Let's go, buddy!" I said, standing between Albert and the fire. "Back this way, Albert, back this way!"

I was never a good football player in high school, but hours of blocking practice suddenly came in handy. I shouldered Albert away from the fire and more or less shoved him back out the kitchen door. When we got to the foyer I pulled the alarm.

Taimi was on the landing with everyone in his or her pajamas. The alarm reverberated through the house.

"I don't like that noise!" bellowed Mike.

"I was sleeping! What the heck is going on! Why are you making me get up!" screamed Lilith.

Taimi had Sophia and Candy's hands.

"Down we go, let's go, this is a fire drill, you know what to do, out the door, out the door. Everybody out the door!" yelled Taimi.

I opened the door and kept Albert moving out onto the porch. Taimi used her body and the human chain she made with Candy and Sophia to herd everyone toward the door. Jake grabbed Candy's hand, and Benny, who seemed more asleep than awake from his medication, grabbed Jake's.

"There are eighteen steps and we have to step on every one of them," said Jake.

The smoke had reached the detectors and they began sounding. I hadn't realized they were separate, but they made a high-pitched, shrill blare that penetrated the home. Between the fire alarm, the strobe lights and the smoke alarm, it was official: The house was on fire.

We had just reached the front lawn when the sound of the nearby engines could be heard. Taimi and I frantically counted heads.

"We got everybody?" I asked.

"They're here, they're all here," she assured me.

I saw Harold running up the hill.

"What the hell happened?" he yelled.

"That noise is making me mad!" yelled Mike.

"The pantry's on fire!" I told Harold. "Watch Mike, will you?"

The first engine arrived.

"Is everybody out?" the first fireman asked.

"I think so," I said.

"You think, or you know?"

"They're all here," said Taimi calmly.

"What happened?" asked the fireman.

"The pantry is on fire. You might want to go around back. The food pantry is there and the door is open."

The word "food" was like a starter pistol. Lilith *flew* into the house.

"NO!" screamed Taimi, but her hands were still locked with Sophia's and Candy's. Lilith disappeared into the smoke billowing out the front door.

"You come back here, missy!" yelled Mike as he dropped his hands from his ears.

Harold stepped in front of Mike, sensing that Mike was about to follow Lilith. With one enormous shove Mike knocked Harold on his back and in two large leaps he too disappeared into the front-door inferno. I charged in behind him but was blocked by one, then another fireman.

"No one goes in."

Harold scrambled to his feet and made a run at the door, but a fireman used his axe as a block. "No one goes in!"

We could hear Mike yelling.

"You get out of here, missy, this is a fire drill and we are supposed to be outside!"

Others came and emergency vehicles were pulling up and hoses were being fixed onto the house. The first responders ran around back and I followed. I was thinking I could go in the back door and get Mike and Lilith out that way. But they had the hoses already attacking the flames.

"My food! My food! I want my food!" we could hear Lilith scream.

Harold and I started running around to the front of the house. We both must have had the same idea: to go in through the front windows.

Firemen were moving in through the front door, then just as suddenly they retreated. "Holy shit!" I heard one of them say.

It was Mike. He was carrying the refrigerator. Lilith was right behind him.

"My food, my food, my food," she yelled as she grabbed at Mike's back.

Mike stopped at the edge of the porch and unceremoniously dropped the refrigerator onto the stairs. The door flung open and the contents tumbled out onto the steps and the front yard. Lilith dove in. She was shoving food into her face as fast as ever.

"Don't go in there again!" warned Mike.

By now there was a crowd. Gwennie was coming up the hill, wearing Harold's bathrobe.

People began helping clear the food and lift the refrigerator. The kitchen was still ablaze.

"Where's Benny?" asked Taimi nervously.

"Benny!" I screamed. "Benny!"

"He's inside!" yelled Harold as he pointed through the window in the front of the house.

Harold took two steps back and, like a human cannonball, hurled himself through the front window. Benny was walking toward the flames. In seconds Harold appeared at the front door huddling Benny in his arms, face-forward, out onto the porch. He ushered Benny down the stairs.

"I wanna see my fahdah. I wanna see my fahdah!"

As they came down the steps, Gwennie pointed at Harold and yelled. "Your shirt's on fire!"

The tail of Harold's shirt had caught on fire. He tore it off, threw it to the ground and stomped on it. It was dark, but everyone there could see flesh-torn scars on his chest. His ebony skin was blotched with off-pigment white scars that looked like three pools of white candle wax had become part of his skin. In that moment, he looked like he had to make a decision of a lifetime. He could be ashamed or proud. He chose proud.

Harold lifted his chin slightly, as if he were letting us all have a good look. His chest opened to us and his strength and courage shone though. The house alarm went off. It was impossible to know how much time had passed since I told Taimi to get everyone out.

Awakenings

I don't know exactly what it was that changed the people who had witnessed all of this. It could have been the caring they saw of the staff for the residents. It could have been seeing Mike save Lilith in the only way he could. It may certainly have been Harold's unbridled bravery. But one thing was certain: there was a shift in the town that night. People witnessed other people in distress and they saw heroes of every size and shape and ability come to their need. The word about all this spread quickly. I'd later learn as a positive psychologist there is a name for this kind of reaction: elevation. The New York University psychologist Jonathan Haidt would conduct research that shows when we see acts of bravery, moral justice, kindness, and the like, we are inspired by the warm feelings we experience. I think elevation is a great word. That's exactly what we felt after the fire—elevated.

We were not allowed to go back into the home because of the smoke and damage. We made arrangements for each of the residents. If they could, they stayed back at home with their loved ones, and two families took in another resident, which greatly helped. Lilith stayed with Candy, and Mike stayed with Benny and his mom. We had support staff to help them out, but just the idea that this was feasible, that people who'd been impossible were now able to stay for a few nights as guests was astonishing. I moved into a studio apartment in a neighboring town and Taimi stayed with her parents. We found high-quality respite for Jake, Sophia, and Albert. It seemed once people learned what had happened, they responded—and that included the town.

An investigation determined that the pantry fire was started in a way deliberately set fires in vacant lots and garbage cans all over town had been set. The town had a firebug. It didn't take long to figure out who it was. A pack of burned matches from Pete's bar were identified— it was Jeffery, Chief Willy's son, who had set the fire. In fact, his pyromania had been responsible for a dozen fires in town over the past year and a half, none of which his father had solved. Soon, a buried box of Pete's matches was found in the corner of the yard. Those awkward movements had been Jeffery practicing match strikes.

Carl, the newspaper columnist, had been the first first responder to reach the group home. He was on the volunteer fire department and lived across the street. He'd witnessed the collective acts of bravery and, since Chief Willy wasn't there, he verified us himself, and we were granted the certificate of occupancy.

We weren't the first home for the people with intellectual disabilities to be burned in a community—and certainly not the last. In December 1987, a Long Island home was being readied for residents to move in when it was set ablaze, and similar crimes occurred in many states. The fires rarely succeeded in doing little more than delaying the opening of the group home and costing more money. As is often the case, hate backfires.

Jeffery had serious problems, and rather than suffer punitive measures, he was set up in an intensive outpatient program in the city. A child learns to hate what his parents hate, and Jeffery was as much of a victim as we were.

The townspeople quickly learned what had happened, and a dozen pool passes were brought to the house, paid for with contributions given at the town hall. Donations for fixing up the house from the smoke damage, and the time and material donated by Chief Willy's hardware store, brought us a steady stream of volunteers for painting and repairs. We had become the cause du jour, and in a short time we were back.

As with many disasters, the kindness and humanity that comes forth is an inspiration, a correction to hatred, bigotry, and meanness. As Elie Wiesel, Nobel Laureate and Holocaust survivor, noted: "Even in darkness it is possible to create light and encourage compassion."

Someone took Mayor Billings to get his photo taken with Mike on the front porch of the house, handing him the key to the city—a concept Mike was unable to grasp—for being a hero and saving Lilith.

To celebrate our certificate of occupancy, we threw an open house. The participants dressed to the nines, as did the staff. Gwennie and Harold looked more like they were attending the Academy Awards. Her long, low-cut black dress and Harold's black suit and bowtie made everyone look twice. We actually found a suit large enough for Mike to wear at a big-and-tall rummage shop, and he escorted Lilith wherever she went around the home. The other ladies, Sophia and Candy, looked splendid in their dresses, earrings, and dress shoes. Candy wore every piece of jewelry she could find, and Gwennie helped Sophia put on some makeup. Sophia had come a long way since my first day with her. She was calm and smiling and signed "Hello" when she walked into the room. Everyone who saw her signed in return.

Jake was impeccably dressed in a suit he'd brought from home. When I took a moment to look at his face, I was struck by the fact that his acne had improved dramatically since the time I tested him. Harold's healthy diet probably had something to do with it. Finally, there was Albert, who, with his dark blue suit, looked for all the world like an accountant. Except, of course, most CPAs don't chew their ties.

Harold insisted on preparing all the food. The entire fire department was there and he regaled them with boxing stories and names of boxers he knew personally. They were impressed.

His food, as always, was perfection, and one of the firemen asked where he'd learned how to cook.

"I got separated from my platoon in 'Nam and we were under heavy fire," he began, "and I don't know what happened. The last thing I remember is a blast that left me with this."

Harold peeled down the back of his shirt collar to reveal nasty scars across the back of his neck.

"The next thing I knew I woke up in a Buddhist temple, a monastery, and these amazing men were attending to me. They removed the shrapnel and nurtured me back to health through diet and herbs. The tenzo took me under his wing, and taught me how to be a mindful cook."

"What's a tenzo?" asked one of the firefighters.

"The tenzo is responsible for every aspect of the food's preparation and readiness. It is a sacred position. You think about the quality, the preparation, the blessing needed to make the food. You realize the responsibility falls all to you to nurture the people in the monastery. The spiritual nurturance comes from the food that nurtures. The job of the tenzo is to prepare reverential offerings. I watched, and learned, and prepared. Preparing food is like life. The more you are prepared, and the greater the variety, the better you feel, and the better you do. The motto of the tenzo is to not be careful about one thing and careless about another."

Each of the men nodded. "It's the same in firefighting," offered one of them. "Don't watch the ceiling when the floor underneath you could give way."

I had been eavesdropping on Harold's story when Taimi came up in front of me.

"I learned a lot from you," she said as she shook my hand.

"How's school?" I asked.

"How'd you know?"

"I had to sign the tuition reimbursement form from Central."

"School's for losers, but I *am* the top loser in the class."

"You know the field needs people like you," I said, looking directly at her.

"What, do you get a fucking toaster if I say I want to be a mental health professional?"

"You're good, you're better than good, and I told Central so in my final report."

"Final report, eh? Gwennie told me you passed your dissertation defense. You are finally going to be 'doctor.' Christ, how long did it take you?"

"My whole life."

"You get that college teaching job you always wanted?"

"It's only a one-year replacement in a community college, but these jobs don't open up unless someone dies. I have to take this to get my foot in the door," I explained.

"You know what cinched it? The fact that I have experience working with . . . working here, and the fact that my dissertation was about people with . . . ya know . . . needs."

The mayor walked in with a frame in his hand and whispered something to the chief. Willy nodded and came over to me.

"Mayor Billings wants to make a toast and wanted to know if it's okay."

I flashed the mayor a thumbs up. He nodded, then picked up a spoon and clanged on the side of a ceramic coffee cup.

"If I may have your attention." He clinked the cup again. "If I may have your attention. This is a very proud day for our fine town. We have come to know each other and work together in ways none of us thought possible a year ago. Man alive! It's hard to believe it's been a year. Right, Dr. Dan—who, as I understand it, is officially Dr. Dan."

The group clapped; I took a half bow.

"It went fast, didn't it? Did it seem like a year?" the mayor said, looking at me.

"Actually, more like ten."

People laughed.

"You don't mean that, do you?"

"Fifteen?"

As people laughed, the mayor took back the floor.

"At my own expense, I have framed this certificate of occupancy, which I hope will hang here in this warm and inviting kitchen as a symbol of our welcoming you, officially, to our humble town."

I glanced around the room. Two months ago, such a scene would have been impossible. Now Sophia was signing "like" to Benny at the sheet cake, Albert was sniffing one of the fireman's badges, Mike was replacing a light bulb handed to him by Gwennie, and the town was in our home celebrating the fact that we were staying, not going. The mayor continued his toast.

Gwennie noticed the mailman at the front door and invited him in for a piece of cake. He had a package in his hand. The mayor concluded his remarks and the group applauded.

"Someone has to sign for this," said the mailman, holding it up. "Special delivery."

Gwennie signed and made her way over to me.

"It's for you," she said, handing it to me. "It's from some institution in upstate New York."

Taimi came over with Harold.

"Special delivery? Man, you rate," said Harold.

I tore the package open. The contents were wrapped in a clear plastic bag. I pulled them out and inspected it. I started laughing and couldn't stop. Taimi grabbed the bag out of my hand.

"What the hell are these?" she said. "They look like . . ."

"Buttons!" I said, laughing. "They're buttons for my leather jacket."

The phone rang as I started explaining my first meeting with Albert to those who would listen. Gwennie answered the kitchen phone, and then handed it to me. She had to shout to be heard above the crowd.

"It's Central; they want to talk to the group home manager."

I took the phone from Gwennie, and, without lifting it to my ear, passed it directly to Taimi.

"Actually," I said, handing it to her, "I get a microwave."

Jesus of Asbury Park

I was offered a one-year replacement position teaching psychology at Brookdale Community College in Monmouth County, New Jersey. I left Walden House with a sense of being part of something larger that had never been done before. There were a few loose ends—such as Candy's revelation about her attackers. Somehow the safety of our home had allowed her memory to come back. This was the beginning, and although it took several years, all of the assailants were brought to justice. Experts came in to help her, and I never had to testify at the trial—but her uttering the names was the beginning. As a group, we witnessed courage, love, kindness, creativity, teamwork, honesty, persistence, forgiveness, self-regulation, gratitude, hope, and humor—all of the very things I would later, as a positive psychologist, realize are essential character strengths. I did get my PhD—in the mail—about two years later. I was $500 short paying my tuition, and while I was at the top of my class, the university wouldn't let me walk at graduation with my classmates because of the debt. It took me two years to pay it off, and a few weeks after I did, a tube with the diploma and a letter inviting me to the next graduation came. I declined. After the struggle and all that I thought it meant, the actual piece of paper and ceremony didn't mean a thing. To this day, I don't know where that tube is, or if I still have it. But the experiences at Walden House and the innumerable homes, workshops, agencies, and hospitals that followed have remained: they are my diploma.

I was lucky to have experiences that most psychologists don't get, and I was ready to put those experiences to use. Moving into a small home near the college with my girlfriend (who later became my wife), I began training in psychodrama, an action-oriented form of psychotherapy that uses elements of theater to help clients, with Bob and Jacquie Siroka.

Moving to Monmouth County was like hitting the reset button on my life: I had the type of job I wanted, a woman in my life, new friends, an army of students I could teach by telling stories, a doctorate degree, and a new fascination with psychodrama. In addition to teaching, consulting jobs were easy to find, and I could start paying off my loans and the $500 I owed to Yeshiva. Life was good. I was presenting at conferences about new ways of working with people with intellectual disabilities and had put together a model known as Interactive-Behavioral Therapy. This was very different than what had come before, as it was a form of group therapy for people with intellectual and psychiatric disabilities that used psychodrama to make therapeutic gains. At that time, I worked with a new colleague of mine, Dr. Al Pfadt, a leader in the field working to devise a model of group that might be successful with people with both intellectual and psychiatric disorders. Al was a serious researcher with direct experience with people from Willowbrook. We met at a conference and became fast friends. We sent in a paper to the APA to present our work on group process. We knew that if it got accepted, it would be the beginning of something important. The notice came in the mail, and you couldn't have found two happier people. We were about to bring a new idea out into the world. There was just one piece of business I'd have to take care of first.

Our presentation at APA was a success, and we were invited to publish in the first journal devoted to the subject of people with intellectual and psychiatric disabilities: *Mental Health Aspects of Developmental Disabilities*, created by Dr. Anne Hurley. The success of and interest following the presentation finally convinced me to get a license in New Jersey as a psychologist. My ongoing training as a psychodramatist combined with my experience with people with intellectual disabilities allowed me to collect my clinical hours. I was trying to take everything I'd learned forward, but I also had to let go of the past: it was time to finalize the divorce.

The entire fee for my lawyer was $175. He told me up front that he didn't specialize in divorces, and that in fact he didn't specialize in anything. "Whatever pays the bills," he said, "is good enough." If things got too sticky, he would refer his clients to more experienced people and took a referral fee in return. He struck me as clearly the kind of person who did the least amount of work he could to still get paid. He also told me he wasn't that great of a lawyer, but that this was simple and that he could get the job done. I believed him.

But what I didn't know was that he also represented Jesus.

* * *

At five feet six inches and 280 pounds, Jesus seemed to waddle more than walk. He stuttered, had bad breath and worse body odor, and when they finally got around to measuring his IQ, it was only fifty-five.

When he was two, Jesus had eaten pieces of lead paint from the baseboard of his parents' apartment. Thinking it was candy, he gobbled up several flakes before his parents saw what he had done. The lead in the paint brought about a type of poisoning in his system that caused a developmental disability. Now, twenty-nine years later, he lived in a used-up Victorian with fifteen other homeless people in Asbury Park along the Jersey shore.

Each day, he'd pace the boardwalk from Asbury down to Belmar blasting a huge boom box on his shoulder. It was always Springsteen, always loud. No one ever complained.

"Here come Jesus, preaching the Boss," was all they'd say.

August at the Jersey shore was no place for the flannel shirt and corduroy pants he was wearing. Jesus made his way along Belmar's

Ocean Avenue as *Born in the USA* poured out of his speakers. As he walked, his belly threatened the buttons of his shirt, and his balding head, topped with long, stringy hair, was beaded with sweat. His legs gave the impression they were independent of each other. One seemed to veer off to the right, the other to the left.

As if he weren't already attracting enough attention, he was stealing money out of parked cars along the street. On this brutally hot day in August, he scanned convertibles, cars with open windows, or those with unlocked doors for change.

He found a target. Stopping to put the boom box down, he tried to squeeze himself through the window of a small black Toyota Camry. His feet lifted off the ground as he pushed himself in, but then his body, more specifically his belly, got stuck in the car's open window.

Jesus had been given his religious persona by cops who arrested him for preaching with his pants down near Convention Hall. This happened years back when his thin frame, long hair, and beard suited his nickname better than now. After his arrest, he was always on probation for something. After his coronation at Convention Hall he'd been arrested for urinating under an escalator at the mall when he couldn't find a men's room; kicking a neighbor's cat down a storm drain because it cried too early in the morning; and stealing a convertible simply because the top was down and the keys were in it. The fact that he didn't know how to drive didn't stop him

Jesus wasn't "bad"; he just didn't think about consequences. Jesus did something because he needed to, wanted to, or thought it was okay. There was really nothing malicious about him. That's what his lawyer, who was also my lawyer, wanted to tell the judge when he was arrested for holding a gun to a policeman's head.

Warren was the plainclothes cop assigned to the beach. He was standing in front of DeeJay's eating his hot dog and watched as Jesus struggled to push himself in through the car window. Warren had seen him coming—who hadn't—and knew Jesus because he'd arrested him twice before: once for the mall incident, and once at a stop sign when he was stealing the convertible.

Warren walked across the street eating his hot dog and shaking his head. He stood behind Jesus but in front of the boom box, and chuckled to himself as Jesus tried to kick and wiggle his way into the car.

"Well, if it isn't Christ Almighty," Warren said, as he took another bite of his hot dog. "It looks like you've had a few too many loaves and fishes for that belly of yours to make that collection there, Jesus."

Startled, Jesus pushed himself out of the window, stumbling backward into Warren. They both fell back, tripping over the boom box and landing like dominos on top of each other. Warren's gun tumbled onto the pavement and, in a panic, Jesus picked it up and pointed it at Warren's head.

With the half-eaten hot dog clenched in his left hand, the veteran cop instinctively held his hands over his head as a sign of surrender. Jesus stood holding the gun, but staring at the hot dog. Finally, Jesus grabbed the hot dog and dropped the gun in a trash basket.

He ran and was arrested three blocks later, completely out of breath, waving the hot dog in his hand while his legs ran in different directions down Eighteenth Avenue.

Although he wasn't really interested in what I did, my lawyer, Rick, made small talk while we waited in the Freehold courtroom for the divorce judge and pretended to look interested. Rick was the kind of guy who looked disheveled even in a $500 suit. He was bright but scattered, always drinking coffee, and always preoccupied. I never offered him my opinion, but I thought he had adult ADHD and that the excessive caffeine consumption was his way to try to manage it. Children with ADHD are usually bright, accident-prone, and easily distracted, and are often given stimulants like Ritalin or Adderall to calm them down. The opposite thing happens to them than would happen to someone without

ADHD: amphetamines will slow them down and help them focus, while central nervous system depressants, like alcohol, can often exacerbate their condition. Although I never shared my diagnostic impression with Rick, I did make a mental note not to be in his vicinity if he were drinking.

"So, I remember you saying you never got along with your wife's family?" he asked, starting the conversation.

"My wife and her family didn't like the fact that I was going to graduate school and working with the intellectually and psychiatrically disabled," I explained. "I was a major disappointment to my wife and in-laws because I didn't join the trades. To them, I had no real skills, and early on they insisted I take an apprentice job in the plumbers, electricians or carpenters union," I told him. Then I told him about my ridiculous plumber's union test.

I thought I might get a chuckle out of him, but once he heard I had experience treating people with intellectual disabilities, he focused, as best he could, his full attention. "You work with retards?" he said.

"People with developmental or intellectual disabilities is the preferred term these days," I corrected him.

"I forgot, you're a shrink, you're a doctor, right? That's gotta be difficult," he said. "I got this one retard now that's gonna get screwed. He put a gun to a cop's head and they're just gonna send him away. My job is to just make sure they don't trample on his rights. It's a slam-dunk. Christ, you've got to be a moron, no pun intended, to put a gun to a cop's head. The judge isn't going to stand for that."

"Is the Division of Developmental Disabilities involved?" I asked.

"Who are they?" he asked.

I was puzzled. How could he be defending a man with a developmental disability and not involve the state agency designed to help such individuals? "The division," I began, "monitors everything from the kind of testing he would need, to finding the kind of *services* that might be available."

"Services?" he said sarcastically. "What kind of services does a retard who holds a gun to a cop's head need? He probably needs to be put in jail: safer for him, safer for society. I'm just window dressing the state pays for to make sure his rights aren't violated."

"What's his IQ?" I asked.

"I dunno," he responded.

"Aren't there tests in his file? Haven't there been some reports and evaluations done on him?" I queried.

"Just a rap sheet," he said. "This is the infamous Jesus of Asbury Park: he's legendary around here. They've been lenient with him in the past, but they are going to burn his ass good this time."

"What would happen if you didn't do your job? If the state hired you to protect his rights and it turned out you didn't? What happens if there was something obvious you missed and his rights were violated?" I asked.

"The judges remember things like that," he said. "You'd get a bad rep pretty quickly."

"What happens if you protect his rights in a way that is thorough?" I said, trying to make my point.

"You'll never be faulted for doing good work—but let's face it. I've got a retar . . . a person with intellectual disabilities. What could be done for someone like him?" he asked.

"To start with, you could have a battery of tests to determine his intellectual capacity and his emotional stability. Then you could find out about social services available for him, vocational services, counseling—"

"Counseling?" he interrupted. "How do you counsel a retard?"

I stared at him.

"How do you counsel a person with intellectual limitations?"

"The same way you counsel everybody else," I told him. "You find out who or what caused their pain, what they need, and how you can help them get it."

"But he stutters, he stinks, and he's violent. He held a gun to a cop's head for Christ's sake," he said, raising his voice.

"I do research on this kind of thing," I told him, "and about eighty percent of people with intellectual disabilities have a coexisting psychiatric diagnosis, and most have undiagnosed post-traumatic stress disorder."

"PTSD? Like the kind of thing people get if they are in a car accident or a bombing?" he asked.

"Exactly," I said. "But they don't express it in the same way as people without intellectual disabilities do, and they need much less of a trauma to trigger it off."

"No shit?"

"No shit," I answered. "Stuff you and I would find no big deal could trigger them."

"Like what?" he asked.

"Like being fired from a job, a sibling going off to college, a parent going into the hospital, consensual sex, even simply being startled could do it," I explained.

"No shit?"

"No shit," I said again. "And that's when they can be aggressive."

"Why would they be aggressive?" he asked.

"Hurt people hurt people," I responded.

"So what do you think my guy is going to need?" asked Rick.

"He will need a social worker and a medical evaluation for psychotropic meds. Has he ever been violent with anyone before?" I asked.

"Only with a cat."

"If the state puts him in jail, it will cost them about $60,000 to incarcerate him for a year. He's likely to get raped and beaten, and when he gets out he's going to need some services from the Division or he will become violent. The statistics are pretty clear on that. Where did he get the gun from?" I asked.

"It was the cop's."

"So he had no plan, right? Will you get paid more if this case goes longer?"

"I might. It ain't much, but everything helps. But if I do okay I'll get tossed a few more cases, which is good," he said.

"So, calling for all these tests, referring him to DDD, trying to set up counseling all will take time," I offered, "and this will become something that will have to be done for him in the future anyway."

"Don't they got special jails for people like him?" asked Rick.

"Yeah, two, each with a two-year waiting list. They will stick him in a regular jail and the rest will be history."

"Sixty grand, huh?"

"If the division gets him into a group home it will cost about $20,000 a year, he'll have a better life and they are likely to be able to help him get a job, so he can pay taxes that will go to pay for, you know, roads, parks, and lawyers."

"You got a point. I could make a few points with the judge," he said. "Do the right thing for the guy *and* get paid for it."

"Imagine that," I said sarcastically.

"It's not a concept I am unfamiliar with."

"I knew you were familiar with the getting paid part. It is the doing the right thing part I was wondering about."

"Very funny, but the truth is I do have a conscience, and I know what it takes to make the system work."

"I am sure," I said. "When is my divorce going to take place?"

"It could be fifteen minutes; it could be in five hours." He checked his Timex against the wall clock. "I hope it's in fifteen minutes," he said.

"Why?" I asked.

"The hearing for Jesus—his real name is Joe Reed, that's the intellectually disabled gentleman I have to represent—is at eleven," he said.

My divorce proceeding wasn't going to happen by eleven, so I followed my lawyer over to the courtroom to watch the case against Joe. As we walked he asked me to fill in the blanks.

"So how the hell did you ever get involved in working with these people? I mean most shrinks just want to work in their private office seeing normal, well you know what I mean, regular people with normal problems. How did you get mixed up with people like Jesus?"

"I consulted up in Paterson at a pre-vocational program for the last year and before I went back to school I ran an experimental group home in New York for people coming out of Willowbrook," I said.

"Willowbrook!" he said with astonishment. "That was the place Geraldo Rivera made infamous, right? Christ, what a snake pit that was!"

"That's exactly what Bobby Kennedy called it. It sure wasn't pretty," I responded.

Rick bumped into someone and his coffee spilled on his briefcase.

"Shit!" he muttered. As he bent down to wipe off the spill, the open coffee cup emptied onto the hallway floor.

"Shit!" he yelled.

He pulled his handkerchief out of his breast pocket and the pen he had in it flew out across the floor.

"Damn it!" he screamed.

As I helped him gather his things I mentally confirmed my ADHD diagnosis.

"You must have seen some pretty depraved people," he offered as he collected himself.

"True," I said, "but to paraphrase Ayn Rand: The most depraved type of human being is the one without a purpose. I just try to help people find their purpose."

"Right, right," he said, as he tossed the coffee cup out and bunched the briefcase up under his arm. "So who was like the wildest, most odd, most peculiar person you've worked with?"

"Wildest? Or most out of the ordinary?" I asked for clarification.

"What's the difference?" he asked as we neared the courtroom.

"Wildest, there are a bunch of contenders, over the last couple of years."

"Okay, so how about out of the ordinary?"

"One guy was amazing," I answered. "It was like he was the most brilliant person I knew, and the most troubled."

We opened the courtroom door and the bailiff told Rick that there was a brief delay in transporting his client from the jail, so we could wait in the hallway until Jesus arrived. We sat on a vacant bench right outside the courtroom.

"Looks like we got a few minutes, so tell me about this guy," he asked with what seemed like genuine interest.

"He was a participant I worked with when I set up the group home," I answered.

"What kind of a disability did he have?" asked Rick.

"He was what was once called an idiot—"

"Oh that's real nice, you're all over me about calling people retards, but you can call this guy an idiot, and it's okay?" he said interrupting me.

"Idiot *savant*," I clarified, "and, for the record, the label has been changed to autistic savant."

"So he was brilliant, right, totally like Rain Man."

"He was one of the smartest people I ever met, and yet had the most difficulty in life," I responded.

"So what was his problem?"

"He had no social skills," I answered. "None at all."

"Kind of like me, huh? So, what kind of work did he do?" Rick asked as he wiped coffee off his briefcase.

"He was a professional bingo player."

At that moment, the bailiff called Rick into the courtroom and I followed.

"All rise," said the bailiff.

The judge read over the charges as Jesus, in an orange jumpsuit and handcuffs, sat next to Rick.

Rick was on it. "Your Honor, there are some extenuating circumstances with my client that I believe warrant further evaluation. I have consulted a psychologist familiar in these matters and there are several suggestions which have been made that I believe are in my client's best interest."

"Such as?" asked the judge.

"Such as the involvement with DDD: that's the Division of Developmental Disabilities, Your Honor. They work with individuals like Mr. Reed, and they can assign a social worker to set up IQ testing and a medical evaluation. I believe Mr. Reed may be mentally incompetent and need a battery of tests to determine his intellectual capacity, his emotional stability, and his competency, as well as his potential for social and vocational rehabilitation," explained Rick. "I also believe Mr. Reed may need counseling, Your Honor."

"Counseling?" the judge said.

"Yes, Your Honor. I believe a skilled counselor could find out why Mr. Reed hurts and what he needs," answered Rick.

"I am impressed with your level of concern for the well-being of your client," offered the judge.

"Thank you, Your Honor. Just trying to do my job."

"This isn't the first time Mr. Reed has appeared in my court. I am inclined to give him some serious jail time, counselor," said the judge.

"Your Honor, hurt people hurt people. I believe if the state puts Mr. Reed in jail, it will cost taxpayers about $60,000 to incarcerate him for a year," Rick said. "Mr. Reed is likely to get abused and beaten while in there, and when he gets out he's going to need some services from the Division or he will become violent. The statistics are pretty clear on that, Your Honor. I think the state's money would be better spent now, because it will cost less and likely be more effective for Mr. Reed. And, as I am sure you know, Your Honor, the specialized jails have a long waiting list."

"You said that you consulted a doctor skilled in these manners. Is this the person available to do the counseling and evaluation?"

"Er . . . why yes, Your Honor, he is," said Rick. My lawyer looked at me, and I answered him with a slight smile and a nod.

"Dr. Tomasulo is his name, Your Honor. He is very familiar with people with intellectual disabilities like Mr. Reed, and has agreed to see him for an evaluation."

"I see," said the judge. "Although Mr. Reed has shown a depraved indifference for the rights of others, I believe your suggestions are good ones, counselor, and I am going to court-order these evaluations."

"Thank you, Your Honor," said Rick. "I believe that the most depraved type of human being is the one without a purpose, and my hope is, with proper treatment, we can help Mr. Reed find his."

In that moment, I realized I had been doing to Rick what I accused him of doing to Jesus. I prejudged him, labeled him, and acted toward him in a way that reflected my prejudice.

Not many people can say they started their private psychotherapy practice with Jesus as a client. I was astonished to find that I could, little by little, supplement my college teaching and agency consulting time with clients. In the beginning, most of the clients were intellectually disabled adults. Various agencies and private parties would pay to have me work with people with a dual diagnosis: someone with both an intellectual and psychiatric disability. With this specialty, it seemed that in no time I had a private practice. By 1986, I became fully licensed by the state. I never would have dreamed you could build a practice with individuals with profound disabilities, incapable of referring or paying for themselves.

Over time, others were referred who had more common problems than holding a gun to a cop's head. Rick became a good referral source. He always sent me someone he thought needed a unique approach. Many years after the divorce, Rick referred Suzanne, a young woman who cut herself and struggled with borderline personality disorder. Suzanne ended up doing very well in life. She eventually became a New York University professor and we stayed in touch sporadically over the years. It was almost three decades after Walden House. Suzanne referred Nick, one of her graduate students. Right from the start, like Walden House, Nick would demand more from me, much more, than I knew I had.

Rock, Paper, Sister
Private Practice: 30 Years Later

June 8

Nick had presence. He was a tall, solid bodybuilder. Sharp, chiseled angles defined his jaw and shoulders. He wore a worn green T-shirt and jeans to his first therapy session. The muscles in his chest and arms were more defined than on anyone I'd ever seen. When he shook my hand, it felt like he wore a catcher's mitt. I could barely get my hand around his.

I don't intimidate easily, but I felt humbled by his size. He seemed a yin-yang blend of power and stillness.

"Hey," he said as his catcher's mitt swallowed my hand.

"Hey."

"Cool." Nick pointed to a large leather recliner.

"It's all yours." I gestured toward it.

If he had asked for *my* chair I wouldn't have batted an eye in finding somewhere else to sit. "Can I take notes?" I asked.

"Knock yourself out, man."

"So what brings you here?" I clicked my pen.

"Took a course at NYU and it was cool. Like I opened up. Group therapy course, and the dude teaching it was cool. I didn't open the throttle on what was percolating, but I asked him, like who knows about this kind of thing, and he said you're the dude, so, like boom." He flicked his fingertips for emphasis. "Here I am."

"I'm the dude for . . ."

"Psychodrama, man. Like, I checked you out, you know, Googled you and like that." He made typing gestures with his fingers on an imaginary keyboard.

"Oh, right." I nodded.

"So, bingo." He turned his palms faceup.

"So, what was percolating?"

He looked at me. Then everything about him changed. This intense, strong, intimidating, powerful man folded into himself. His large frame had been squarely positioned in the chair, fingertips resting gently on his kneecaps. Now his hands retracted. He looked down and away. His straight back and magnified chest seemed to have withered. Like a life-sized balloon, his air had been let out.

"Wow."

"Yeah," he muttered into his hand.

"It's okay. We don't have to do this all today."

"Right."

"But it seems powerful."

"Yeah, right," he continued, looking away. "It's like, everything."

"Everything?"

He shook his head slightly. "Wow, man. Wow, this is more fucked up than I thought. Can you handle this?"

How was I supposed to answer that type of question? I didn't even know what we were talking about. "Like I said, we don't have to do this all in one day. Don't push yourself."

"Yeah, well, that's the whole fucking problem, isn't it?" His intensity surprised me. "That's all I fucking do is push my fucking self so I don't have to deal with this shit, right?" He didn't wait for an answer. "I've got to deal with this or I'm just going to stay fucked. I'm just going to be living the life I think I should, instead of the life I was meant to live."

"You're dealing with it now in the most direct way possible. You brought yourself in here to do the work. Right now, you're in this moment and you're doing it. There's no more direct way to deal."

It appeared as if he was slowly being filled with helium. His body unfolded and he inflated back to his original stance and presence. The transformation was palpable. Wherever he had gone, he had returned. The conversion took a full minute. A slight smile crossed his face as his fingertips returned to his kneecaps. "Cool."

"Very cool." What else could I say?

As if the helium had reached the liftoff point, he rose out of his chair and stuck out his catcher's mitt. It felt like an unspoken game of Simon Says. I stood up and shook his hand.

"Same time next week?" he asked.

"There's still a lot more time, you know."

"Nah, I'm cool."

"You sure?"

"Yeah, I got it. I'll leave a check with your secretary."

I was stunned, and a bit intimidated. Was I going to try to stop this guy from leaving? Not a chance. "She'll set you up for next week," I said as he let go of my hand.

Nick turned to the door, then stopped and turned toward me. "Read your book, man."

"And you decided to come anyway?"

"This chick I know, Suzanne, I think she knows you, gave it to me to read. Just wanted to see if you could handle it."

"How'd I do?"

"I think we both passed the audition." He smiled.

I laughed.

"Later." Nick walked through the door.

Nick had been in my office four minutes.

* * *

His hand swallowed mine again as he shook it and sat down in the same chair.

"So last week was a blast, eh? What do you do, pump special gas in here so people can feel shit they don't want to feel so they can heal up?"

"My secret is out."

"So what made you want to write a memoir?"

"It was just in me," I offered. "It felt like something I had to do."

"That's cool. I get that. That part about your cousin with his chicken-shit habit and your channel-swimmer patient with the White China overdose blew me away, man. Blew. Me. Away."

"Thanks. Sounds like you know the language of heroin addiction. Do you write?"

"Me? Nah. Well, like lyrics and shit, but not like write-write."

"Lyrics? You write songs?"

"Yeah, you know, it just felt like something I had to do."

"I've heard that before."

Nick smiled.

"What kind of music?"

"Whatever." He shrugged his shoulders. "Sid, Kurt, Neil, Bruce, Bowie, Amadeus, whatever."

"That sounds like a range."

"Yeah, actually taught a class a while back on variations and similarities in composer styles."

"Where did you teach it?"

"Harvard."

I smiled at what I thought was a joke.

"They have their heads pretty fucking far up their asses there, but it was cool. The students dug it."

"Harvard?"

"Yeah, it's a college up in Boston."

"Oh, that Harvard." Was he auditioning me again? "Any other places?"

"Juilliard, but only strings. Stanford, percussion. That was a sweet gig." He rapped off a series of drum riffs on the edge of the chair. "Back then down and around to NYU, Tisch, doubled back there to do the PhD thing . . ."

"PhD thing?"

"Yeah, but the dissertation stalled me, and I couldn't figure out a reason to finish. So, wham-bam back to England and in love," he paused to hold his right hand to his heart with his eyes closed and his left hand up in the air, "and then did the lighting for the Globe Theater. Then the young lady said she couldn't live with a fucking addict, so I shot up, OD'd, and awoke ten years later as a tenzo in a Zen monastery in Massachusetts."

"You've taught at Harvard, Juilliard, Stanford, and NYU. *And* you were the cook in a Zen monastery?"

"So you know about the tenzo, cool. Learned the ultimate mantra there too, *Om Mani Padme Hum*," he chanted with his eyes closed. "Praise to the jewel in the lotus, man. Also, did a summer gig at Princeton one year and two semesters at Cornell. You know what I like about Cornell?"

"Tell me."

"Abso-fucking-lutely nothing."

"Is there an Ivy League school you haven't been to?"

"U Penn."

"How'd you miss them?"

"You've got to drive through the war zone, man, to get there. Fuck them. They probably wouldn't dig my groove anyway. But I do love Ben Franklin."

"What instruments do you play?"

"Trick question, man, we'll be here all day. Shorter answer is what don't I play."

"I'll bite."

"The hung, man. I *can* play it, but it's too intense for me. I trip out."

"I don't even know what that is."

"It's a drum, man, looks like a spaceship and sounds like one. Forget it. If I play that, it's like I'm on acid."

"Wait until you see this segue; you're gonna love it."

"Go, man, go." He box-punched the air.

"What kind of drugs did you, or do you, use?"

"Smooth, man. Picked right up on the acid thing. Well, you're gonna get the same answer as the instruments, man. The shorter list is what I didn't take."

"And that would be . . ."

"Belladonna, man. Once I heard Manson did that, I just freaked for some reason and kept it off the list." He looked at me intensely. "But let me anticipate your next question. My drug of choice? Heroin, man, the occasional speedball, but man, for a little rush-o-mundo and to keep from crashing, but there is nothing like the poppy, man. That was it. Hence why I liked that bit about you, and your cousin, and your patient."

"Right," I said. "How bad?"

"How bad?" he said, letting himself laugh. "How bad is there? I mean I'd do anything, give anything to get it. *Anything.*"

"Okay, how about the flip side: Why'd you stop?"

"'Cause I lied."

"Lied?"

"There was one thing I would give to get it."

"And that would be?"

"My life, man. I realized it was taking it a dime at a time and that just woke me the fuck up."

"How'd you quit?"

"Planned an OD, wrote down the dosage, history, got all my medical information together, blood type, admission forms, signatures. Everything. I even made a recommendation about what drug they should use to revive me. Shot up, walked into Columbia Presbyterian and passed out with the information stapled to my shirt. They saved me and then got me clean."

"Wow."

"I had no money. I knew it would work."

"Then what?"

"Then I stayed sober—still clean, mind you. Eleven years."

"How long were you in the hospital?"

"A month or so. Never looked back. It took me ten years to pay them back for saving my dumbass life."

"How much?"

"48,611 dollars and twelve cents." Nick launched into a perfect a cappella version of the song by the Who: "I call that a bargain, the best I've ever had."

"You *can* sing."

"Thank you very much," came the Elvis imitation. Then he turned serious again. "Hey, you know what that song 'Bargain' is about?"

"Tell me."

"Most people think it's about a drug or a person, but it ain't."

"Then what?"

"God," he said. "Pete was talking about God."

"That actually makes sense. You know, most people wouldn't have even thought to pay that back."

"Right intention, right action," he said matter-of-factly.

"The eight-fold path?"

"Buddhism is where it's at, but I'm just chipping away at the mountain."

"How so?"

"I still got a long fucking way to go with right speech."

* * *

July 20

"So?" Nick sat down.

"So," I echoed, "bring me up to speed."

"Actually, man, I think I'm ready. I am definitely tired, but I'm ready."

"Do I know what for?"

"What is this, like the sixth session?"

"Eighth, actually."

"Then I'm definitely ready."

I had learned to let Nick find his way. I answered him by opening my palms slightly toward him.

"My fucking mother, as opposed to just some mother-fucker, came to see me last night."

"I was wondering when we would get around to your mother."

"Yeah, if it's not one thing it's your mother, right?"

"Right."

"So my fucking mother comes last night and I tell her I'm in therapy, and she laughs."

"She isn't very empathic, is she?"

"You don't need therapy, Nick," he said in a mock woman's voice.

"How did you respond?"

"Stared at her for like two minutes, and she stared back. Then I simply said: I will need therapy for the rest of my life. Then I burned a hole in her eyes with mine."

"What did she do?"

"She had a fucking shit-fit, and started going off on me," he said, making gestures with his fingers poking into the air in front of him.

"When are you going to grow up?" he said, poking to emphasize each word with an air jab.

"What did you do?"

"She poked me in the chest and I really had the image of just grabbing and breaking her finger," he said, biting his lower lip.

"What stopped you?"

"I knew I wouldn't stop until I broke every bone in her fucking body."

"Good choice, then."

"She said some other shit about me not needing it. Then she asked the six-million-fucking-dollar question."

"Which was?"

"'Why do you need therapy? You had a good childhood.' I lost it, man," he said, raising his voice. "I wanted to slap her silly, but as I was thinking how I would do that, she dropped a bomb."

"What'd she do?"

"She got all quiet. In a rage, she started screaming at me what a piece of shit I am, what a loser fucking drug addict I am, then she started poking me and trying to kick me."

"Nick, I'm sorry that happened to you. What did you do?"

"I had a split second where I envisioned breaking her fucking neck with one fucking snap, but decided I would kill her with my words."

I nodded.

"I said, 'I'm in therapy because of what you fucking did to me.'"

I kept nodding.

"She sank into a ball on the floor and started rocking, scream-crying, and I didn't do a fucking thing but watch her crinkle on my kitchen floor. I hoped she would die from the awareness. I watched her like you watch road kill flop around after it's been hit by a car."

"Then what happened?"

Nick was now burning that hole into my eyes. He deflated again. Right in front of me he folded up, just as he had done in our first session. He wasn't sucking his thumb, but he could have been.

"This is that spot, huh?"

"Not today, man. I can't do this today," he mumbled into his fist. Nick almost seemed to liquefy and leaked off the chair and toward my office door.

"Don't push yourself, Nick."

"I gotta go."

"I understand."

"Next time, man." He slunk toward the door, head down.

"Next time," was all I said.

* * *

July 27

"When I was six, something happened," Nick said the moment he sat down.

"Do you want to tell me about it?"

"I guess we'll see, man."

"You probably can't tell me everything; it's almost certainly too much for one session. But what would you be willing to share with me?"

"I was running around, just being a kid. Making noise, freaking out, whatever. I was six, man. So, I was doing whatever the fuck six-year-olds do. I had no idea my mother was a borderline with bipolar disorder. She was intense; I knew that, but I didn't realize how fucking crazy.

"She ran at me with scissors in her hand, grunting, being a wild woman. Crazy shit. Most of the time she didn't even pay that much attention to me, so I thought she was playing. When I saw her coming at me I thought it was a game."

I nodded.

"But it wasn't no fucking game, man."

Nick let the air out of him once again, and slowly moved his right hand up to his heart. His shoulders, like the huge wings of an eagle tucked in, rolled forward, and surrounded his heart. His bottom lip began to vibrate, then quiver. Finally, his hand moved from his heart to cover his eyes. He sobbed. Through his tears he whispered, "It was no game."

* * *

August 1

"How'd you do after our last session?"

"Yeah, man, thanks for the call. I got the voice mail. I was like, freaked for a while. I hate talking about this shit, but I guess this is why they call it the talking cure."

"I suppose if Freud were a bit more creative he would have come up with the singing cure."

Without missing a beat, Nick began tapping his right foot and performing a funeral dirge drumbeat on the arm of the leather chair. His powerful voice filled the room with the opening line to John Lennon's song: "Mother, you had me but I never had you."

His drumbeat switched to his fingers tapping out the piano accompaniment.

"'I wanted you—but you didn't want me.' Fuck, man, you know that screaming part at the end of the song?"

"Sure," I said, appreciating his performance.

"I used to perform that every night I played out and the screams at the end would go on for like three minutes. Sometimes I'd get a standing fucking ovation, other times people would walk out. One night Lennon actually came in to see me perform and two months later he records 'Mother' with those awesome screams."

"Sounds like you had an influence."

"We all have influence over everything—the butterfly effect, right? So, how does this work?"

"What are we talking about now?"

"Hey, man," Nick flashed a sly smile, "do I have to spell everything out for you? Aren't you paying attention?"

"I'm sorry, I wasn't listening. Could you repeat that?"

He threw his head back. It was the first time I had seen him laugh so hard. "You are a trip, man."

"Thank you. I've . . . I've always wanted to be a trip."

"Well then, you have achieved your goal."

"Excellent."

"I was talking about doing a psychodrama. How do we do that?"

"Can you tell me what happened when you were six?"

Nick stared at me as if deciding what he would say, or if he would speak. He rotated his palms upward and opened them wide. "I ran toward her, smiling, thinking it was a game. She came right at me, grunting and gritting her teeth. I thought it was funny. But at the last second all I could see was the scissors. There I was, running toward her with my arms open to her, and in that split second I knew something bad was about to happen. I was panicked *and* still running toward her with my arms open. It happened so fast."

"Oh my God."

"I remember hearing the scissors go into my chest. It sounded like what you hear when you rub a rubber balloon. It kind of squeaked. I didn't feel the pain in my heart until she pulled it out. I opened my mouth—but nothing came out. My arms were still open when she plunged the scissors in so deep the second time that I remember looking down after she let go and seeing them stuck in my fucking chest—right up to the grips, man. The blades were buried inside me. My T-shirt ripped and all I could think was how mad my mother is going to be that it's torn. I knew I would get blamed for it. How fucked up is that?"

* * *

August 8

"Have a seat, Nick."

"Thanks, man."

"That was an intense session last time."

"Really? I forgot. What did we talk about?" He smirked.

"If you're ready, I think we could do a little work around this in a psychodrama today."

"Let's do it, man."

"First, let me say that we can stop anytime. Just let me know and we just stop. There isn't any place we have to get to; there isn't anything we have to do but make this process safe for you."

"I'm cool."

"Just tell me if something's off, or you need a minute, or just want to stop. Just keep letting me know where you're at."

"Got it."

"So you've been keeping that journal all week doing that dialogue between you and the six-year-old Nick."

"Yeah, we been hangin' out. He's a cool kid."

"No doubt. Has he told you anything we might want to know about today?"

"Nah, not really. He's just glad I came to get him out of this place and he's thrilled I brought somebody with me."

"Brought somebody with you?"

"That would be you, Dr. Dan. I think he would have freaked if he thought I was coming in to get him alone. He likes the fact that you got a map about how to get there, and how to get us back home. Tour guide." Nick knew I was in it with him.

"Well, let's see what that map looks like."

"Do it, man."

"Where do you see six-year old Nick sitting?"

"He would be right over there in that swivel chair. He loves moving around, probably has ADHD."

"Right. So, can you go over there and sit?"

"Like, you mean, be him?"

"Yep."

"He's a little scared."

"Naturally."

"Just sit over there?"

"And become six-year-old Nick."

There were two empty swivel chairs in my office, plus the recliner the adult Nick was sitting in. The swivel chair he chose was to my left. The recliner he was sitting in was to my right. I sat between the adult Nick and the six-year-old Nick.

As Nick walked over to the other chair and sat down, I stood up next to the side of my chair.

"So, Nick," I said beginning the drama with little Nick, "thank you for coming to talk to me."

Nick got into it. He folded his legs up under him and, for the entire world, looked like he was six. "Hi!" he said, wiggling around, using his hands to swivel himself back and forth from the walls. "I'm Nick. Who are you?"

"I'm Dan."

"Hi, Dan."

"Hi, Nick. Can I ask you some questions?"

"Sure. You can ask me anything."

Little Nick reached over and picked up a small stone on my table, a keepsake from some work I'd done in Holland. I pick up stones from the places I've traveled and trained. Over the years I've displayed one or two from the more memorable trips. That stone was from a particularly good training event, but now it had become little Nick's security blanket.

"Big Nick wanted me to talk to you to help him feel better."

"Okay," he said, getting into the rhythm of the swivel.

"Is it okay if we talk about your mom?"

"Sure," he said, not thinking about his answer.

"Your mom sounds like she was kind of crazy sometimes."

"All the time," he said, keeping the rhythm.

"It must be hard to deal with her."

"Sometimes."

"Do you remember a time when it was really hard to deal with her?"

He kept swiveling, but there was no answer.

"Nick?"

"Uh-huh?"

"Is it okay for me to keep talking to you and asking questions?"

"Uh-huh."

"Can I still talk about your mom?"

"Uh-huh."

"Was there a time when it was very hard to deal with her? You don't have to tell me anything you don't want to. Any time you want to stop, we can."

"Okay."

"Are you okay?"

"Uh-huh."

"What do you want me to know about your mom?" I said, shifting away from the uncomfortable question.

"She doesn't like me."

"How come?"

"I make too much noise."

"I thought six-year-olds were supposed to make noise."

"Not me. She doesn't want me to make noise. She says it gives her a headache."

"So what do you do?"

"I make noise."

"Naturally." I smiled. "What does she do?"

"She gets angry and sometimes hits me, but then she gives me cookies or buys me ice cream and says she's sorry and we have a good time." Little Nick fingered the stone in his hand.

"What's a good time?"

"I don't know." He swiveled back and forth.

"But whatever it is, it feels good, so it must be worth getting her angry."

"Uh-huh."

"What happened that time with the scissors?"

Nick stopped the chair. It was time for Nick to do what he'd come to do.

"Nick, if it's okay, I'm going to come over and stand by you, stand behind you, and say some of the thoughts and feelings you might be having. Would that be okay?"

"K," he said, head down.

I stood up and walked to where little Nick sat, taking my place slightly behind him. This is the double position in psychodrama. In this position you say, first person, as if you were the protagonist, the thoughts and feelings the person may be having that they may not be able to say on their own.

I settled myself in behind little Nick and adopted his posture. Doing this got me into his frame of mind. After a moment, I spoke as Nick, "I'm scared to think about all of that," I began in a soft voice. "I thought we were playing a game. Then she hurt me, hurt me bad." I stopped and checked in with Nick. "Does that sound right, Nick?"

He nodded his head.

"Then I'm going to continue, okay?"

He nodded. I put my hand on his shoulder and went back to doubling for him.

"She scared me so much. Those scissors hurt so much. I couldn't believe it. It's my mother! Mommy . . . Mommy . . ." I shifted my breathing and mimicked beginning to cry. In a scared voice, I continued. "Mommy . . . Mommy, no . . . no . . . stop . . . Mommy . . . no . . ."

I watched as Nick's lip began to quiver. I covered my face with my hands and continued doubling, using my hands to mute my screams. "No! Mommy . . . NO! . . . MOMMY! . . . NOOOOOOOO!"

My scream induced a deep wailing in Nick. His whole body shook; his massive shoulders bounced like they were in the back of an old pickup truck. His crying was guttural. He pressed his face with his fists, the small stone held inside his right hand. After several minutes his breathing became more rhythmic, and his body relaxed and softened.

As the crying subsided, I asked Nick to reverse roles and go back to his chair, leaving the stone with the little Nick role. He placed it back on the table as I sat back down in my chair. I asked big Nick to say something to little Nick. He took a moment centering himself. Finally, he took in an enormously deep breath that filled him up to capacity. He seemed whole. The slightest smile crossed his face. "We're going to be okay, kiddo," he said, nodding slightly. "We're going to be okay."

* * *

August 15

"I slept like a baby when I got home after last session," Nick began. "I guess I should say I slept like a six-year-old."

"It was very powerful. How did it feel to do your first drama?"

"Like I said, when it was over, it was like a dream, or a drug state. It was like I was watching someone else's life play out, not mine. But then it was mine! Very cool process."

"Welcome to psychodrama."

"How do you cope with doing that kind of shit? I mean, man, I'm just your eleven o'clock." He tapped his nonexistent wristwatch. "How the fuck do you deal with it?"

"I use a little heroin lite, just to take the edge off." I tapped the inside of my forearm as if looking for a vein.

"That's probably why I didn't finish the PhD. If I had to do this all fucking day I know it wouldn't be heroin lite. I'd be doing some China Cat or an A-bomb at lunch."

"I never asked: What kind of PhD were you working toward?"

"Clinical psych, man. I knew listening to this shit all day would fuck me up."

"I know what you mean. If I were listening to all this stuff this job would be hell."

Nick laughed again. "You're a fucking trip and a half."

"Well, let's see if we can make this one a round trip. Are you ready?"

"Ready, man." He pointed at me with his pinky.

"It might be time to have a little chat with Mom."

"I'm cool." Nick rested his fingertips lightly on his kneecaps.

"Where would your mom sit?"

"Right there." He pointed to the other swivel chair across from where little Nick sat.

I turned the chair slightly so it would be facing adult Nick directly.

"How does it feel to be sitting across from her in this moment?"

"I hate her," he said. "I hate who she is, who she was, and how she treated me."

"I'm going to stand behind you, double you, like I did six-year-old Nick."

"I'm cool with that."

"And remember we can stop any time."

"Got it."

I stood up and walked over behind Nick's chair, slightly to the left side, and began to double.

"Man, I hate you. I hate everything about you. You are one crazy mother," I said as Nick.

"You got that right," Nick chimed in.

"Now, I'm going to add something here. Let me know if it sounds right. If it does, then you can repeat it, okay?"

"I'm with you."

I hadn't done this part with little Nick because he was in a nonverbal state—so I just provided the words for him. This time I hoped I understood things well enough that big Nick would repeat my words. "I'm sick and tired of living like this," I began. "You can't even take care of yourself. You had no idea how to be a mother to me," I said as him.

"I'm sick and tired of living like this," he echoed. "You can't even take care of yourself. You had no idea how to be a mother to me."

"I want this to change, and I know the change has to come from me. I can't rely on you to follow through with anything," I said with conviction. "This feeling inside me has to change."

"I want this to change, and I know the change has to come from me. I can't rely on you to follow through with anything," he said with the same conviction. "This feeling inside me has to change."

"Is this okay?" I asked Nick directly.

"Perfect, man, perfect."

"Good, then reverse roles and become your mother."

"Be her?"

"Yep."

"Sit over there and be her?"

"That's what they say to do in the psychodrama manual."

"Then let's do it." Nick got up, spun himself around, and then dropped into the other chair. "I suddenly feel bipolar and a borderline rage coming on." He smiled as he sat.

"You're warmed up to her; that's for sure."

"Fuck her."

"Actually, now you're going to become her."

"Right, sorry." He paused. "Fuck me."

I laughed. "That's the spirit."

Nick adapted himself to the chair and fussed with himself. "What's this all about?" he said as his mother.

"Your son has some things he wants to talk to you about. He has some things bothering him," I said as me.

"He always has something he's angry about," Nick said as his mother. "He's a drug addict, you know."

"Yes, I know," I said to her standing behind Nick's previous seat.

"He's been a little shit since he was a child, always getting into trouble and making noise."

"Do you like Nick?"

"He was not an easy child."

"But do you like him? What do you feel for him?"

"I was the only person in the world who loved him. He knows that. Don't you, Nick?"

"Reverse roles and answer your mother," I said to Nick as he sat in his mother's chair.

Nick stood up, turned around, took two steps backward, and sat in his recliner. He gathered himself and let his fingertips rest on his kneecaps, and spoke right up. "You're an evil woman."

"Reverse roles."

"What is this?" Nick said as he stood up. "Aerobic psychodrama?"

"Just trying to keep you in shape."

Nick sat in his mother's chair and started. "You see, you see! There's no call for that!" he said as he pointed back toward where he had been sitting. "You're a freak, a drug addict. You caused me nothing but grief. Your father left because you were such a miserable little kid."

"Reverse roles," I said to Nick, but it was hardly necessary. He was halfway to the other chair to become himself.

"How fucked up are you to blame a six-year-old for your husband leaving? You were the one cheating on him: going to bars, picking up men, fucking them in our house, telling me they were friends of yours, and yelling at me not to come near the fucking bedroom. You think that might have something to do with Dad leaving? I don't blame him. If I had a wife like you, I'd have been gone the first time I caught you being a whore. He only stayed with you because I didn't have the fucking balls to tell him what you were doing." Nick's veins were protruding, his body on full alert.

I stopped him. "I just want to make sure I got what you're saying, Nick." He nodded.

"She blamed you for your father's leaving and the divorce."

"Totally."

"Okay, then, reverse roles with little Nick."

"I didn't even know he was in the room."

"He is now."

"I'm not sure I can do that."

"I appreciate you feeling safe enough to tell me you don't want to do that."

"No, man, I *do* want to do it," he said, pausing. "It is just that I can't. I'm so pissed right now, and I can't become little Nick because I can't be angry."

"That would explain it," I said, nodding.

"That would explain what?"

"Why you did so many drugs, and drank so much alcohol."

"I don't follow."

"Little Nick was never allowed to feel angry, so he could never be integrated. Instead of feeling anger, you make him numb to those feelings."

"That sounds right, man. I feel it in my gut."

"But I don't understand *why* he wasn't able to get angry."

"Because if he got angry something even worse than being stabbed in the heart would happen."

This caught me by surprise. My face wrinkled up and I cocked my head to the side. "What could be worse than being stabbed in the heart by your mother?"

* * *

August 22

"Sorry I bailed on you last time and couldn't get back into the little Nick head."

"Nothing to be sorry about, Nick. You knowing your limits is a very good thing, and being able to tell me those limits is even better."

"Yeah, man," he said with a half-snort, half-laugh, "I was never a fan of limits. If some is good, more is better."

"And if more is better, too much ain't enough."

"Jimmy Barnes, Seduce, and Tom Petty."

"Lost you on that one."

"They each did a song titled 'Too Much Ain't Enough'."

"You know that off the top of your head?"

"I am like a Googlepedia for music."

"Wow."

"So where do we go today?"

"Are you willing to go back to the scene—"

"Of the crime?" Nick interrupted.

"Well, I guess that's true."

"Let's do it."

"Where would you like to start? We can begin with you, little Nick, or your mother."

"Let me be the bitch."

Nick got up and sat in the seat representing his mother. I took the opportunity to move deeper.

"Thanks for returning. I think little Nick has something to say to you. Can you turn your chair toward him?"

"What now? What's this little fucker saying I did now?" Nick said as he became his mother.

"Do you remember what you did to him?" I asked.

"Who are you going to believe? Me, his mother, or a six-year-old crazy fucking kid?"

"Something really bad happened to Nick. Can you tell me what you remember?"

"Why don't you ask him?" she asked condescendingly.

"Reverse roles. Can you come back over to the recliner and be adult Nick?"

Nick got up and left the role of his mother. But the moment he sat down in his recliner he had a puzzled look.

"What's the matter?"

"It's like it's both of us sitting here. It is both little Nick and big Nick. We're like finally together, man."

"Then let's make it official," I said, reaching for the Holland stone he had held as little Nick. "Here." I handed big Nick the stone as he sat in the recliner.

He and little Nick were going to be integrated as he confronted his mom. He held the stone in his hand and stared over at the chair where his mother had been sitting.

"You crazy bitch," he said softly.

I moved over behind him to begin doubling. But Nick was already talking.

"You never cared about me. When I fell to the floor with the fucking scissors in me, I lay on my back and there was blood everywhere. My shirt was red, my hands were around those scissors, and I couldn't pull them out. You were just so fucking crazy. I could hear you on the phone calling 911," he said, looking at her chair. "You told him that your six-year-old was bleeding to death. I heard you give the address. Then I was blacking out."

I began to speak as his double. "I didn't know what was happening to me. It hurt so much, and I was scared. I was afraid to do anything. I was afraid of you," I said as his double. "I was afraid and had to protect myself from you."

"No," Nick said, surprising me. "That's not what I was thinking."

This confused me. I thought for sure he would want to protect himself from his mother. I stopped and talked to him as he held the stone in his fist. "Good," I said. "If what I say doesn't sound right, please correct it. Stand here in the double position and say what you were thinking."

Nick stood up behind his chair to the right of me. Then he said something I wasn't expecting. "I had to protect you," he said clearly and deliberately. "All these years I've been protecting you, and it's fucked me up more than you will ever know."

"You were protecting *her*?"

Nick turned to me. "She called 911, then came back in as I was fading in and out trying to stay conscious. I must have been in shock. She told me that when they came I had to tell them my sister did this. My eight-year-old sister was just playing in her room and didn't know anything about what was going on," he said. "My mother bent down and looked at me in my face and told me that if I said my mother did this they would take her away and lock her up forever. She said I had to protect her and say my sister did this."

"Oh my God." I felt my breathing quicken.

"She said if I didn't protect her they would lock her up and I would be responsible for putting the only person that loved me in jail." Nick held his right fist with the stone in it to his head.

"God, Nick."

"So I lied." He shook his head.

I was speechless.

"My mother ran down to Lilith's room and brought her back to me. She was eight and my mother stuck her hand on my shirt. While Lilith was screaming, Mom held her little hand and made it like my sister was holding the scissors."

My mouth was agape. I couldn't believe what I was hearing.

"I don't remember everything, but I told them my sister stabbed me." Nick knocked his head with his fist. "I didn't know what else to do."

Nick turned toward the empty chair representing his mother. "You fucking sick bitch," he began. "Lilith was never right after that. That was nearly forty years ago and she spent her whole life in and out of institutions. She ended up at Willowbrook. I've been protecting you my whole life, and it's ruined my life and Lilith's, you sick fuck."

"Willowbrook? The institution in Staten Island?"

"That very hell-hole. Because I couldn't man up and tell the truth, they institutionalized my sister."

"You were six and in shock."

"Good point."

"What else do you need to say?" I covered my mouth.

Nick focused back on the empty chair representing his mother. "No more, man. The truth is out now. I don't want to see you, let you near my kid, or ever talk to you again," he said as loud as he could while still being in control. "If you ever try to come near me again, I'll tell the whole world what you did."

Then Nick lost it. He lifted up his shirt. His sculptured body was perfect in every dimension except for the horrific blotch of scar tissue spattered in the middle of his chest. "You did this!" he screamed at the top of his lungs. "Look at what you did to your own child!" As Nick stood with the bottom of his T-shirt under his chin, he let out a wailing scream at his mother's empty chair.

The horrific keloidal scar on Nick's chest opened a portal in my mind.

Sophia turned toward me. I see her self-inflicted wounds once again: A vulgar slash on her heart. Blood everywhere as she rips her arm from the window. Harold's bullet wounds. I'm in the shower. There is Albert and Gwennie, and Mike, and Jake, and Benny, and Candy and . . .

The parade in my mind was interrupted. Dolores, my secretary, banged on the door.

Nick blew out his breath, then breathed deeply. He was calming himself. Dolores and I had an understanding. If something didn't sound right coming from my room, she knocked. If I didn't answer, she knew to call 911. The last thing I wanted was the police coming to my office to complete the drama. I reached over and cracked open the door. "I'm okay. We're okay," I said, looking into her saucer-sized eyes.

"You sure?"

"I'm sure, thanks." I closed the door.

Nick had calmed himself and sat back down in the chair. It was done. A forty-year secret had come to an end. I sat back down in my chair.

For a long, long time we sat. Neither of us said a word.

* * *

Six months later

Nick sat down across from me in his usual chair. He started the conversation.

"Hey."

"Hey, long time no see."

"Thought you'd like this." Nick handed me a CD with the drawing of a tarot deck fool with an oversized heart in his chest. The title was in black and at the bottom: "Fool of Hearts."

"I've been working on this for a couple of years. I play every instrument. I do all the vocals. I mixed it, produced it. I even did the drawing. It's mine top to bottom."

"Wow," I said, holding it, admiring the artwork.

"You know what the symbol of the fool is in Tarot?" He stuck his tongue out, wiggling his hands in the air.

"Tell me."

"The fool is worthless, zero, the first and the last. The end and the beginning. Wise because he knows his own ignorance. A reminder of all things sacred that we've forgotten."

I nodded.

"I was working on it before we did our thing, man. But it never came together," he said, fingers resting on his kneecaps. "Thanks, man."

"Nothing to thank me for," I said with a shrug. "I was just here when it happened."

Nick nodded his head. "How about you? You writing anything these days?"

"I'm putting together some stories about people that made some extraordinary transformation in their lives."

"Cool."

"In fact I'm writing about some people I worked with who were coming out of Willowbrook. You said your sister, Lilith, was put in there for a while, right?"

"Yeah, man. Don't know exactly whatever happened to her. She got bounced around pretty good. Last I heard she was being moved out into a group home or something, but shit, that would have been twenty-five or thirty years ago."

"Really?"

"Yeah, man," he said slightly shaking his head. "I think if things had not gone the way they went she'd have been a musical prodigy. Anything I got, she already had it in spades, man. She was into the classics before she could walk, man."

"What do you mean?"

"She really dug listening and soothing herself to music. I could tell, man, she had the gift inside her. Maybe someday I'll go track her down and make things right. She had a freaky disease called Williams syndrome, which meant she had like an intellectual disability in one area, but was like savant when it came to music. I would always play her some music every day, but before she went to bed I played her favorite."

"What was that?"

"Chopin's *Sonata no. 3 in B Minor.*" Nick stood up.

That was it. That was what Lilith played for us in the basement so long ago.

I stood up as well. Nick shook my hand. "Later," he said.

"Thanks for this," I said, lifting the CD.

"Nothing to thank me for, man," he said as a smile began. "Just felt like it was something I had to do."

Love and Civil Rights

"We are more alike, my friends, than we are unalike."
—*Maya Angelou, 1994*

Largely due to Willowbrook, mental health treatment for the institutionalized became a civil right in the United States through the Civil Rights of Institutionalized Peoples Act (CRIPA). In 1980, the year I left Walden House, the Department of Justice sought to protect the rights of people in state or local correctional facilities, nursing homes, mental health facilities, and institutions for people with intellectual and developmental disabilities. The nursing home segment alone is worth understanding the impact of Willowbrook. As baby boomers live longer, the chances we will end up in a nursing home are high. In fact, some estimates are that 50 percent of us will end up in one. In other words, many of us will be the direct beneficiaries of the resilient, courageous lives of the people in Willowbrook.

In the more than thirty-five years since our group home began, over 40,000 other homes have been opened around the country. In 1983, Dr. Robert J. Fletcher developed an association called the National Association for the Dually Diagnosed (NADD), an association for persons with developmental disabilities and mental health needs. Chiefly due to this organization, the field has thrived and advanced to its current status where newer work, such as the START program from the University of New Hampshire under the direction of Dr. Joan Beasley, has taken an evidence-based approach to positively impact the well-being of individuals with intellectual disabilities throughout the country.

The bottom line is that because of the few experimental homes like Walden House, people have stayed out of institutions and moved successfully into the community. This has saved millions in taxpayer dollars—while providing a higher quality of life for the residents. The home this book is centered around is still thriving, and the people have greatly improved lives. Some are still alive and working in the community. They live rich lives, pay taxes, and have hopes and dreams—just like the rest of us. None of these outcomes would be possible had they remained in Willowbrook.

Although I searched for verification that Lilith was Nick's sister, I could not find supporting documents. I learned that she had passed away in the group home a few years back, and I never told Nick that I thought she might have been his sister. But in my investigation for information about her, I stumbled upon a highly unique couple.

On December 15, 2010, I met two extraordinary people, Michael and Amy (not their real names). They live in a supported residential program with ancillary services. They have a wonderful and rare, love story. It is filled with the challenges of circumstance and desire. Amy is nearly thirty years older than Michael. At the time of the interview, she was ninety-two; he was sixty-three. But it isn't their age difference that makes their story the only one of its kind.

The couple has been married thirty years, and together for forty. I had a chance to interview them for about an hour courtesy of the YAI/National Institute for People with Disabilities (NIPD). I still had some dear friends there, Perry Samowitz and Bobra Fyne, two of the most dedicated professionals I've known. Bobra arranged the interview, which took about two months to set up. The meeting took place in front of a small group of staff and was videotaped by Jerry Weinstock of YAI/NIPD for their archives. Amy had on a lovely black and red dress with very tasteful jewelry. Michael was dressed in slightly mismatched shirt and pants, with a good-quality jacket that clashed with both. They were well groomed, in good spirits, and very excited for the interview. It would be hard not to notice that the color choices of Michael's shirt and pants could have been better, but his exuberance and energy more than compensated.

For the most part, Michael spoke for the couple. They held hands and slowly made their way into the interview room. Michael guided Amy and helped her get situated in a chair. He sat down next to her, and both smiled at Bobra and me. Two aides were nearby for assistance if needed.

As we began to talk, I thanked them for making the trip out from Long Island to talk with us. They were pleased to have come, and Michael explained that Amy now needed a little more time to prepare herself for travel. They smiled and held each other's hands as they began talking about their lives.

They'd recently returned from a vacation in Boston, and chatted about the sights they'd seen and the food at the restaurants. They talked about what we all talk about when we come back from a vacation: the vistas, the travel complications, and the new foods. All as normal as can be.

Then they gave a small rendition of their physical maladies, their aches and pains, and the fact that they can't always do the things they used to do. Michael shrugged and smiled. "But what else are you going to do?" he said. Chatting with an aging couple about a vacation and citing a list of ailments shouldn't be cause for a videotaped interview. But this was no ordinary couple.

As we now know, Willowbrook was the largest and most infamous institution of its kind in America. With forty-three buildings, the "school" housed nearly 6,000 residents—sixty-five percent over capacity. More than seventy-five percent of the residents had IQs below fifty, and most had been residents for more than twenty years. Just to give you some understanding of the jeopardy the inmates were in: in an eight-month period in 1972, there were over 1,300 reported incidents of assaults, fights, and injuries.

That is not a misprint: 1,300 incidents in an eight-month period: "Hell on earth" described it well.

Michael and Amy met as inmates in Willowbrook. What makes them so exceptional is they are the only couple from the institution ever to get married.

Beneath the unspeakable horrors, inhumane and unsafe conditions, and the traumatized lives was an incredible resilience of spirit and of mind. My intent was to have them talk about their experiences in Willowbrook and of their transcendence. I asked them how they met.

"I was over on the men's side; she was over on the women's side," began Michael. "There was a staff member that liked me, and he brought her over to me."

"Did you like Michael right away?" Bobra then asked Amy.

"No," she said with a slight smile.

Michael was incredulous. We all laughed. He put his hand gently on Amy's shoulder and spoke directly to her. "Bobra asked if you liked me right away," he said, smiling.

Amy smiled back. "I like you now!" she said.

More laughter.

Then they talked about their time in the institution.

"I was there for sixteen years," said Michael. "In buildings four and five, then building ten."

"Do you remember things from Willowbrook?" I inquired.

"Geraldo Rivera," he said right away. "And then pictures of the babies in their own feces."

"What was your time in Willowbrook like?" I asked.

"It was the worst place to be. I didn't like the way people were treated. There was a man that had his hands in the food. He didn't have no gloves on. That's not how you serve food."

Amy was still thinking about how they met. "I seen him when they would bring together the boys' side and the girls' side," said Amy.

Bobra picked up on Amy's comment. "What did you notice about him?" she asked.

Amy paused and smiled at Michael and looked back at Bobra and me. With the slightest of shrugs, she closed her eyes in a reverie of recall. "He was a snappy dresser," she said, smiling.

Michael beamed. It was not lost on Bobra or I or the onlookers that Michael might be described as many things, but "snappy dresser" wouldn't be the first thing that comes to mind.

Except Amy's.

We then pressed Michael for confirmation. "Is that true?" asked Bobra. "Were you a snappy dresser?"

In true New York style, complete with the hand gestures that conveyed total self-assurance, Michael turned his palms out in front of him and moved them up and down his torso to reveal his wardrobe. He didn't utter a word, but his actions said it for him. Could there be any doubt he was a "snappy dresser?"

Amy nodded.

In the words of H.G. Wells, "Beauty is in the heart of the beholder."

Michael is on the New York State self-advocacy board and has a long list of involvement in advocacy. He and Amy were part of the original transferees in the Willowbrook Consent Decree. Had that decree not been made, they both would have died after nondescript lives, been buried in pine boxes, and forgotten. Their love for each other would never have flourished.

Toward the end of the interview, I asked Michael if he had any advice for people who want to have a successful marriage. With the unconscious timing of the great comedic sensitive Art Carney, Michael slowly, deliberately, and painstakingly removed a small folded paper from his pocket. The unfolding of this paper and the anticipation of its message by the gathered audience was spellbinding. It was a palpable pull on our attention. As I looked at Bobra and the staff, it was clear we all wanted Michael's secret to be revealed. Once out of his pocket and unfolded, he made known the contents.

It was a picture of Amy and Michael kissing.

He held it up for the camera, leaned over and kissed Amy, duplicating the photo. In that moment, the interview ended and thirty years dissolved.

I am at the group interview for candidates for the job as manager of Walden House. Gerry has just asked the group: "What if you found two residents kissing in one of their bedrooms?"

I remembered my answer—the one that got me the job.

"I'd apologize and close the door."

Epilogue

"If any organism fails to fulfill its potentialities, it becomes sick."
—William James

The story behind *American Snake Pit* is not only one about the resilience of the human spirit, but also the conditions under which lives can flourish. William James, the founder of the field of psychology, knew that each of us needs to fulfill our potential as human beings to function properly, yet he also declared that "the soul is stronger than its surroundings." Both of these axioms are important in understanding what allows people to transform.

The souls of the individuals inside Willowbrook were indeed stronger than their surroundings, and the effort to move people into a community where they could reach their potential with an emphasis on dignity and well-being proved a valuable experiment. We are now able to enhance the lives of individuals at much less cost than is required to house people in institutions. But in doing this, we also learned something about the strategies and thinking that make lives thrive and worth living. Moving forward, it is important to understand the principles that guided these positive developments—and what has happened in psychology since Willowbrook closed.

I didn't know it back in 1979, but I was part of a nascent movement that sought to understand the possibilities life could hold beyond simple survival. We wanted to know what makes people flourish and thrive. In hindsight, that time in my life was the beginning of my career as a positive psychologist.

I've always had a positive, optimistic view of life, but I've never really understood exactly what that means. Trying to understand what motivates optimism has led me, particularly over the past decade, to turn my attention to the field of positive psychology and the practice of intentional well-being. My current interest in the field began with the vision of Martin Seligman who, in 1998, as president of the American Psychological Association, declared that psychology was half-baked. Central to his platform was an effort to transform the APA into an organization that worked to develop positive psychology, in addition to its usual efforts to help ameliorate suffering and alleviate pain. But not being depressed isn't the same as being happy, and as a science we had focused only on what's wrong with people. While all of Dr. Seligman's initiatives are illuminating, two are particularly relevant for understanding the mental health needs of all people, especially those with intellectual and psychiatric disabilities.

First is his emphasis on character development. Rather than limiting our work to assessing and developing IQ or skills, focusing on character development has shown to be an even better predictor of an achievement. While developing character isn't a new idea (similar suggestions are found in the writings of Buddhism, and in Aristotle and Montessori) the current effort by Chris Peterson and Martin Seligman to identify character strengths and virtues has resulted in a database that includes over 5 million people. Their research categorizes six virtues and twenty-four character strengths as valued by human beings. (In this list, the virtues are followed by their respective character strengths.)

WISDOM AND KNOWLEDGE: creativity, curiosity, open-mindedness, love of learning, perspective, innovation
COURAGE: bravery, persistence (grit), integrity, vitality, zest
HUMANITY: love, kindness, social intelligence
JUSTICE: citizenship, fairness, leadership
TEMPERANCE: forgiveness and mercy, humility, prudence, self-control

TRANSCENDENCE: appreciation of beauty and excellence, gratitude, hope, humor, spirituality.

The publication of *Character Strengths and Virtues: A Handbook and Classification* (APA 2004) has been a game changer. The book offers a compendium of what is right and virtuous in human beings and was created to balance out the *Diagnostic and Statistical Manual* (a compilation of what mental health clinicians use to diagnose what is wrong with people.) Thinking back over the stories of each of the residents (and staff, for that matter) of Walden House, it is their development and exhibition of the character strengths of bravery, grit, citizenship, hope, and a little bit of humor that allowed them to become agents of real change.

The character strength survey has radically changed how character is understood and used around the world. The development of a free online survey by the VIA Institute on Character (viacharacter.org) allows people to uncover their strengths and begin using those them in new and different ways. I encourage readers to go to the site. Because of the efforts of Ryan Niemiec, Director of Education for VIA, and his colleagues, there are provisions for administering the character strength survey to people with intellectual disabilities. Indeed, many programs for people with intellectual disabilities are now training their staff in using this classification system to enhance the lives of people with intellectual or developmental disabilities, or IDD. The national START program, one of the largest organizations serving people with intellectual disabilities, has partnered with the VIA Institute on Character to help both staff and individuals with IDD learn about their unique character strengths.

Understanding your own character strengths and spotting them in others has become central to advances in business, education, and psychotherapy. In my graduate, undergraduate, workshop, and certificate courses, all of my students take the survey. And when training mental health workers or coaches, this is always the first bit of information we ask them to learn.

The second of Seligman's initiatives I'd like to emphasize is the concept of positive interventions. These are intentional acts that have been scientifically proven to help improve well-being and alleviate suffering. Such interventions are important to understand because the evidence shows, among many other things, that happier people live longer, are kinder, more successful, and have better relationships. This is not just true for people with intellectual disabilities, but for those in college, grade school, corporations, the military, or in families. Everyone can profit from the right kind of intervention, and Seligman notes that these are the "bottom line of work in positive psychology." It is no longer enough to ask what will relieve misery. It is now just as important to consider what makes life worth living.

To this end, Seligman identified five universal sources which he maintains (and many others agree) are the portal through which flourishing can be achieved. Using the acronym PERMA (Positive Emotion, or Pleasure; Engagement; Relationships; Meaning; and Accomplishment), he presents a process for becoming more self-aware and tapping into our strengths. Being aware of our own habits, thoughts, feelings, and motives is the crucial ingredient for applying positive interventions. It is important to know what needs changing—and then find the right interventions to change it. Positive psychology has shown a remarkable ability to decrease negative reactions in stressful situations, and in psychotherapy, it has had a powerful impact on reducing depression relapse while increasing well-being. The interested reader can find additional reading and references on my website, dare2behappy.com.

For the purpose of deconstructing some of the events in *American Snake Pit*, it may be helpful to map the five elements of PERMA to some of the experiences of the patients and staff in the book.

POSITIVE EMOTIONS (PLEASURE)

The simple pleasure of sleeping without fear of attack, of being able to take a warm shower with soap and a clean towel; the joy of savoring food that you don't have to horde or fight for; a warm bed, television, and juice to drink. All of these simple pleasures are part of the transitional experience.

ENGAGEMENT

Focusing long enough to learn sign language to communicate, acquiring the skills to prepare a meal, setting the table, cleaning one's room, or applying make-up—all take concentration. The ability to learn new skills, such as those seen in the protracted training for the fire drill, also required a higher degree of engagement.

RELATIONSHIPS

Taking turns, helping each other put food away, worrying about others, alerting others if there is danger, exhibiting teamwork, pitching in, and eating meals together. Learning sign language so you can understand someone. Learning to trust each other, as when Lilith and Mike formed a new appreciation for each other.

MEANING

What is it like to go from battling for survival every day to some degree of contentment? What is it like to have a new or greater sense of belonging, to cheer together, to be disappointed together, to laugh together, cry together? What is it like to celebrate group achievement? All of these experiences were important to the residents in the story, and changed them in uncountable ways.

Setting goals for the first time, such as not hurting yourself and not hurting others. Not eating inedible objects. Communicating your needs, stating your preferences: these are simple actions to be sure, but monumental in the lives of people who've never had a chance to achieve them.

William James's statement—"If any organism fails to fulfill its potentialities, it becomes sick"—couldn't be a more accurate way of describing what happened in Willowbrook. Philip Zimbardo's *Lucifer Effect: Understanding How Good People Turn Evil* (Random House 2007) provides a good framework for how a Willowbrook can happen, a framework augmented by a 2017 study by Pavel Freidlin, Hadassah Littman-Ovadia, and Ryan M. Niemiec that demonstrates that not being able to use your strengths regularly may be the central factor in being mentally unwell. Isn't this what happened at Willowbrook? By depriving people of what has become a civil right, a right to realize their potential, they became sick. Theory and research would indicate that when we can't live a life that incorporates our strengths, we will resort to baser elements of our emotions and behaviors. In the simplest of terms, this is the change that takes place in *American Snake Pit*: As more of each person's potential was realized, the residents became happier, more productive, and healthier. Through 2009, more than 40,000 group homes serving fifteen or fewer residents have been created for people with intellectual disabilities. This accommodates over eighty percent of the population in need of services.

There is a simple way for all of us to carry this work forward. When you encounter anyone—whether they have an intellectual, psychiatric, or physical disability, or none at all—one character strength in particular will always help you both: The kindness you show to others helps them, helps you, and helps anyone who is witness to it. Kindness creates a strong ripple effect due to the phenomenon I spoke of earlier known as elevation. Finding a way to be kind has real value—it is the fastest way to bring you out of your negative mood, and the most direct way of helping someone else. As the story of Walden House shows, we are intricately woven together in a delicate balance. In the end, we are all responsible for helping one another live happier lives.

American Psychiatric Association, *Diagnostic and Statistical Manual of Mental Disorders, Fifth Edition* (Washington, D.C.: American Psychiatric Publishing, 2013).

Freidlin, Pavel, Littman-Ovadia, Hadassah, and Niemiec, Ryan M., "Positive Psychopathology: Social Anxiety Via Character Strengths Underuse and Overuse," *Personality and Individual Differences*, vol. 108 (2017): 50-54.

"Institutions: Definitions, Populations, and Trends," National Council on Disability. https://ncd.gov/publications/2012/Sept192012/ Institutions.

Mechanic, David and Rochefort, David A., "A Policy of Inclusion for the Mentally Ill," *Health Affairs*, vol. 11, no. 1 (1992): 128-150.

Peterson, Christopher, and Seligman, Martin E. P., *Character Strengths and Virtues: A Handbook and Classification* (Oxford: Oxford University Press, 2004).

Seligman, Martin E. P., and Csikszentmihalyi, Mihaly, "Positive Psychology: An Introduction," *American Psychologist*, vol. 55, no. 1, 5-14.

Seligman, Martin E. P., *Flourish: A Visionary New Understanding of Happiness and Well-being*, (New York: Atria Books, 2012).

Zimbardo, Philip, *The Lucifer Effect: Understanding How Good People Turn Evil* (New York: Random House, 2007).

Acknowledgements

Dedicated to the courageous and inspiring residents of Willowbrook

In the more than four decades since my initial experiences in the field of intellectual disabilities, creative writing, and now positive psychology, I have been fortunate to work with and learn from some of the very best and most innovative thinkers in their respective fields. Each has been an exemplar and source of inspiration and support in some important way. It is daunting to realize the sheer volume of knowledge, conveyed in such a loving way, that has been passed on from this collection of great teachers, friends, and mentors. The most recent support has come from the people at Stillhouse Press, who helped develop and shape this book with great care and attention. Scott W. Berg, Marcos Martinez, Meghan McNamara, Katie Ray, Douglas Luman, and Mateusz Nowakowski have all contributed selflessly to this project. I am greatly indebted.

Marty Seligman, the father of positive psychology, has helped to transform my life most directly by creating the branch of psychology with which I now most closely identify. He has allowed me to grow personally and professionally in ways I could not have imagined. Since 2012 he has invited me to work alongside him at the University of Pennsylvania in the Master of Applied Positive Psychology (MAPP) program to help teach his course. His support for my work as a psychologist and my growth as an individual has opened me to experiences I would not have been able to create on my own. I've also been lucky to have James Pawelski, Director of Education and Senior Scholar at the Positive

Psychology Center at Penn as a mentor and exemplar. James's capacity as an awakener—not merely a teacher—combined with the caliber of his writing, has created a standard for excellence that has served to inspire my own. The framework of the teachings of the MAPP program have informed the central message of this book: Given the right conditions and opportunities, every individual, regardless of his or her struggles in life, can flourish and thrive.

The MAPP community reaches far beyond the normal academic program of study, and since 2011 I've had instructors, colleagues, and friends who have continually supported, challenged and nurtured my development as a writer and person. Leona Brandwene, Johannes Eichstaedt, Dan Bowling, Dan Lerner, Reb and Amy Rebele, Elaine O'Brien, Jennifer Cory, Cory Muscara, Scott Asalone, Andrew Soren, Robert Rosales, Donna Hemmert, Mika Keener Opp, Faisal Kahn, Julia King, Sophia Kokores, Henry Edwards, Mike Hayes, Yashi Srivastava, Gloria Park, David Yaden, Anne Bradford, Naomi Arbit, Emily Esfahani Smith, Jer Clifton, Suzann Pileggi Pawelski, Laura Taylor, Mary Bit Smith, Kayleigh Vogel, Kathryn Britton, Lisa Sansom, Pete Berridge, Martha Knudson, Virginia Millar, Daniel Torrance, Shannon Polly, Caroline Adams Miller, Louisa Jewell, Kunal Sood, Emilia Lahti, Yumi Kendall, Benjamin Jones, Jan Stanley, Amy Holloway, Sydney Rubin, and Aaron Boczkowski all represent the essence of what has been called "the magic of MAPP." I am a better person for having each of them in my life.

Leaders in the field who have been beacons of light in carving a path of influence for me include Ryan Niemiec, Barbara Fredrickson, Bob Vallerand, Scott Barry Kaufman, Adam Grant, Angela Duckworth, Tal Ben Shahar, Jonathan Haidt, David Cooperrider, Meredith Myers, Judy Saltzberg Levick, Tayyab Rashid, Lisa Miller, Ralph White, and Alan Schlechter, Each brings with them a dynamic quest for understanding, combined with a balanced love of life that makes being in their presence and learning from them a treasured and remarkable experience. For each, I have a memory of a nuanced moment of dialogue and conversation that has ignited a line of thought or creative endeavor that has been as intriguing as it has been fulfilling.

In the world of psychodrama, Nina Garcia, Bob and Jacquie Siroka, Dave Moran, Adam Blatner, Louise Lippman, Nancy Kirsner, Phoebe Atkinson, Tian Dayton, Dale Buchannan, Sue McMunn, Rebecca Walters, Judy Swallow, and Bob and Bernice Garfield all bring to their work an inspiring level of warmth, dedication, and care for the human condition that continues to inform my professional and personal life.

In the world of creative writing, my teachers and mentors have provided challenges to strengthen my ability and capacity for storytelling. Christopher Durang, Paul Muldoon, and Jack Klaff from my time at Princeton; Dani Shapiro, Hilton Als, Lucy Grealy, and Robert Polito from the New School's stellar MFA writing program; John Grohol, Marie Hartwell-Walker, and Candy Czernicki from PsychCentral.com whose support and enthusiasm for my work is ever-present; and Robert McGee's and Paul Pettito's deep work and instruction in screenwriting have each introduced new ways of thinking and writing for which I am eternally grateful. I am indebted to my book coach, Lisa Tener, for her help on the book proposal and pulling the manuscript into shape, and Barbara Spence, for her careful and thoughtful edits on various drafts over time. And through it all, I've relied on my crossover writing heroes, Oliver Sacks and Irvin Yalom, who've set a high bar.

I have grown up with the field of intellectual and developmental disabilities and have watched its continual progress through the leadership, commitment, and professionalism of some exceptional agencies, such as the Bergan-Passaic Unit and Monmouth Units of the ARC, ServiceNet in Massachusetts, START at the University of New Hampshire, YAI National Institute for People with Disabilities, and NADD—an association for persons with developmental disabilities and mental health needs. The individuals in these agencies and the many others I've had the privilege to work with make the difference.

Anne Desnoyers Hurley, Steve Marcal, Nancy Razza, Rob Fletcher, Perry Samowitz, Tina Sobel, Ben Niven, Bobra Fyne, Jane Toby, Tara

Ferrante, April Stein, Al Pfadt, Joan Beasley, Deborah Trub-Wehrlen, and my Canadian friends, Dave Hingsburger, Frances Owen, Dorothy Griffiths, Bruce Gordon, Rosanne Kerr, Kate Day, John McGettigan, and Vicky Neufeld, have been leaders and avid supporters of my work in many arenas.

Finally, there are those closest to me: Devon Tomasulo, my dynamic and inspiring daughter, who gave continuous honest and dynamic feedback on this manuscript; Joel and Marilyn Morgovsky, life-long friends whose presence in my life remains a constant treasure; and Andrea Szucs, my love and muse, who not only helps me cope with the rejection letters of life but also celebrates those moments that make life worth living.

DAN TOMASULO is the author of two previous titles, most recently *Confessions of a Former Child: A Therapist's Memoir* (Graywolf Press, 2008), winner of the 2009 Rebecca's Reads Written Arts Award in Creative Nonfiction. He co-authored *Healing Trauma: The Power of Group Treatment for People with Intellectual Disabilities* (2005), the American Psychological Association's first book on psychotherapy for people with intellectual disabilities, and is also the author of *Action Methods In Group Psychotherapy: Practical Aspects* (Taylor & Francis, 1998). His second memoir, *American Snake Pit*, was selected as a finalist for *The Southampton Review*'s 2016 Frank McCourt Memoir Prize and the screenplay has received over 20 awards at international film festivals since June 2017.

This book would not have been possible
without the hard work of our staff.

We would like to acknowledge:

KATIE RAY   *Managing Editor*

TODD GONDA   *Copy Editor*

MEGHAN McNAMARA   *Director of Media*

DANIELLE MADDOX   *Intern*

SARAH LURIA   *Intern*

Our Donors

ANONYMOUS

THERESE HOWELL

DALLAS HUDGENS

WAYNE B. JOHNSON

WILLIAM MILLER

stillhouse
press

CPSIA information can be obtained
at www.ICGtesting.com
Printed in the USA
LVHW041456210423
744924LV00003B/350

9 781945 233029